SOUL EATER

ATSUSHI OHKUBO

21

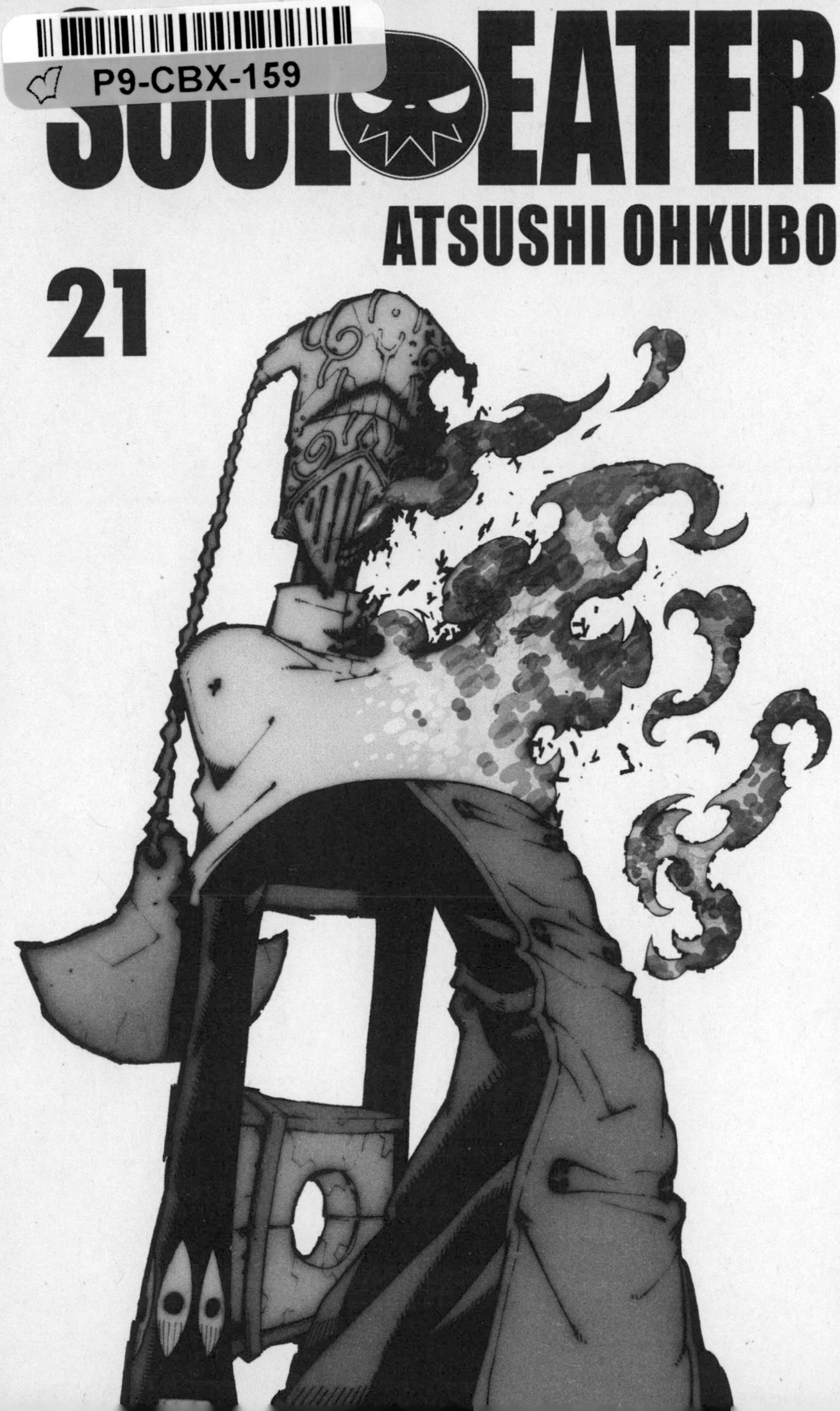

SOUL EATER

vol. 21
by ATSUSHI OHKUBO

Keep the discipline all over the world

SOUL EATER 21

CONTENTS

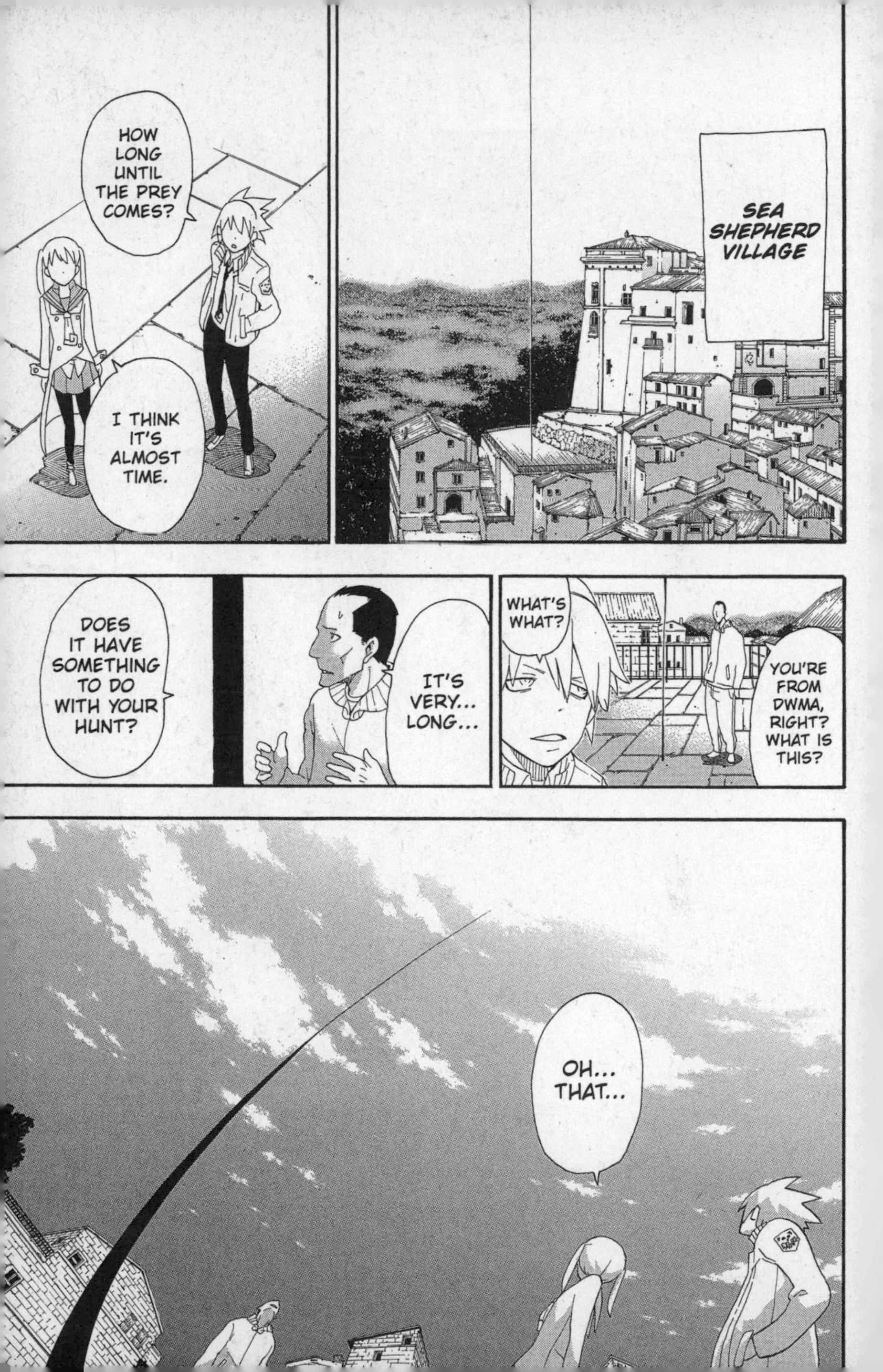
SEA SHEPHERD VILLAGE
HOW LONG UNTIL THE PREY COMES?
I THINK IT'S ALMOST TIME.
YOU'RE FROM DWMA, RIGHT? WHAT IS THIS?
WHAT'S WHAT?
IT'S VERY... LONG...
DOES IT HAVE SOMETHING TO DO WITH YOUR HUNT?
OH... THAT...

SOUL EATER

CHAPTER 88: HUNT

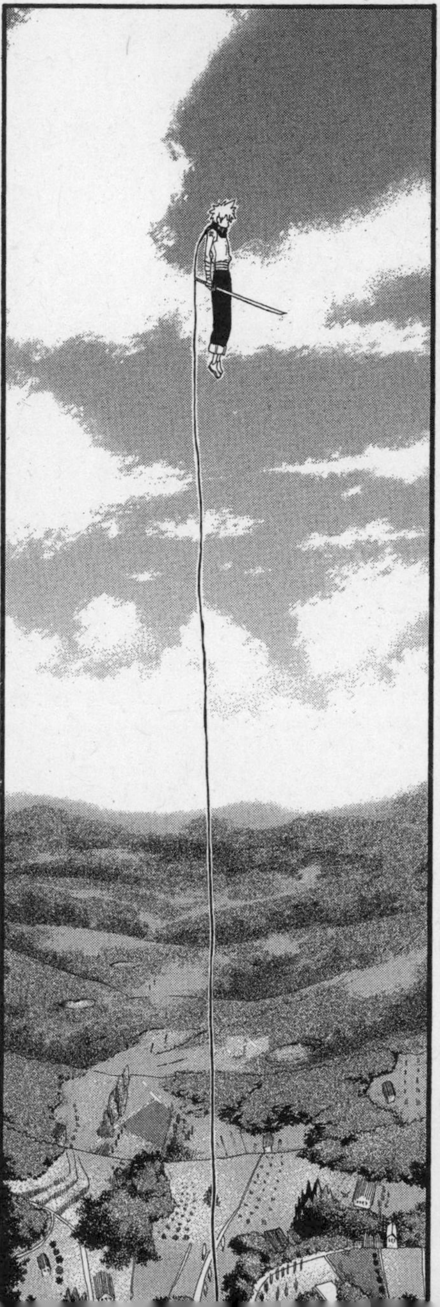

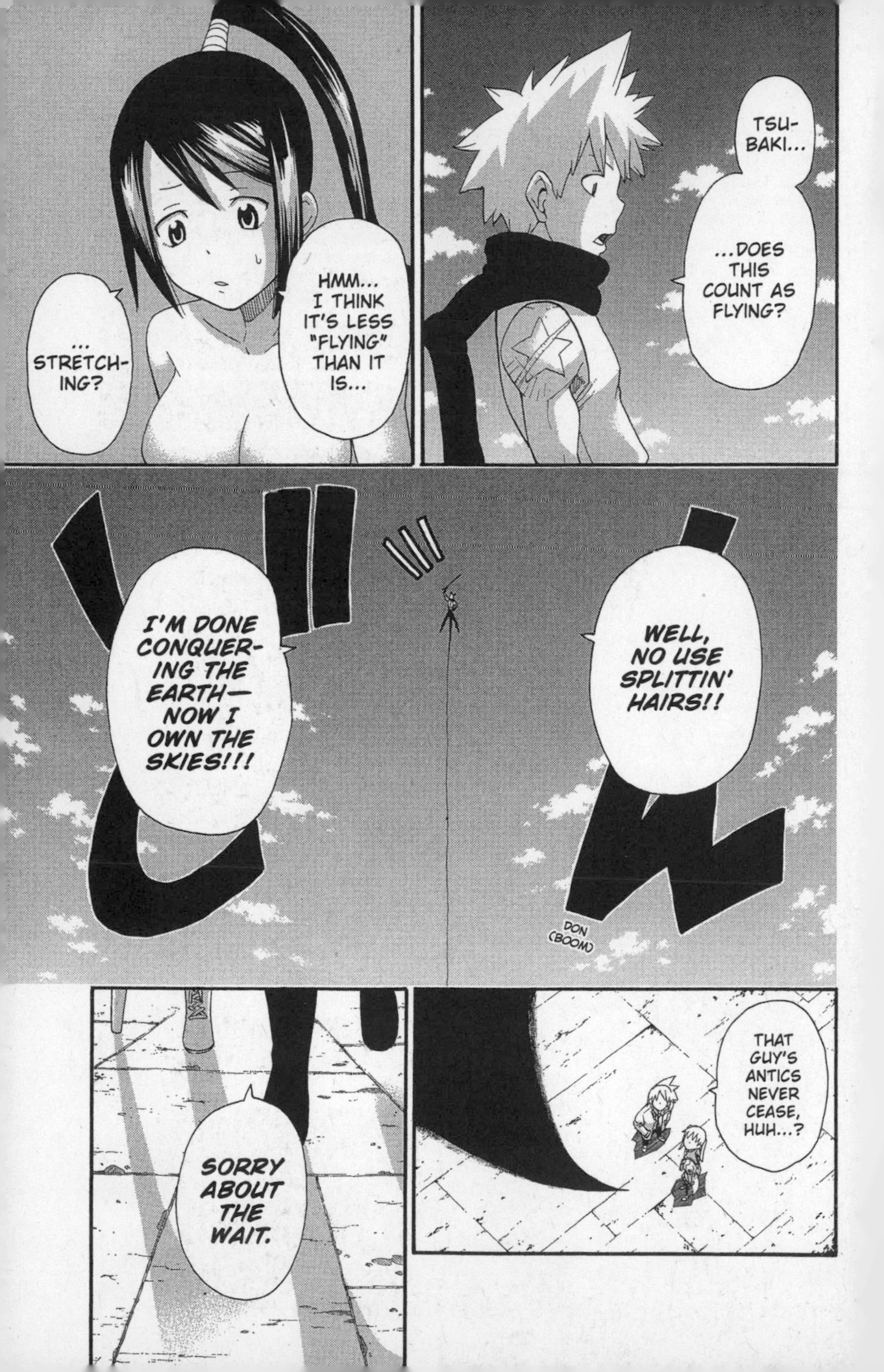
TSU-BAKI...
...DOES THIS COUNT AS FLYING?
HMM... I THINK IT'S LESS "FLYING" THAN IT IS...
...STRETCH-ING?
WELL, NO USE SPLITTIN' HAIRS!!
I'M DONE CONQUER-ING THE EARTH—NOW I OWN THE SKIES!!!
DON (BOOM)
THAT GUY'S ANTICS NEVER CEASE, HUH...?
SORRY ABOUT THE WAIT.

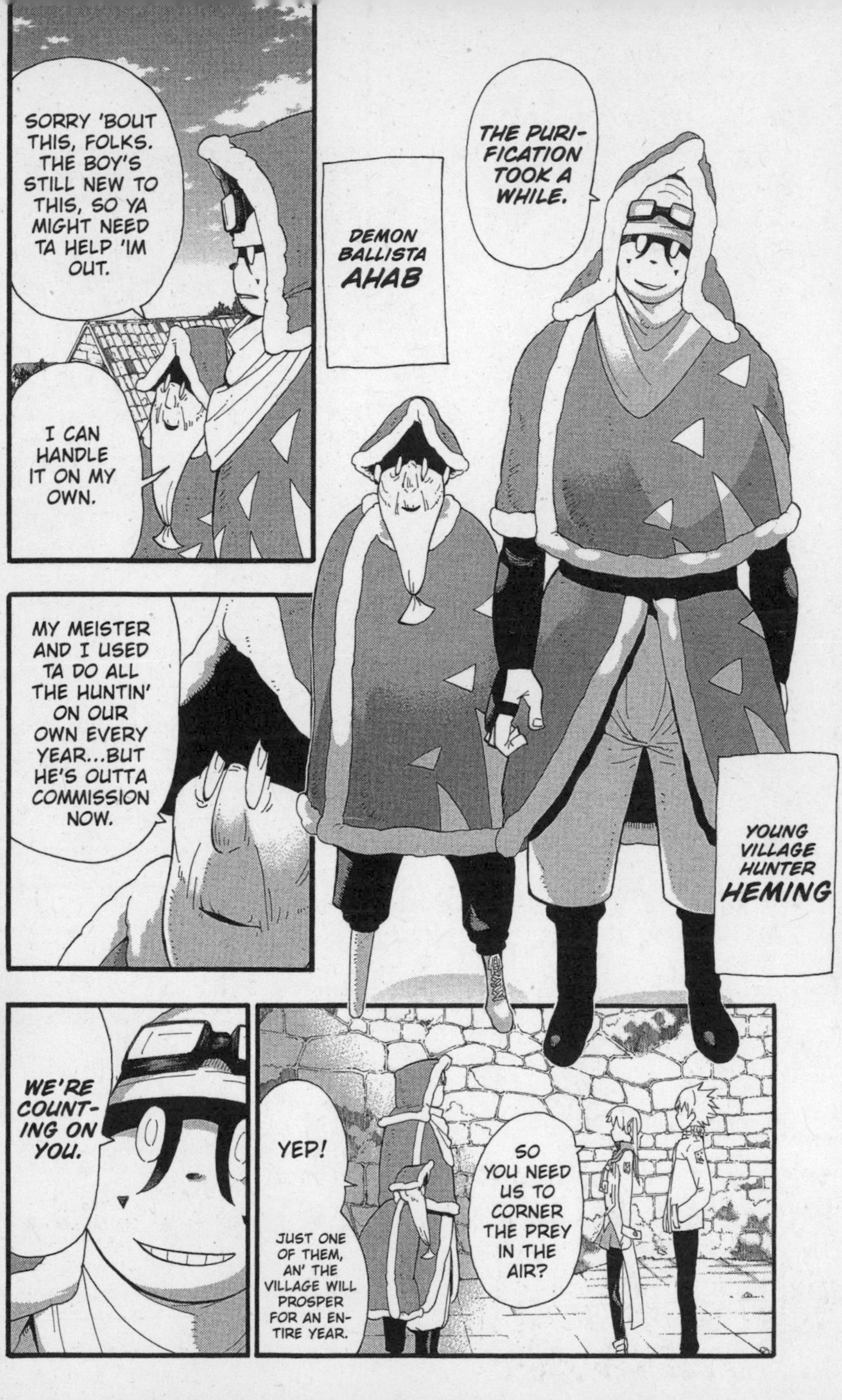
THE PURIFICATION TOOK A WHILE.
DEMON BALLISTA AHAB
YOUNG VILLAGE HUNTER HEMING
SORRY 'BOUT THIS, FOLKS. THE BOY'S STILL NEW TO THIS, SO YA MIGHT NEED TA HELP 'IM OUT.
I CAN HANDLE IT ON MY OWN.
MY MEISTER AND I USED TA DO ALL THE HUNTIN' ON OUR OWN EVERY YEAR...BUT HE'S OUTTA COMMISSION NOW.
SO YOU NEED US TO CORNER THE PREY IN THE AIR?
YEP!
JUST ONE OF THEM, AN' THE VILLAGE WILL PROSPER FOR AN ENTIRE YEAR.
WE'RE COUNTING ON YOU.

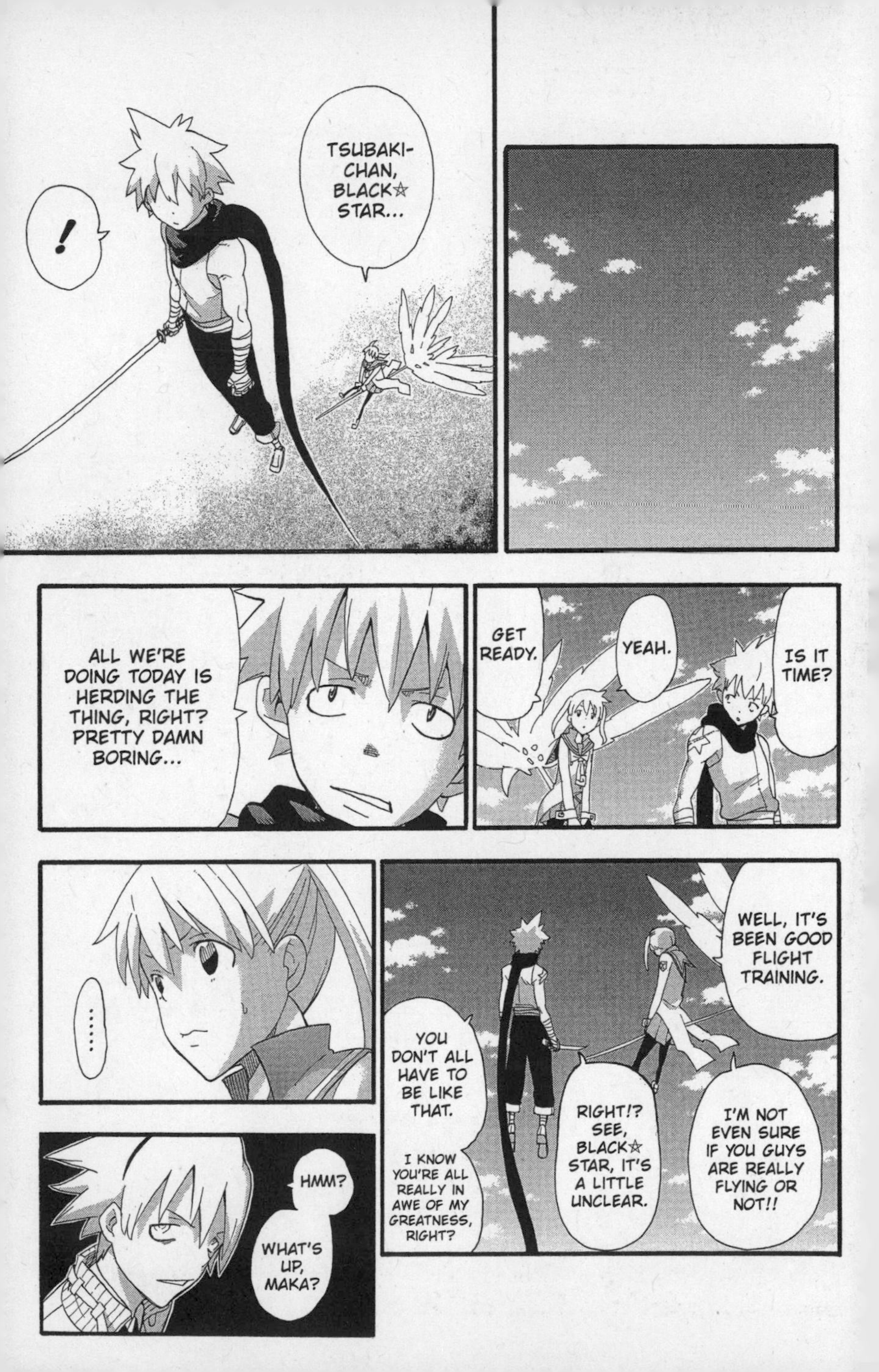
TSUBAKI-CHAN, BLACK☆ STAR...
!
IS IT TIME?
YEAH.
GET READY.
ALL WE'RE DOING TODAY IS HERDING THE THING, RIGHT? PRETTY DAMN BORING...
WELL, IT'S BEEN GOOD FLIGHT TRAINING.
I'M NOT EVEN SURE IF YOU GUYS ARE REALLY FLYING OR NOT!!
RIGHT!? SEE, BLACK☆ STAR, IT'S A LITTLE UNCLEAR.
YOU DON'T ALL HAVE TO BE LIKE THAT.
I KNOW YOU'RE ALL REALLY IN AWE OF MY GREATNESS, RIGHT?
......
HMM?
WHAT'S UP, MAKA?

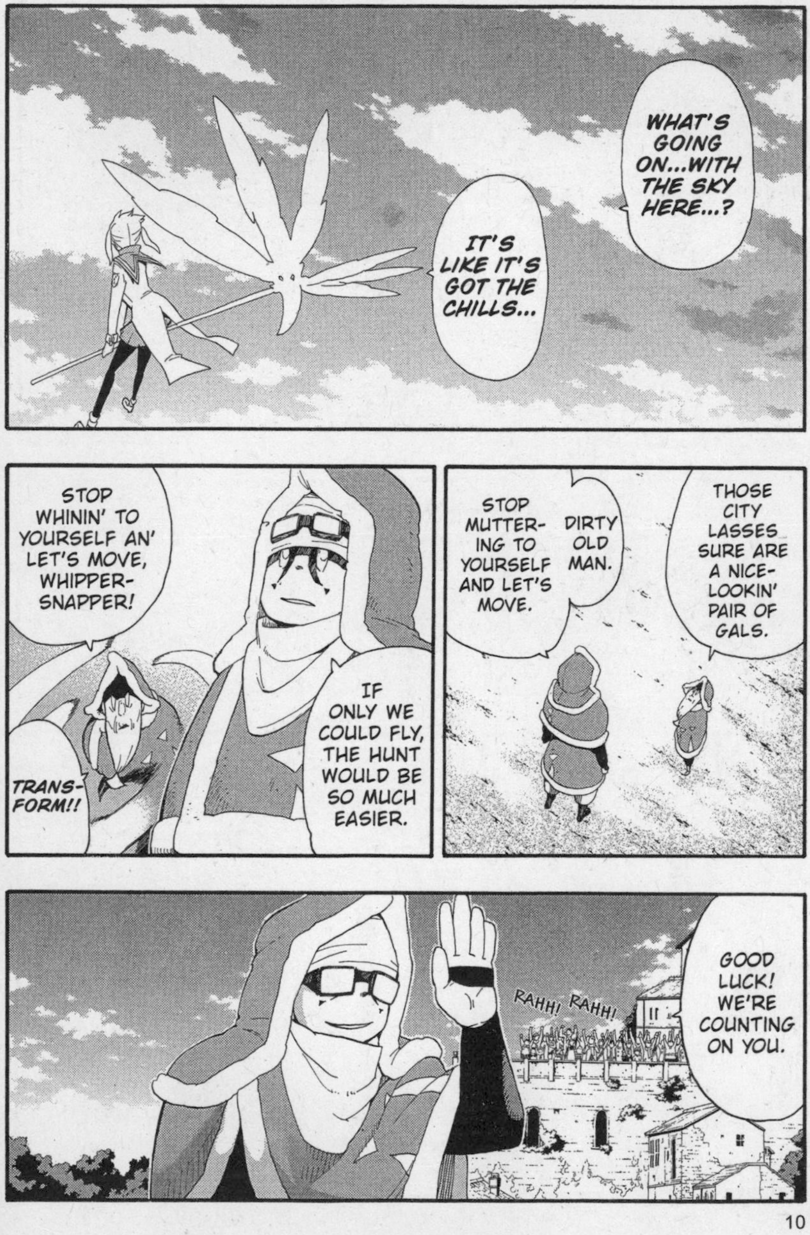
WHAT'S GOING ON...WITH THE SKY HERE...?
IT'S LIKE IT'S GOT THE CHILLS...
THOSE CITY LASSES SURE ARE A NICE-LOOKIN' PAIR OF GALS.
DIRTY OLD MAN.
STOP MUTTER-ING TO YOURSELF AND LET'S MOVE.
IF ONLY WE COULD FLY, THE HUNT WOULD BE SO MUCH EASIER.
TRANS-FORM!!
STOP WHININ' TO YOURSELF AN' LET'S MOVE, WHIPPER-SNAPPER!
GOOD LUCK! WE'RE COUNTING ON YOU.
RAHH! RAHH!

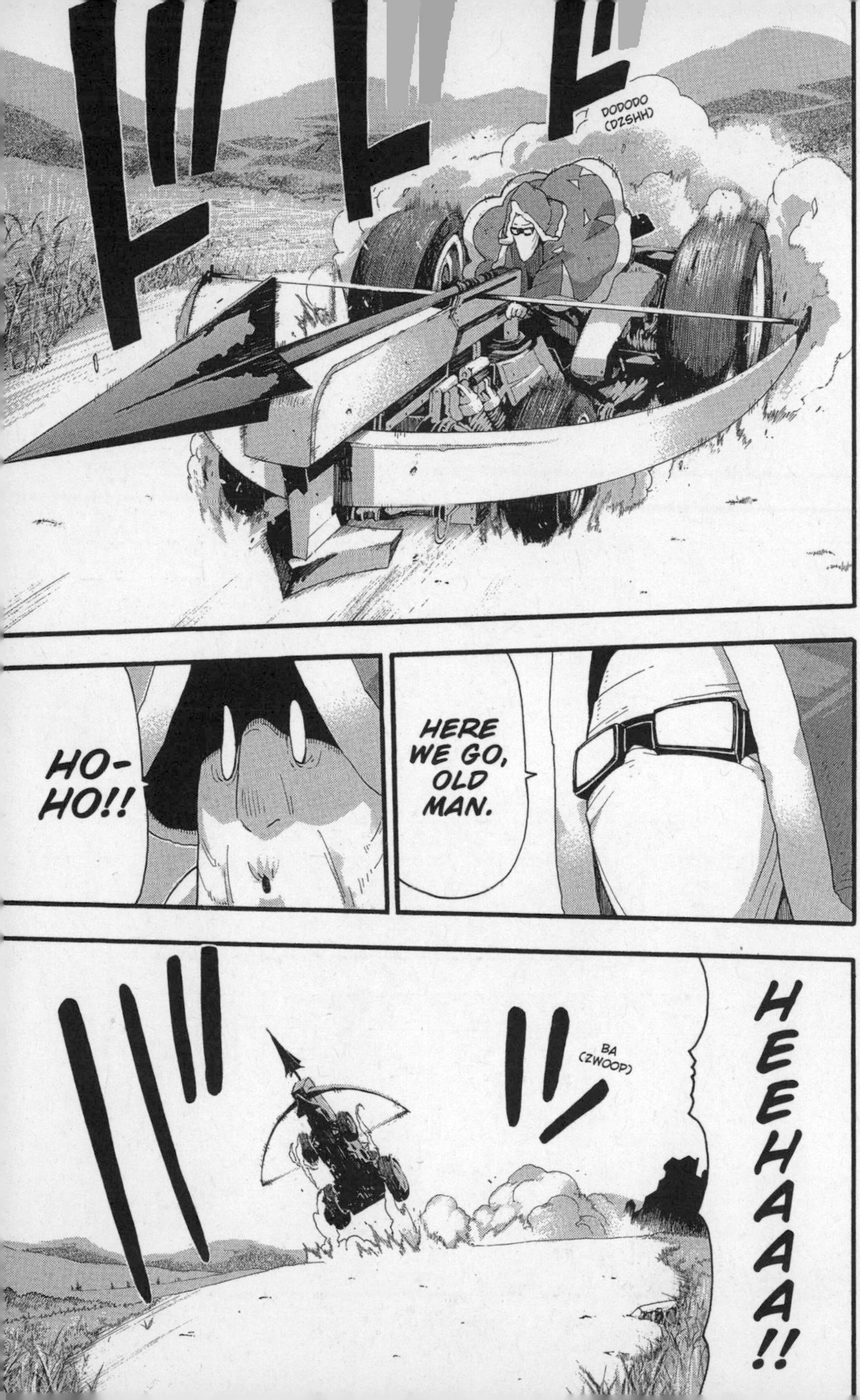
DODODO (DZSHH)
HERE WE GO, OLD MAN.
HO-HO!!
HEEHAAAA!!
BA (ZWOOP)

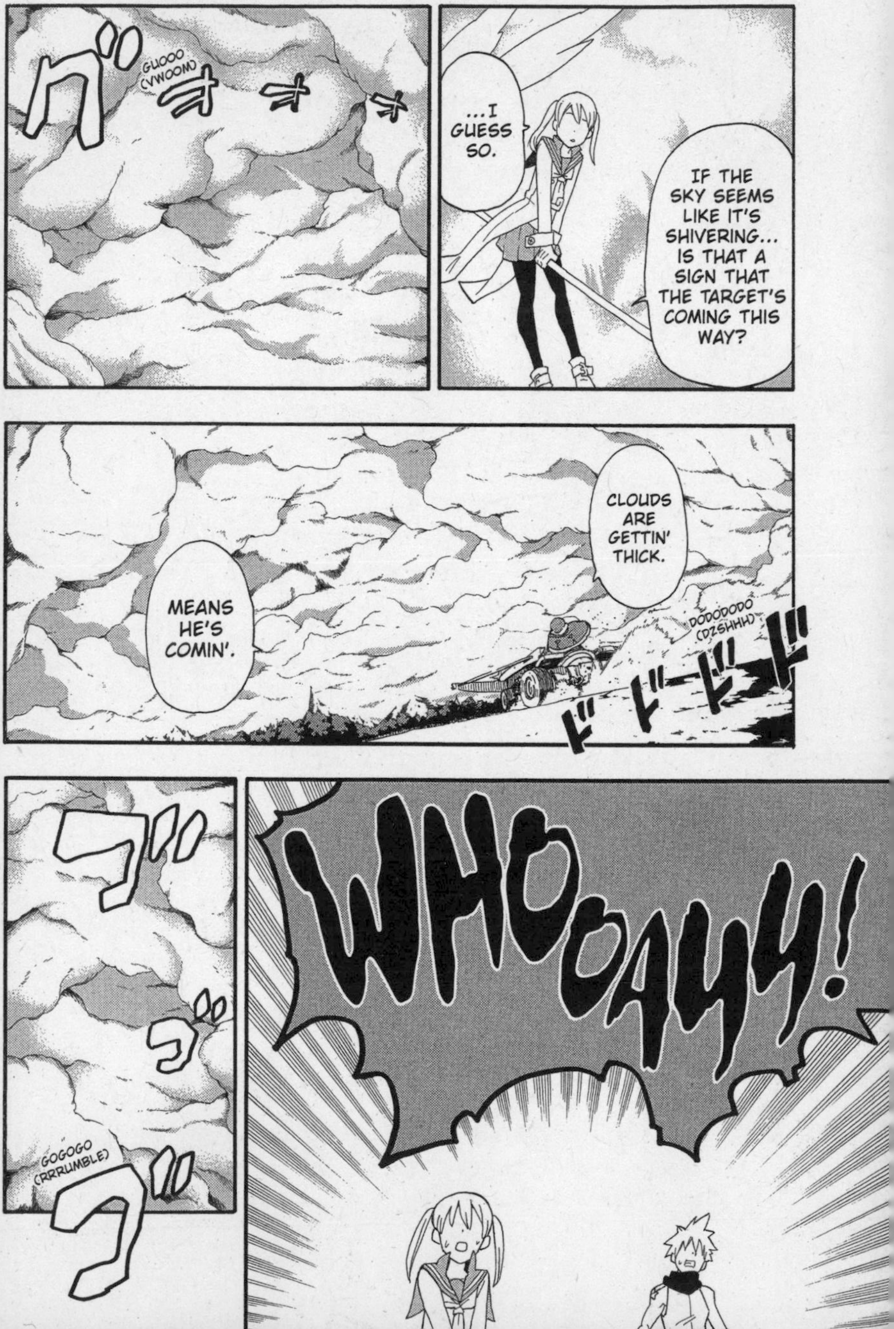
IF THE SKY SEEMS LIKE IT'S SHIVERING... IS THAT A SIGN THAT THE TARGET'S COMING THIS WAY?
...I GUESS SO.
GUOOO (VWOOM)
CLOUDS ARE GETTIN' THICK.
DODODODO (DZSHHH)
MEANS HE'S COMIN'.
WHOOAYY!
GOGOGO (RRRUMBLE)

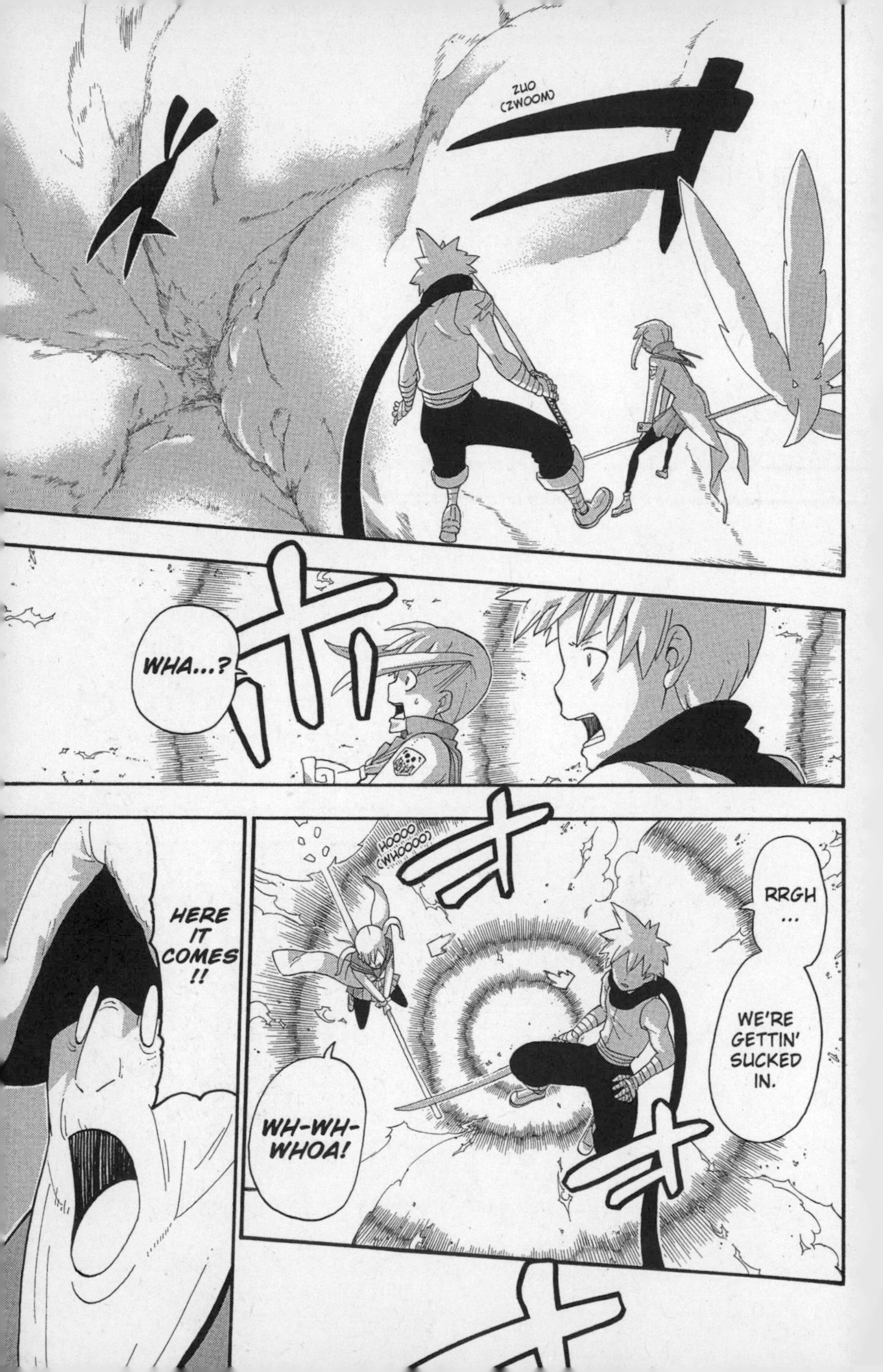
ZUO
(ZWOOM)
WHA...?
RRGH ...
WE'RE GETTIN' SUCKED IN.
HOOOO
(WHOOOO)
WH-WH-WHOA!
HERE IT COMES!!

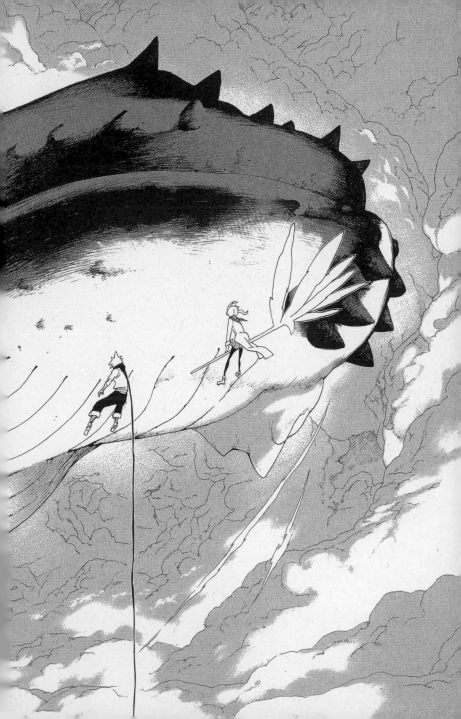

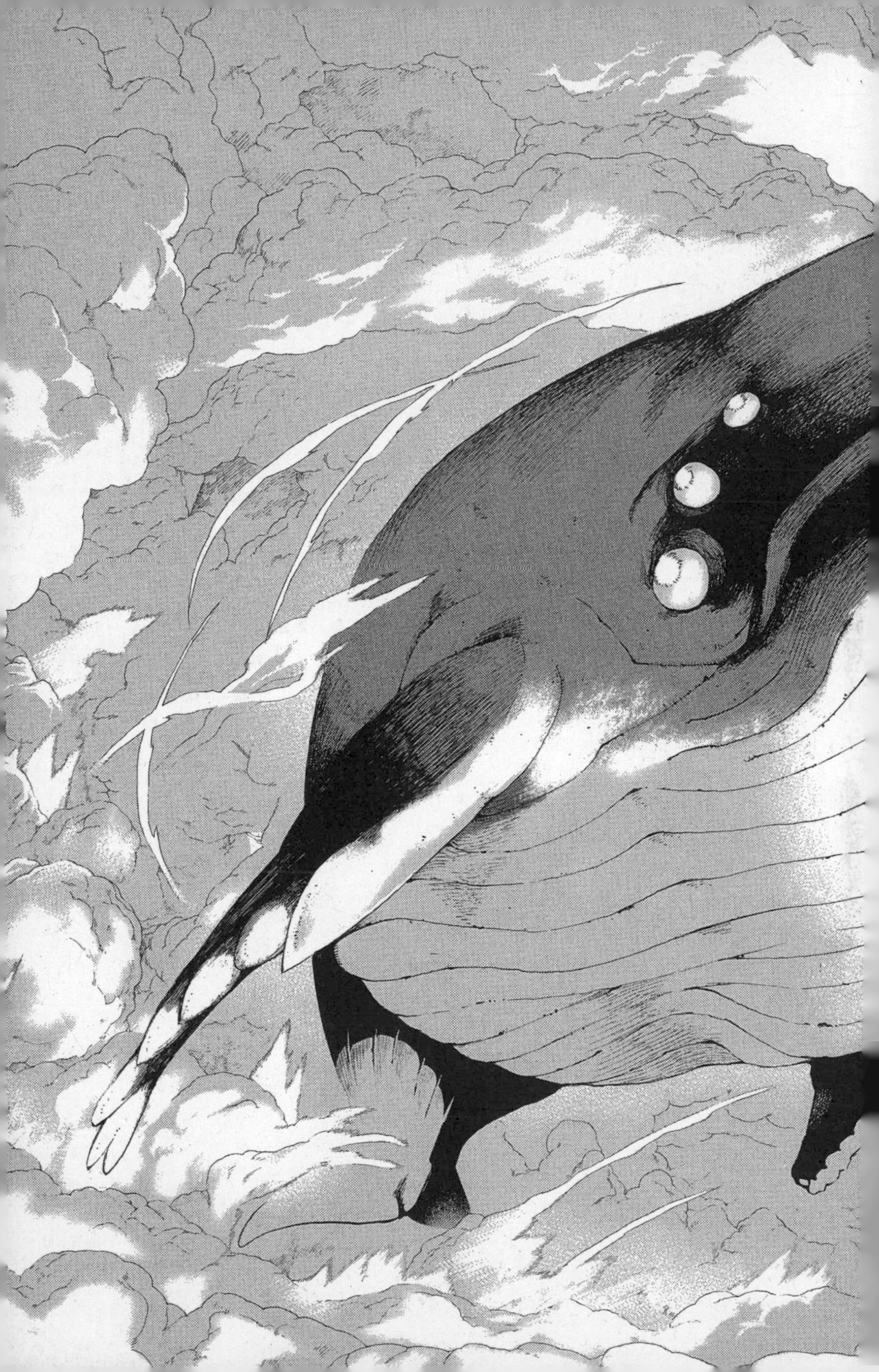

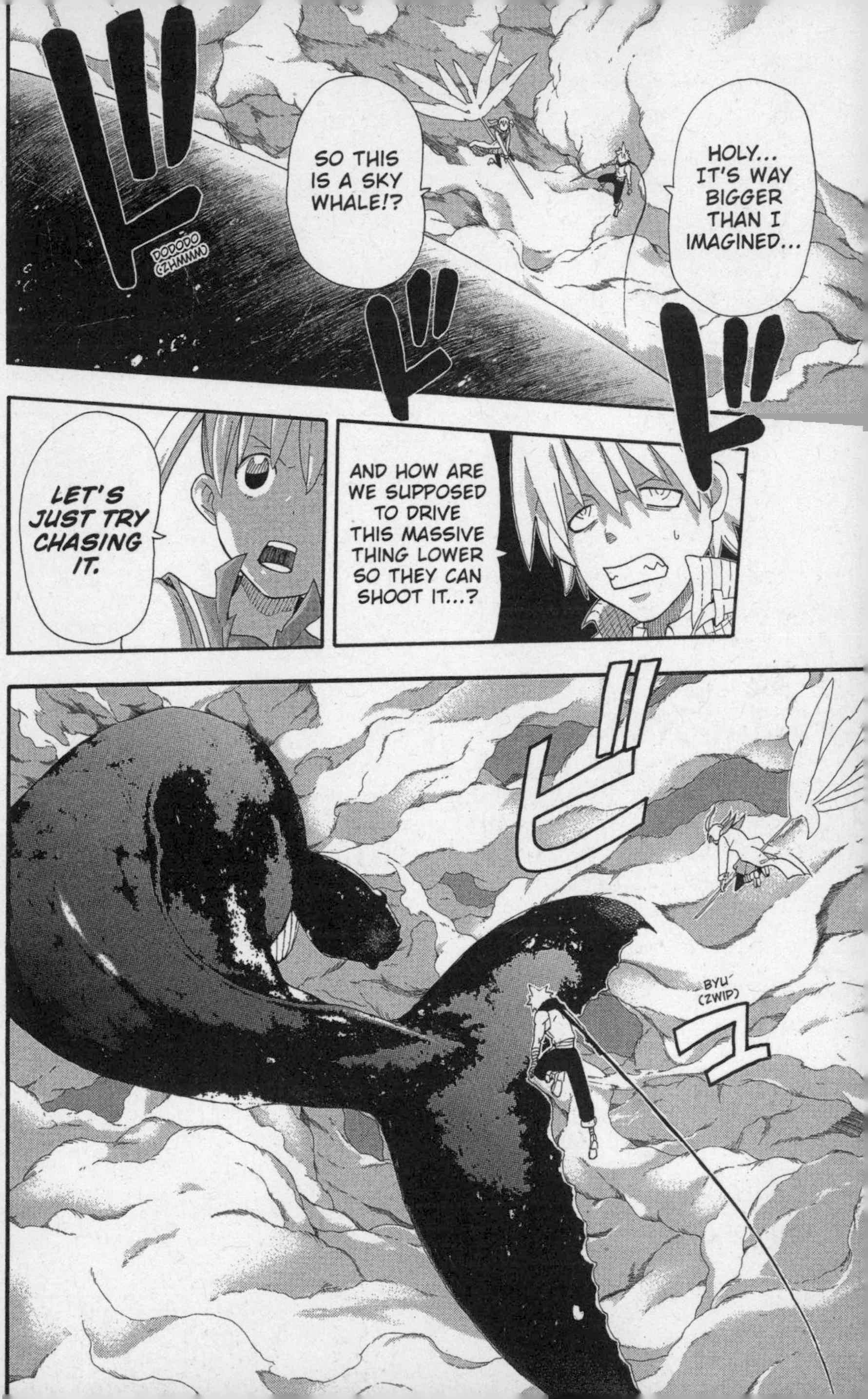
HOLY... IT'S WAY BIGGER THAN I IMAGINED...
SO THIS IS A SKY WHALE!?
DODODO (ZHMMM)
AND HOW ARE WE SUPPOSED TO DRIVE THIS MASSIVE THING LOWER SO THEY CAN SHOOT IT...?
LET'S JUST TRY CHASING IT.
BYU (ZWIP)

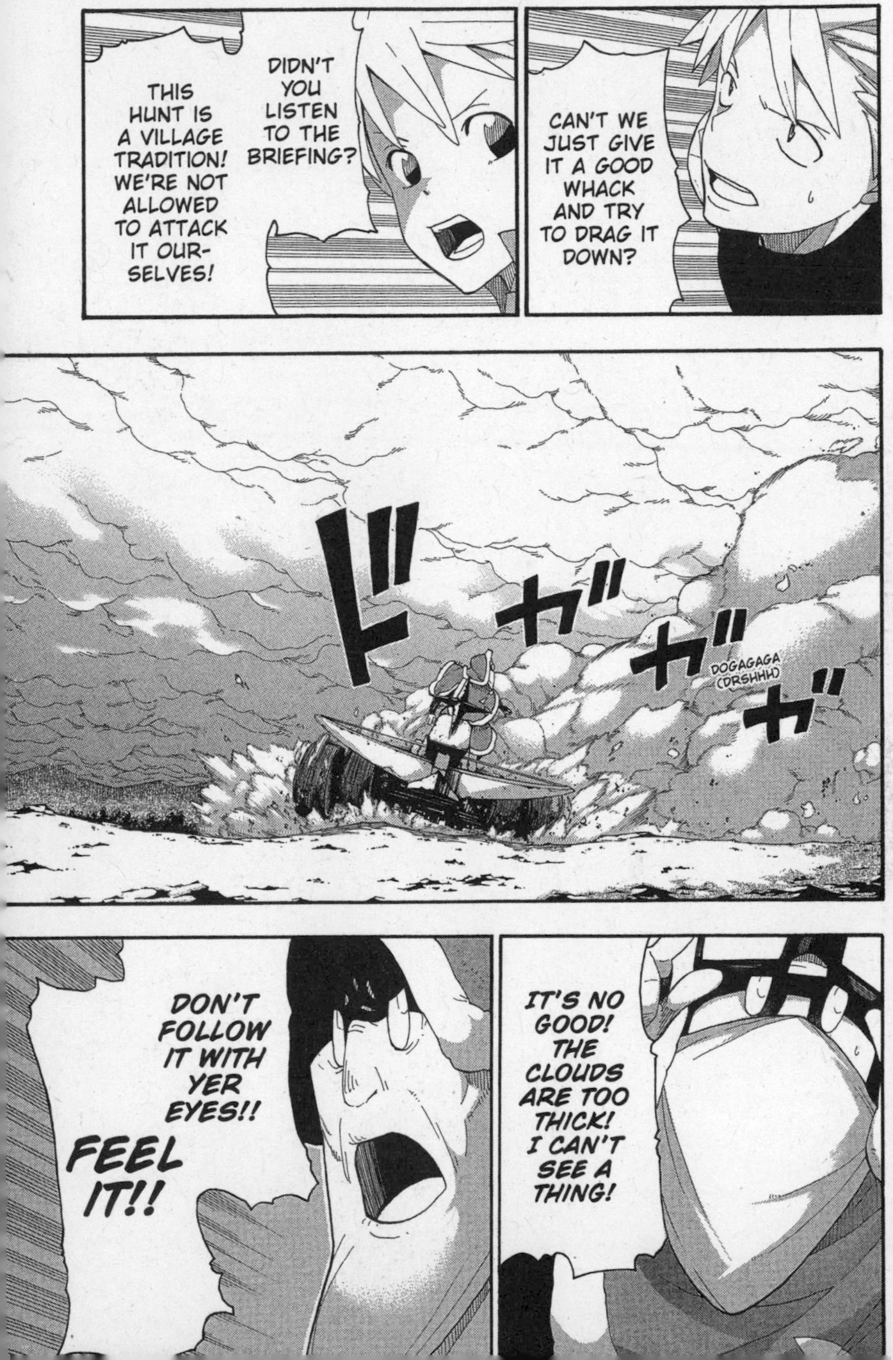
CAN'T WE JUST GIVE IT A GOOD WHACK AND TRY TO DRAG IT DOWN?
DIDN'T YOU LISTEN TO THE BRIEFING?
THIS HUNT IS A VILLAGE TRADITION! WE'RE NOT ALLOWED TO ATTACK IT OUR-SELVES!
ドガガガ
DOGAGAGA (DRSHHH)
IT'S NO GOOD! THE CLOUDS ARE TOO THICK! I CAN'T SEE A THING!
DON'T FOLLOW IT WITH YER EYES!!
FEEL IT!!

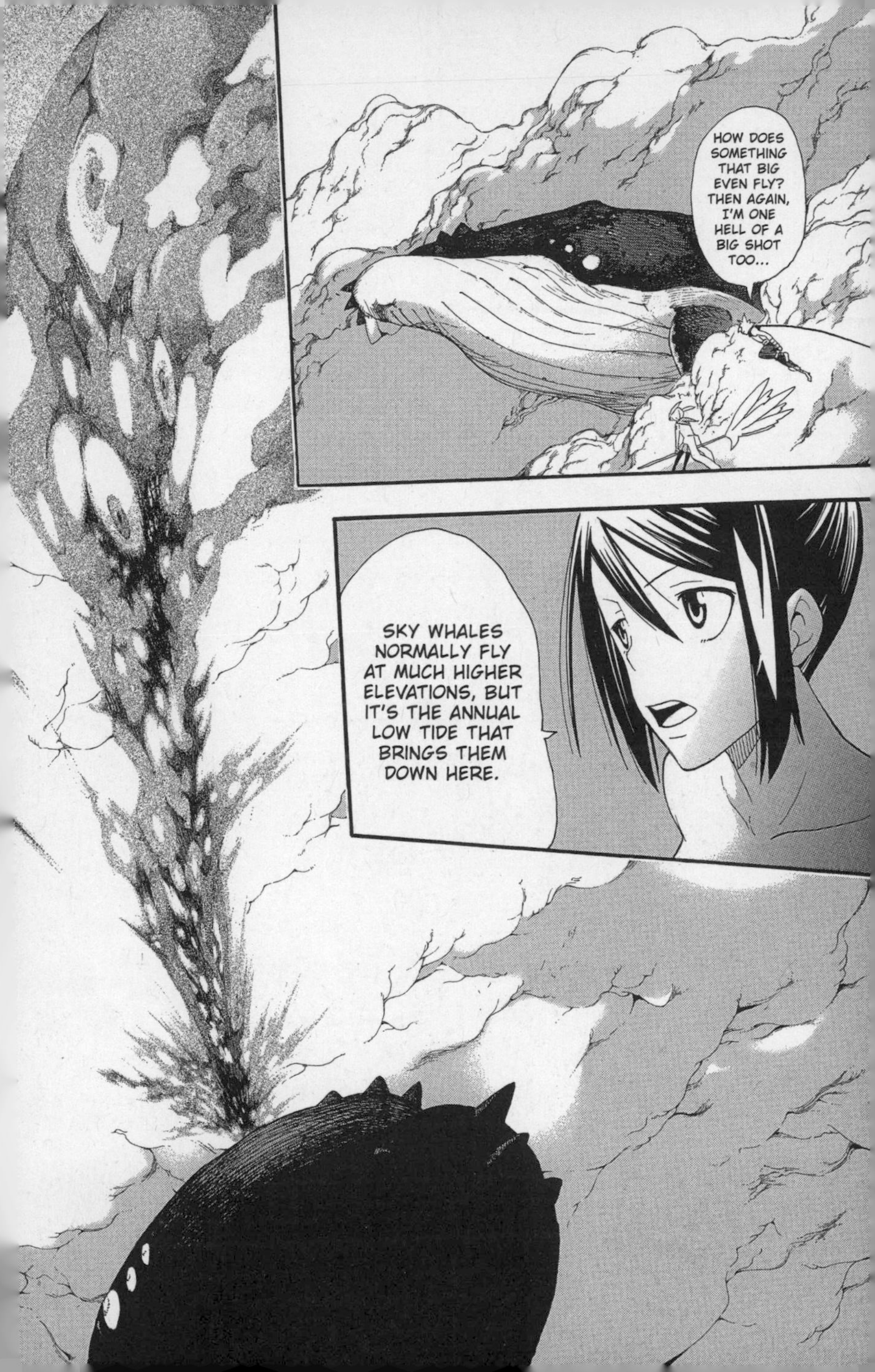
HOW DOES SOMETHING THAT BIG EVEN FLY? THEN AGAIN, I'M ONE HELL OF A BIG SHOT TOO...
SKY WHALES NORMALLY FLY AT MUCH HIGHER ELEVATIONS, BUT IT'S THE ANNUAL LOW TIDE THAT BRINGS THEM DOWN HERE.

WHOA!! THAR SHE BLOWS!!
!
IT'S...
...MAD-NESS...
!?
I THOUGHT IT MIGHT BE... I COULDN'T TELL FOR SURE FROM THE GROUND...
...BUT THE MADNESS IS MUCH THICKER UP HERE...
WHAT DOES IT MEAN...?

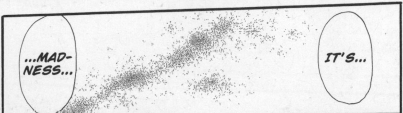

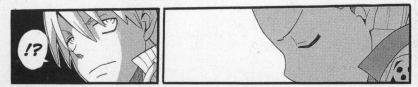

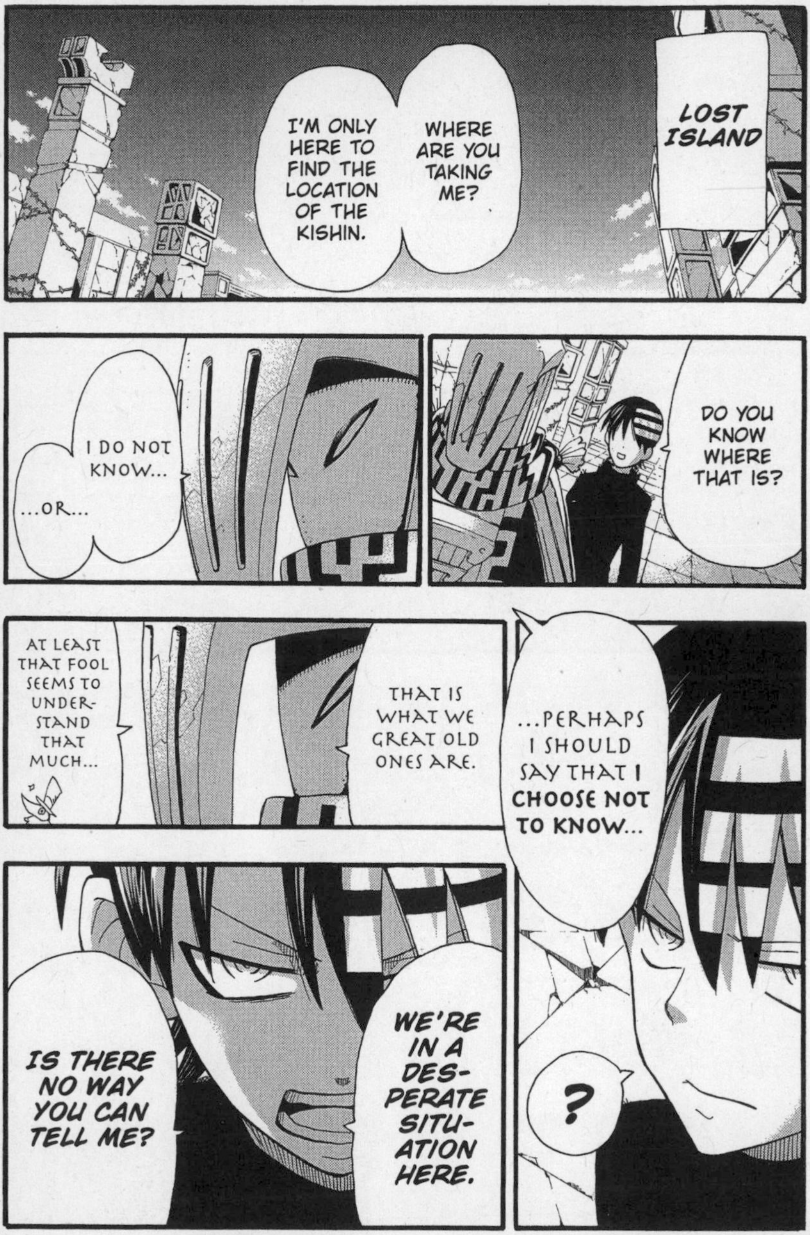
LOST ISLAND
WHERE ARE YOU TAKING ME?
I'M ONLY HERE TO FIND THE LOCATION OF THE KISHIN.
DO YOU KNOW WHERE THAT IS?
I DO NOT KNOW...
...OR...
...PERHAPS I SHOULD SAY THAT I CHOOSE NOT TO KNOW...
?
THAT IS WHAT WE GREAT OLD ONES ARE.
AT LEAST THAT FOOL SEEMS TO UNDERSTAND THAT MUCH...
WE'RE IN A DESPERATE SITUATION HERE.
IS THERE NO WAY YOU CAN TELL ME?

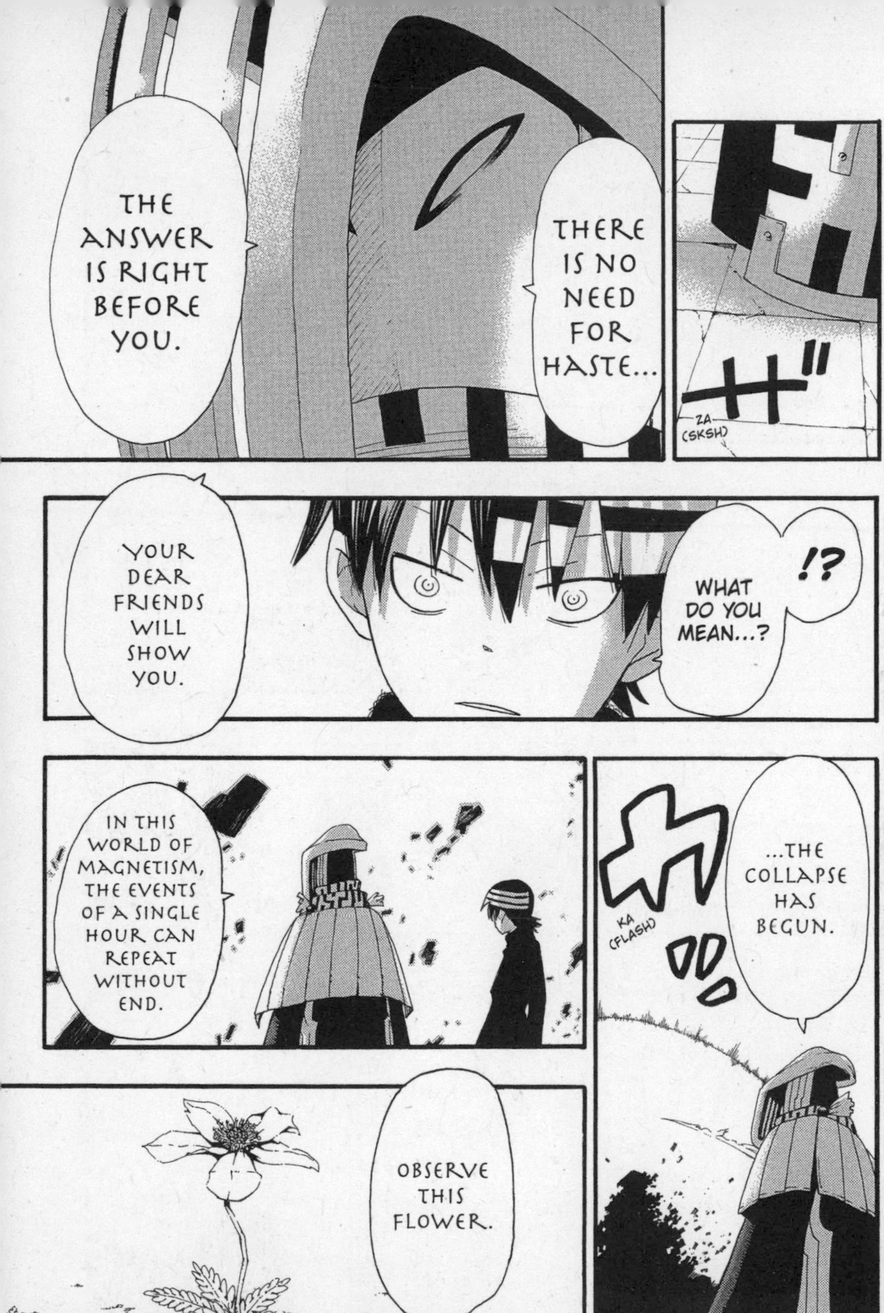
ZA (SKSH)
THERE IS NO NEED FOR HASTE...
THE ANSWER IS RIGHT BEFORE YOU.
!?
WHAT DO YOU MEAN...?
YOUR DEAR FRIENDS WILL SHOW YOU.
...THE COLLAPSE HAS BEGUN.
KA (FLASH)
IN THIS WORLD OF MAGNETISM, THE EVENTS OF A SINGLE HOUR CAN REPEAT WITHOUT END.
OBSERVE THIS FLOWER.

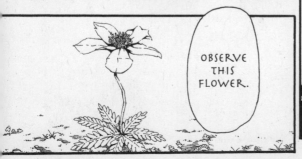

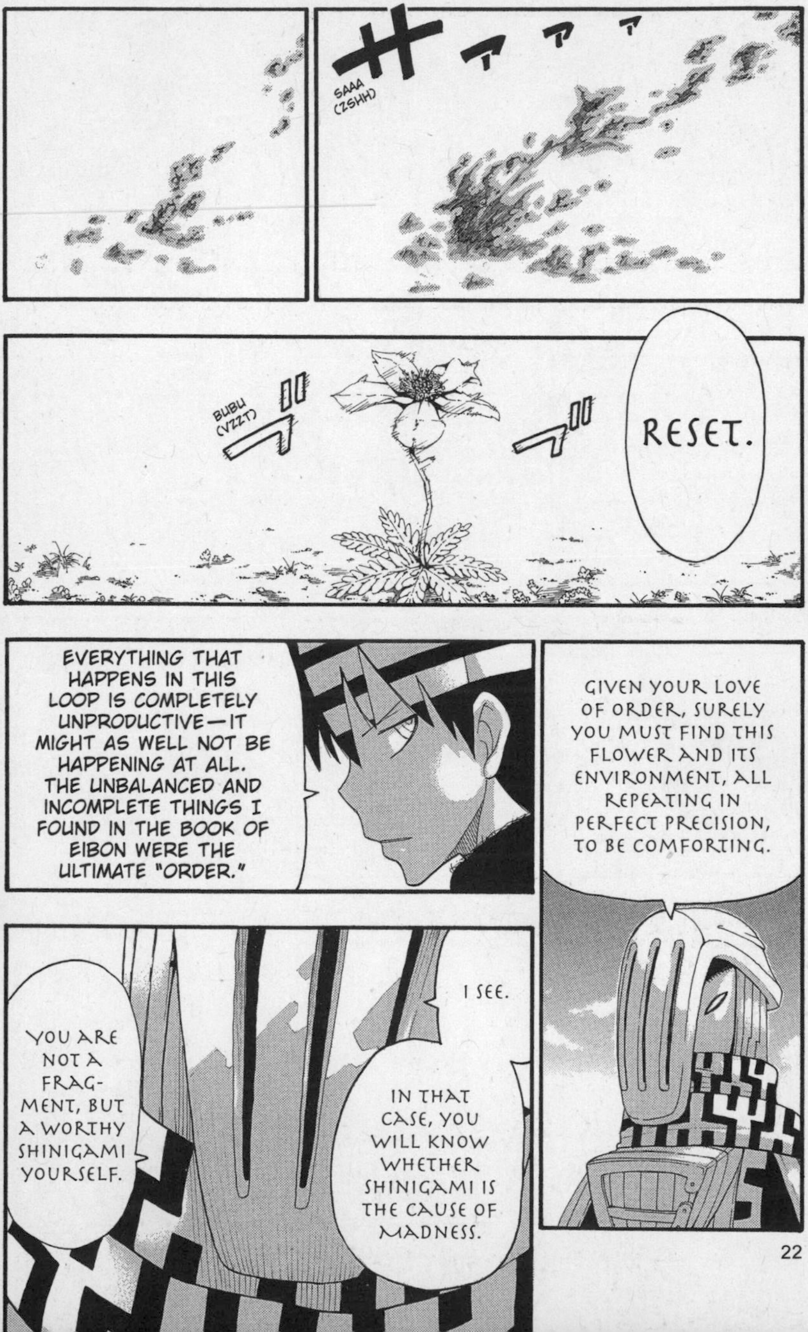
SAAA (ZSHH)
RESET.
BUBU (VZZT)
GIVEN YOUR LOVE OF ORDER, SURELY YOU MUST FIND THIS FLOWER AND ITS ENVIRONMENT, ALL REPEATING IN PERFECT PRECISION, TO BE COMFORTING.
EVERYTHING THAT HAPPENS IN THIS LOOP IS COMPLETELY UNPRODUCTIVE—IT MIGHT AS WELL NOT BE HAPPENING AT ALL. THE UNBALANCED AND INCOMPLETE THINGS I FOUND IN THE BOOK OF EIBON WERE THE ULTIMATE "ORDER."
I SEE.
IN THAT CASE, YOU WILL KNOW WHETHER SHINIGAMI IS THE CAUSE OF MADNESS.
YOU ARE NOT A FRAG-MENT, BUT A WORTHY SHINIGAMI YOURSELF.

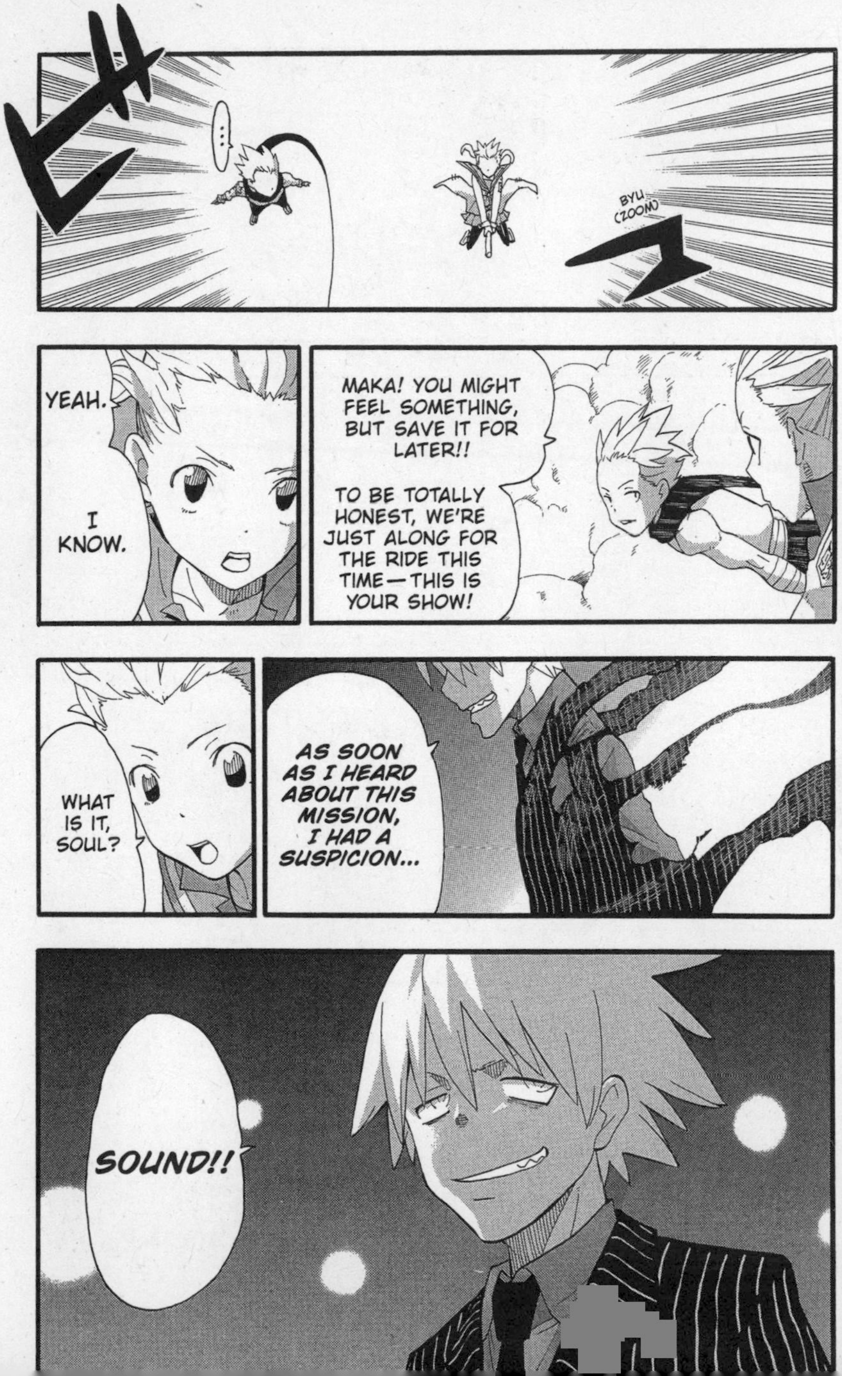
BYU (ZOOM)
...
MAKA! YOU MIGHT FEEL SOMETHING, BUT SAVE IT FOR LATER!!
TO BE TOTALLY HONEST, WE'RE JUST ALONG FOR THE RIDE THIS TIME—THIS IS YOUR SHOW!
YEAH.
I KNOW.
AS SOON AS I HEARD ABOUT THIS MISSION, I HAD A SUSPICION...
WHAT IS IT, SOUL?
SOUND!!

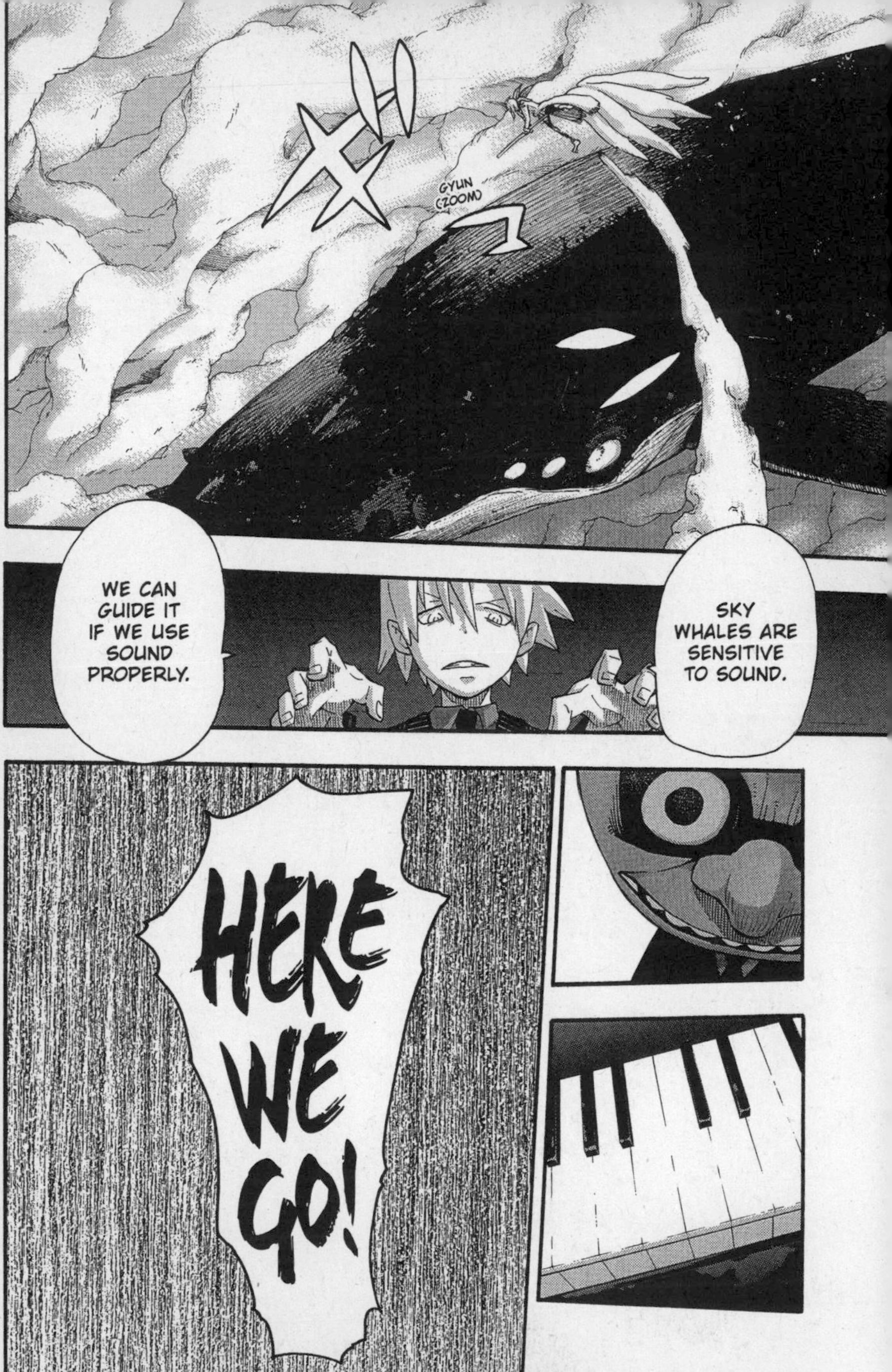
GYUN (ZOOM)
SKY WHALES ARE SENSITIVE TO SOUND.
WE CAN GUIDE IT IF WE USE SOUND PROPERLY.
HERE WE GO!

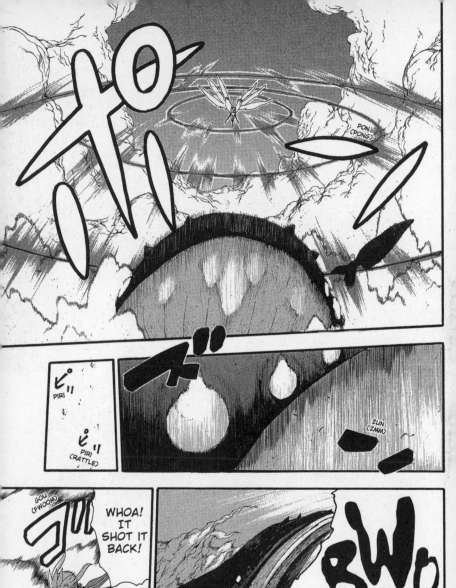

PON
(PONG)

PIRI

PIRI
(RATTLE)

ZUN
(ZMM)

GOU
(FWOOM)

WHOA!
IT
SHOT IT
BACK!

BWOHH!

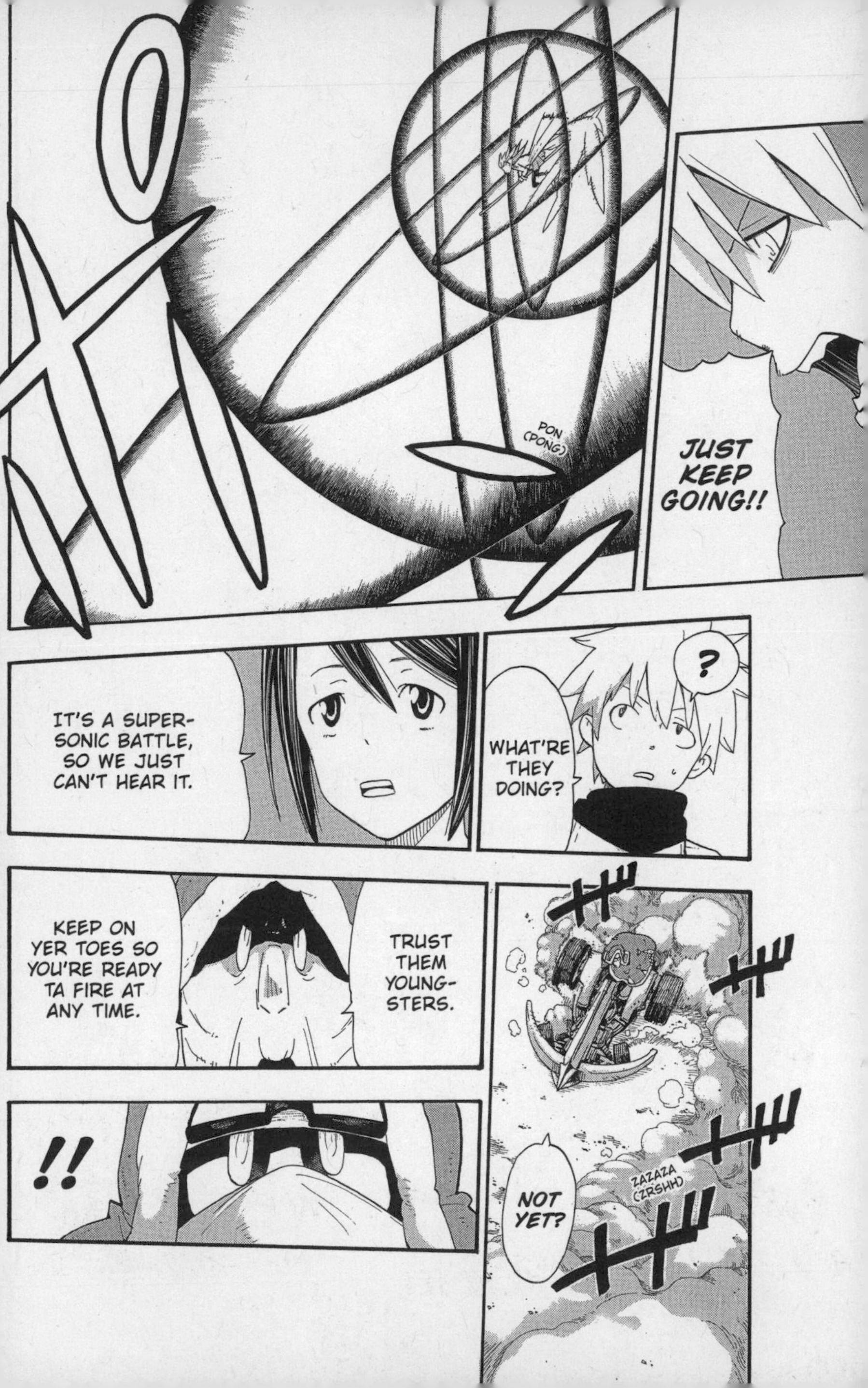
JUST KEEP GOING!!
PON (PONG)
?
WHAT'RE THEY DOING?
IT'S A SUPER-SONIC BATTLE, SO WE JUST CAN'T HEAR IT.
ZAZAZA (ZRSHH)
NOT YET?
TRUST THEM YOUNG-STERS.
KEEP ON YER TOES SO YOU'RE READY TA FIRE AT ANY TIME.
!!

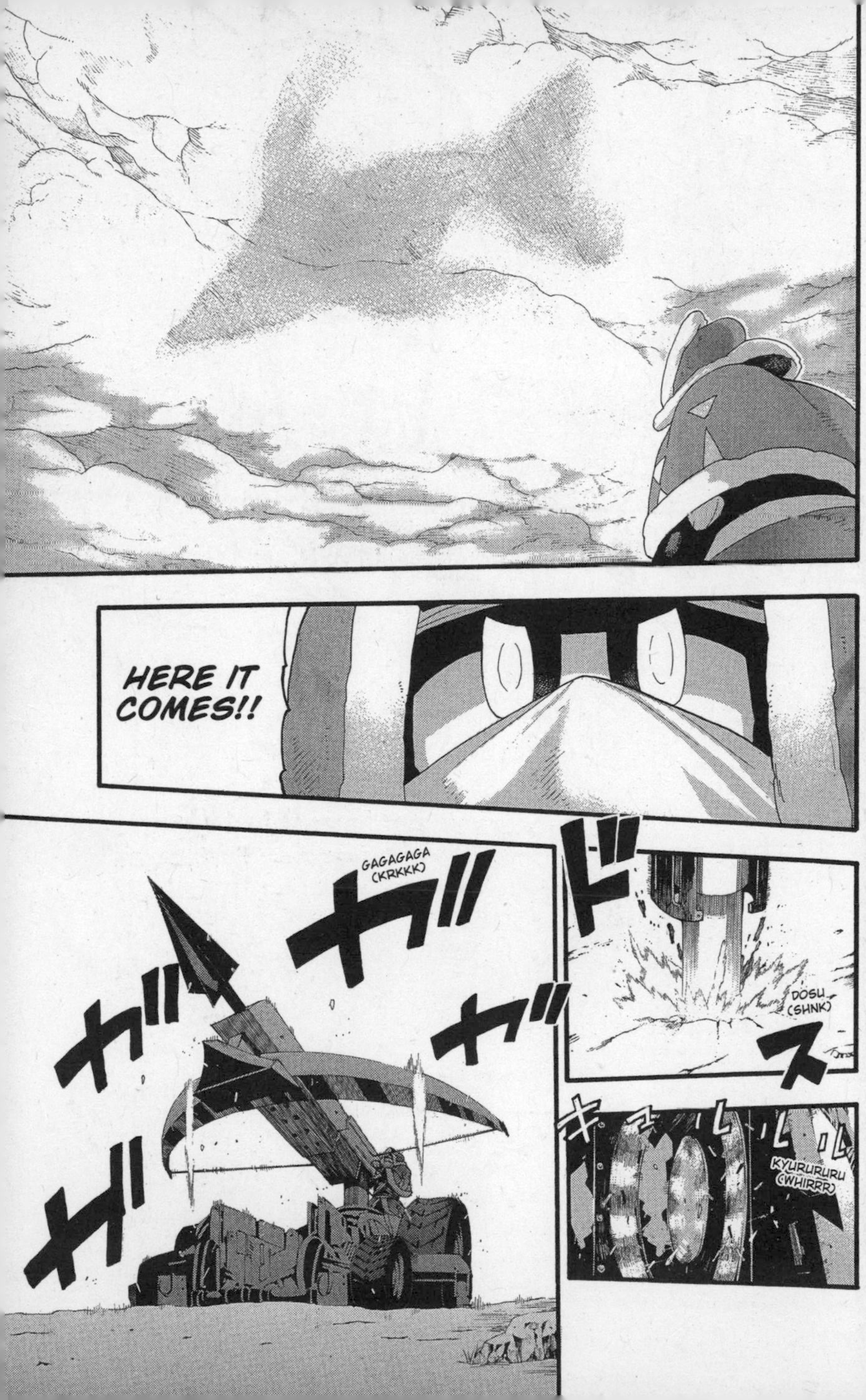
HERE IT COMES!!
DOSU (SHNK)
KYURURURU (WHIRRR)
GAGAGAGA (KRKKK)

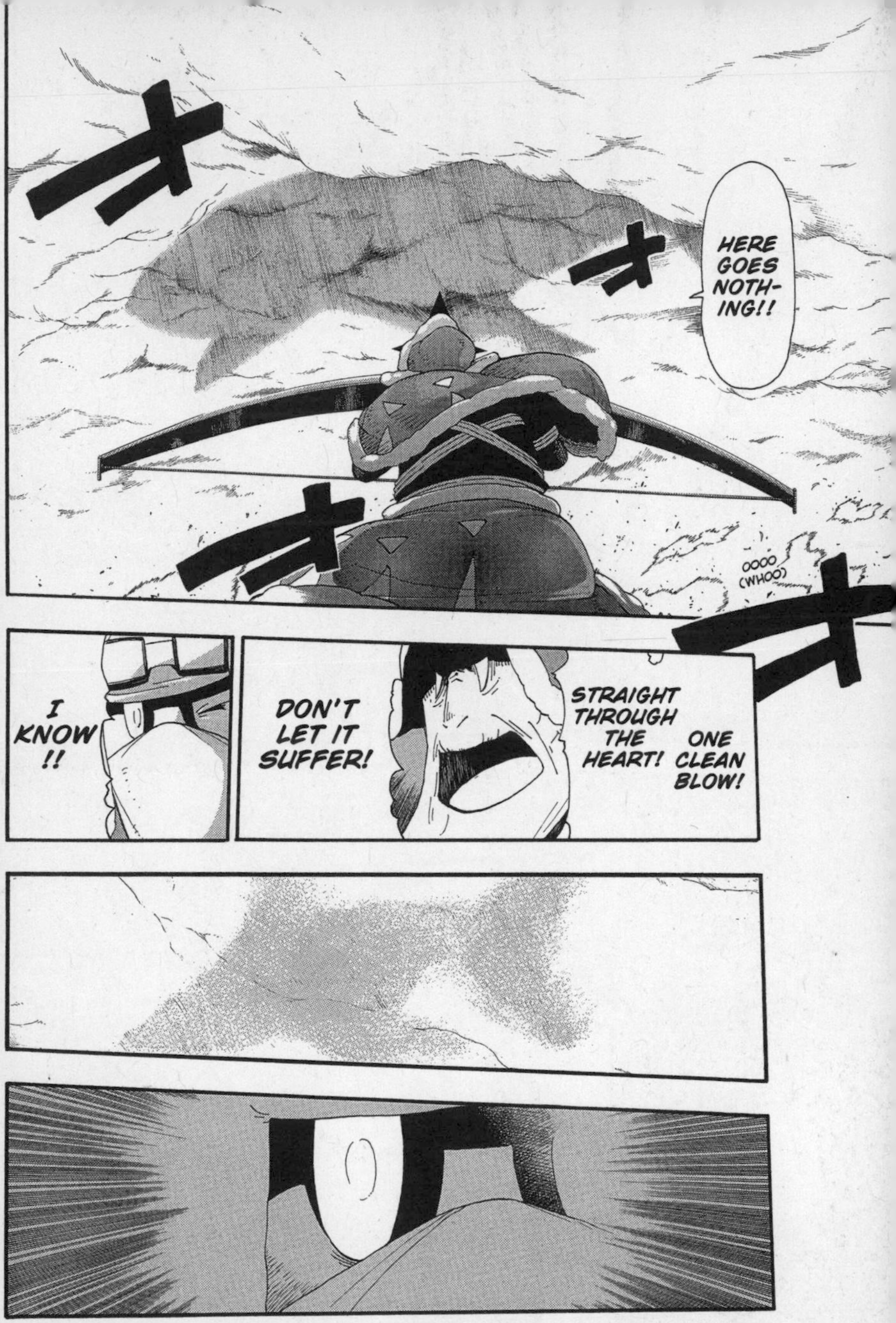
HERE GOES NOTH-ING!!
OOOO (WHOO)
STRAIGHT THROUGH THE HEART!
ONE CLEAN BLOW!
DON'T LET IT SUFFER!
I KNOW!!

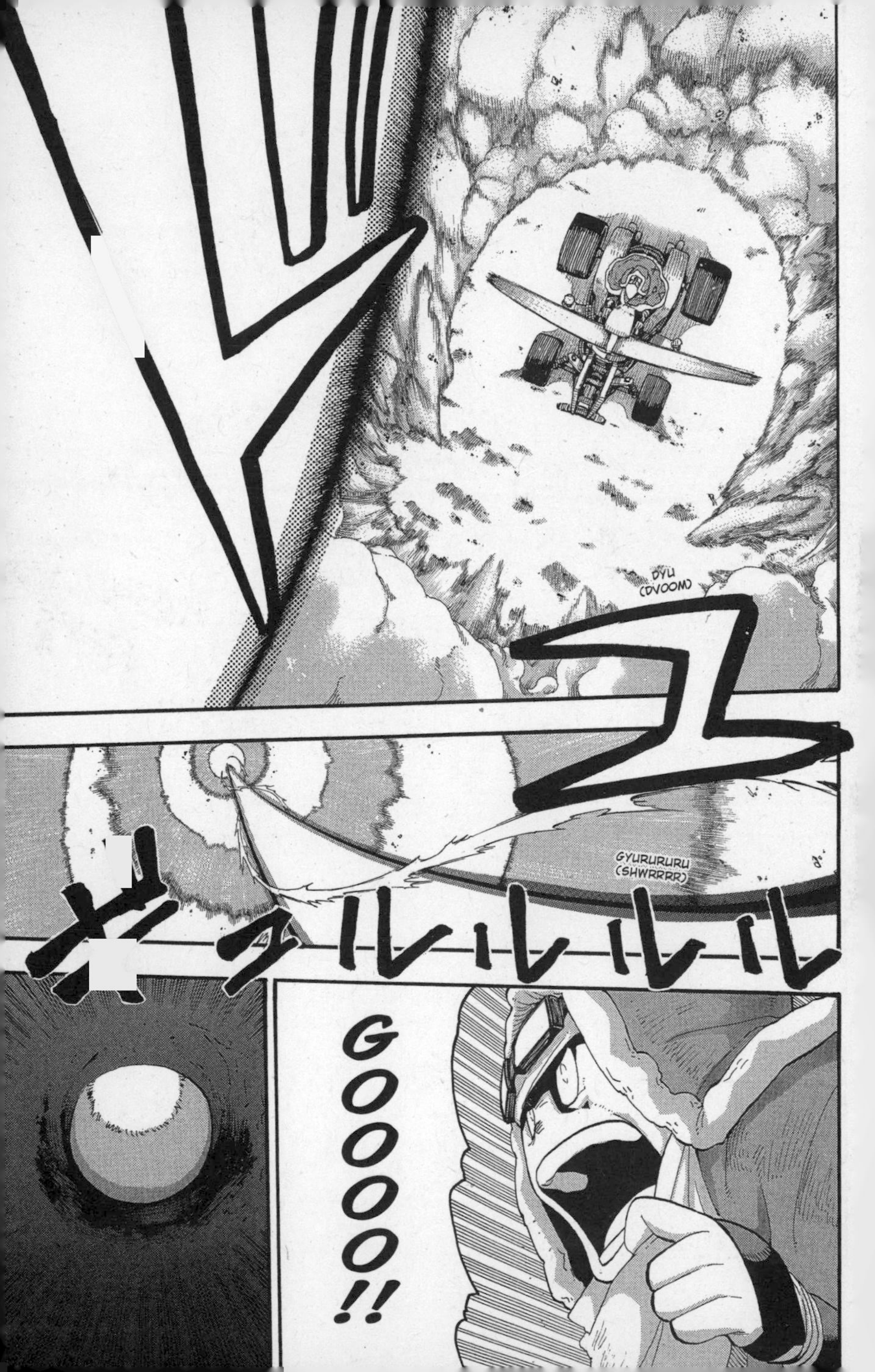
DYU
(DVOOM)
GYURURURU
(SHWRRRR)
GOOOOO!!

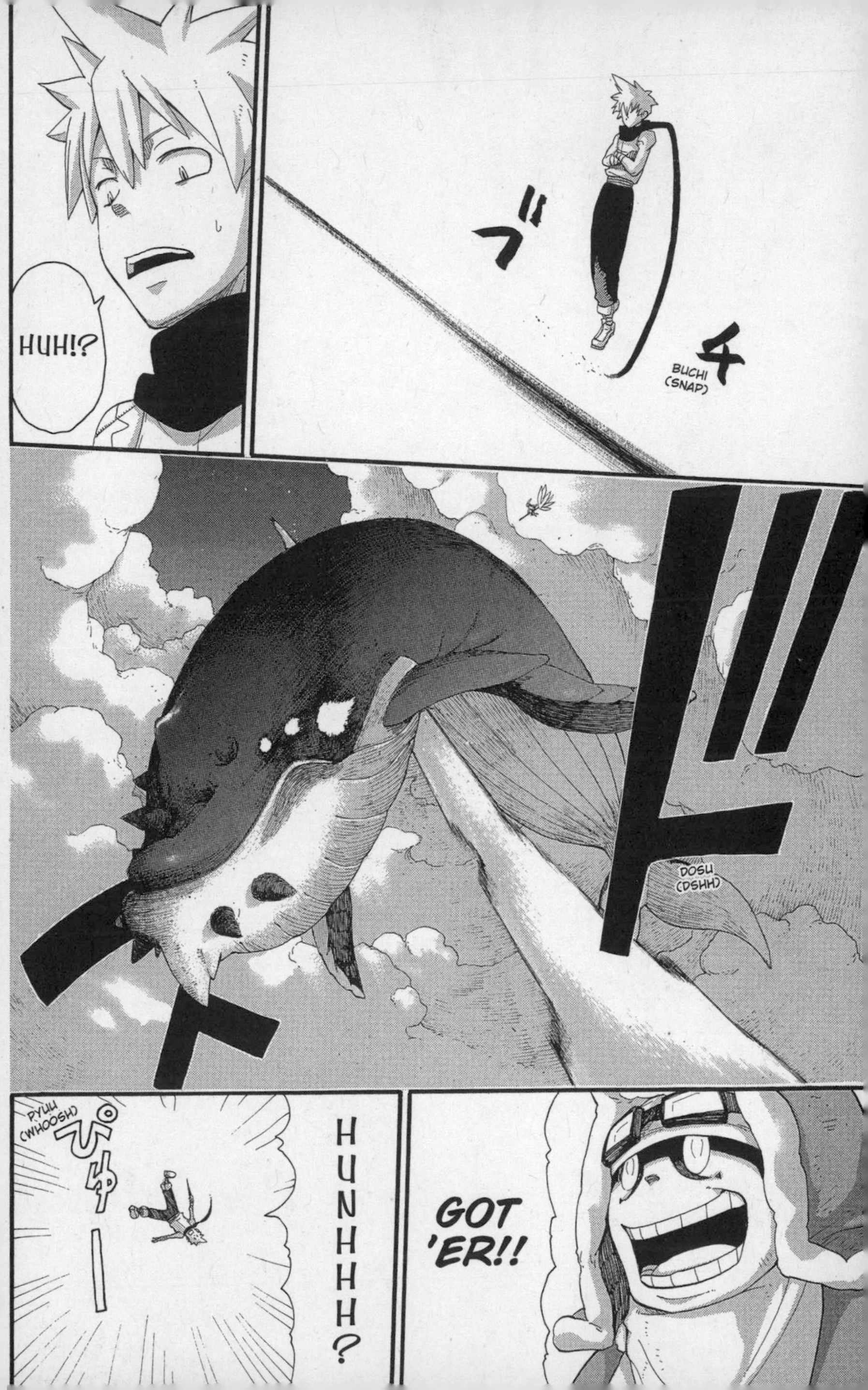
BUCHI (SNAP)
HUH!?
DOSU (DSHH)
GOT 'ER!!
PYUU (WHOOSH)
HUNHHHH?

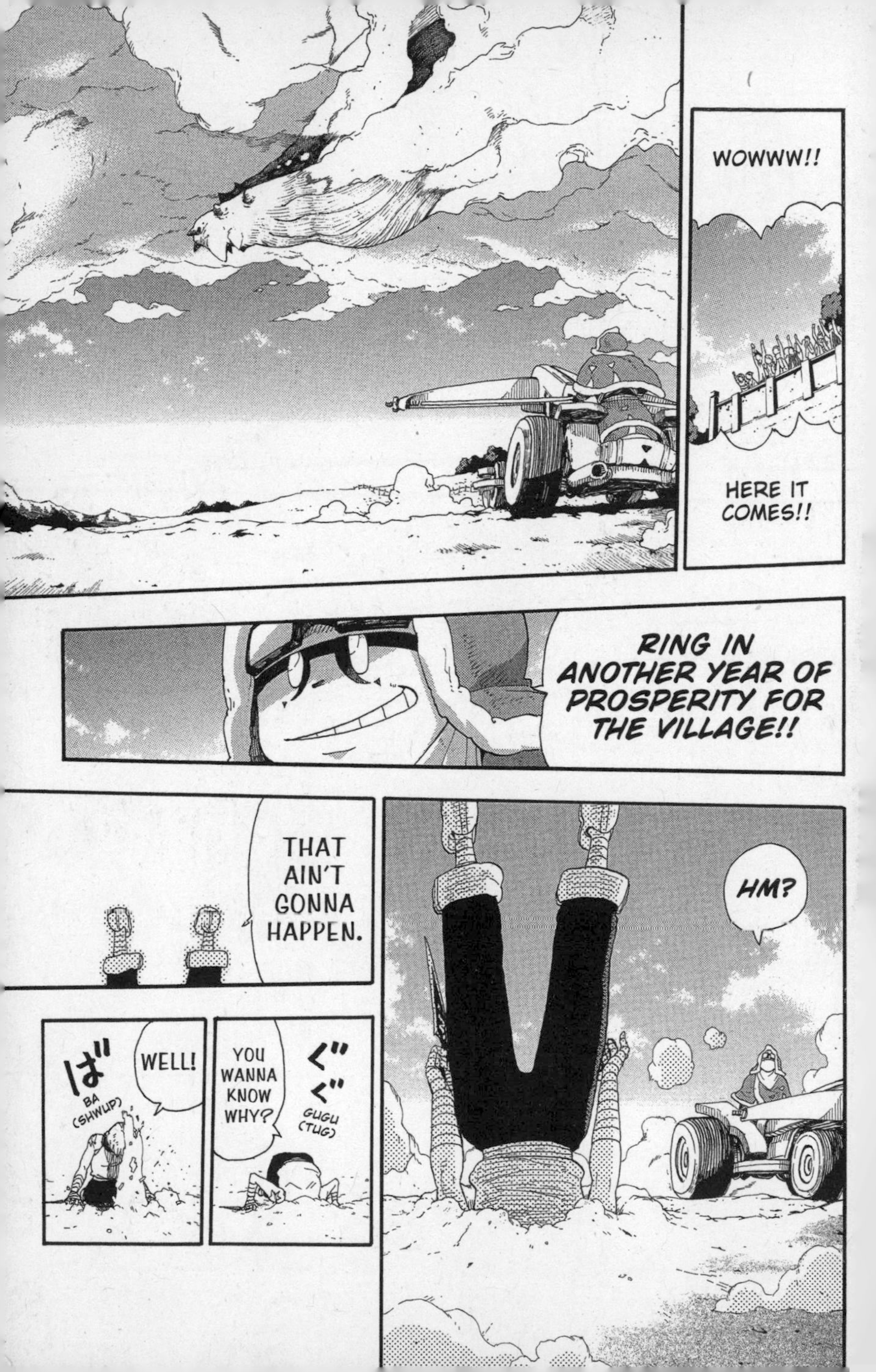
WOWWW!!
HERE IT COMES!!
RING IN ANOTHER YEAR OF PROSPERITY FOR THE VILLAGE!!
HM?
THAT AIN'T GONNA HAPPEN.
YOU WANNA KNOW WHY?
ぐぐ
GUGU (TUG)
WELL!
ば
BA (SHWUP)

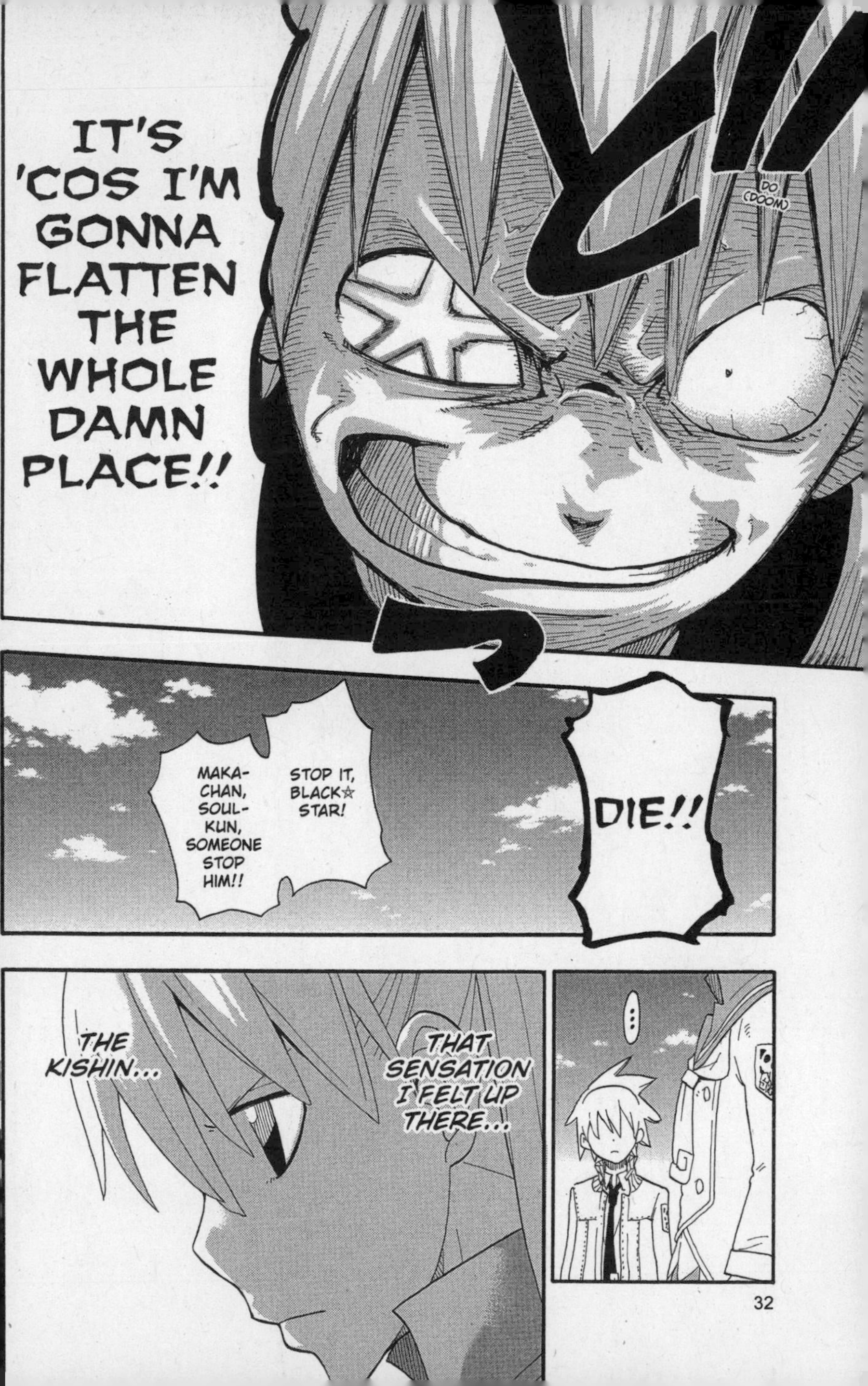
DO (DOOM)
IT'S 'COS I'M GONNA FLATTEN THE WHOLE DAMN PLACE!!
DIE!!
STOP IT, BLACK☆STAR!
MAKA-CHAN, SOUL-KUN, SOMEONE STOP HIM!!
...
THAT SENSATION I FELT UP THERE...
THE KISHIN...

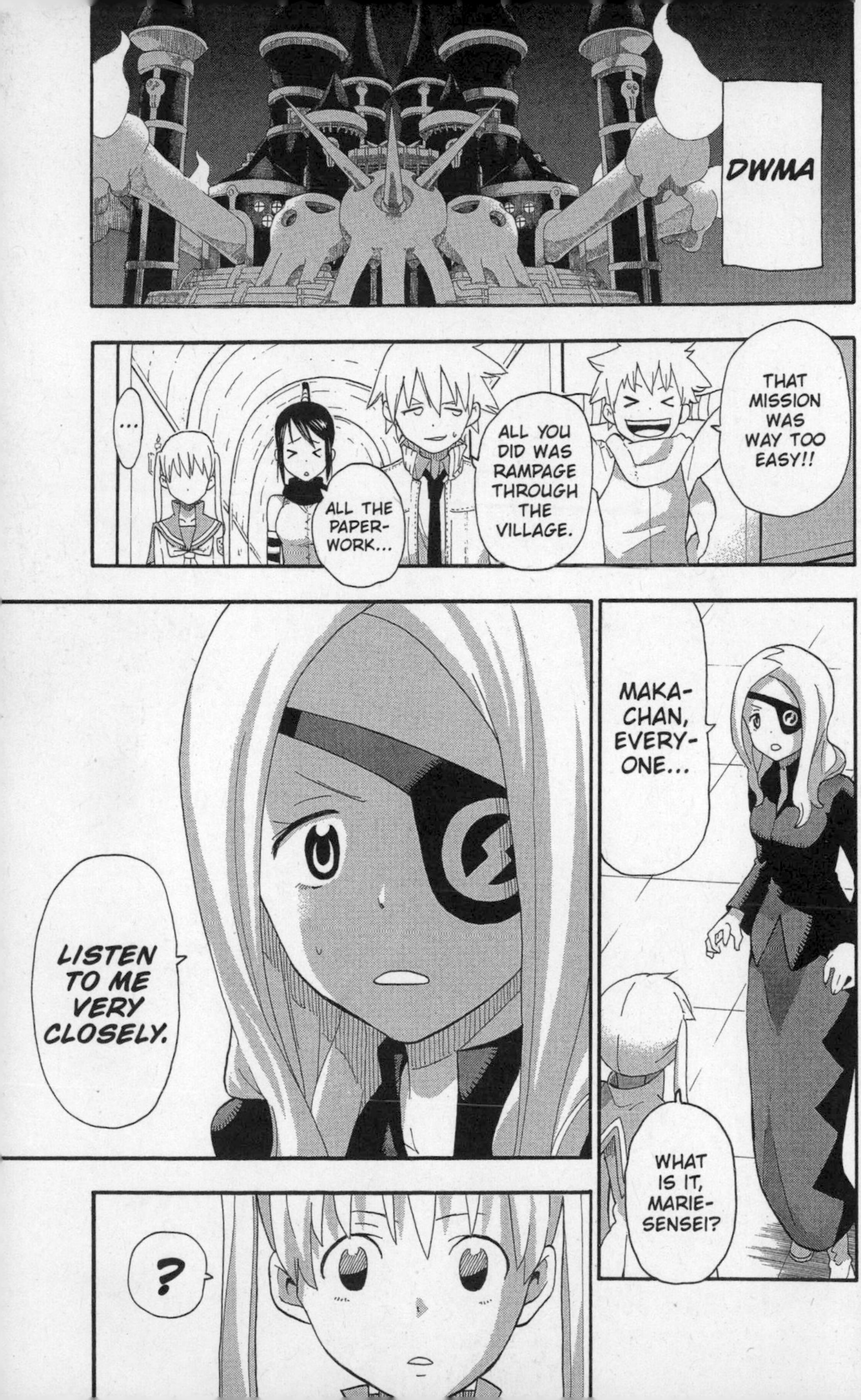
DWMA
THAT MISSION WAS WAY TOO EASY!!
ALL YOU DID WAS RAMPAGE THROUGH THE VILLAGE.
ALL THE PAPER-WORK...
...
MAKA-CHAN, EVERY-ONE...
WHAT IS IT, MARIE-SENSEI?
LISTEN TO ME VERY CLOSELY.
?

AND THAT WAS WHEN WE LEARNED...

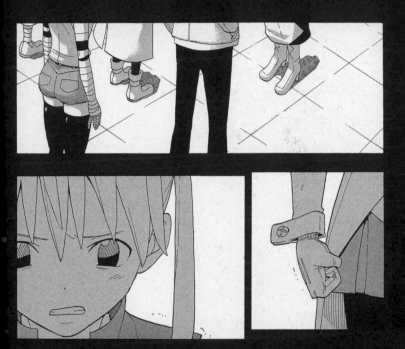

*...THAT CRONA
HAD BEEN PUT ON
SHINIGAMI-SAMA'S
LIST AND THAT
SPARTOI HAD BEEN
GIVEN THE TASK OF
ELIMINATING HIM.*

SOUL EATER

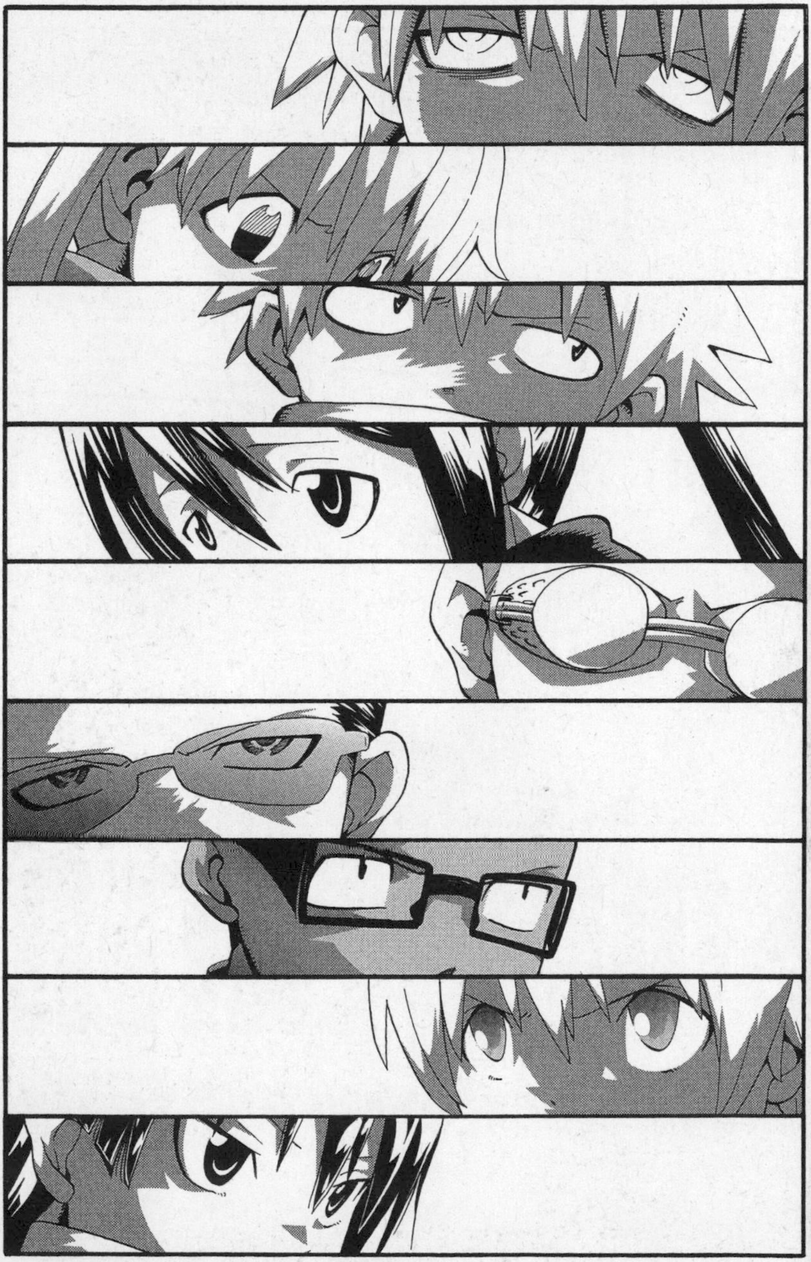

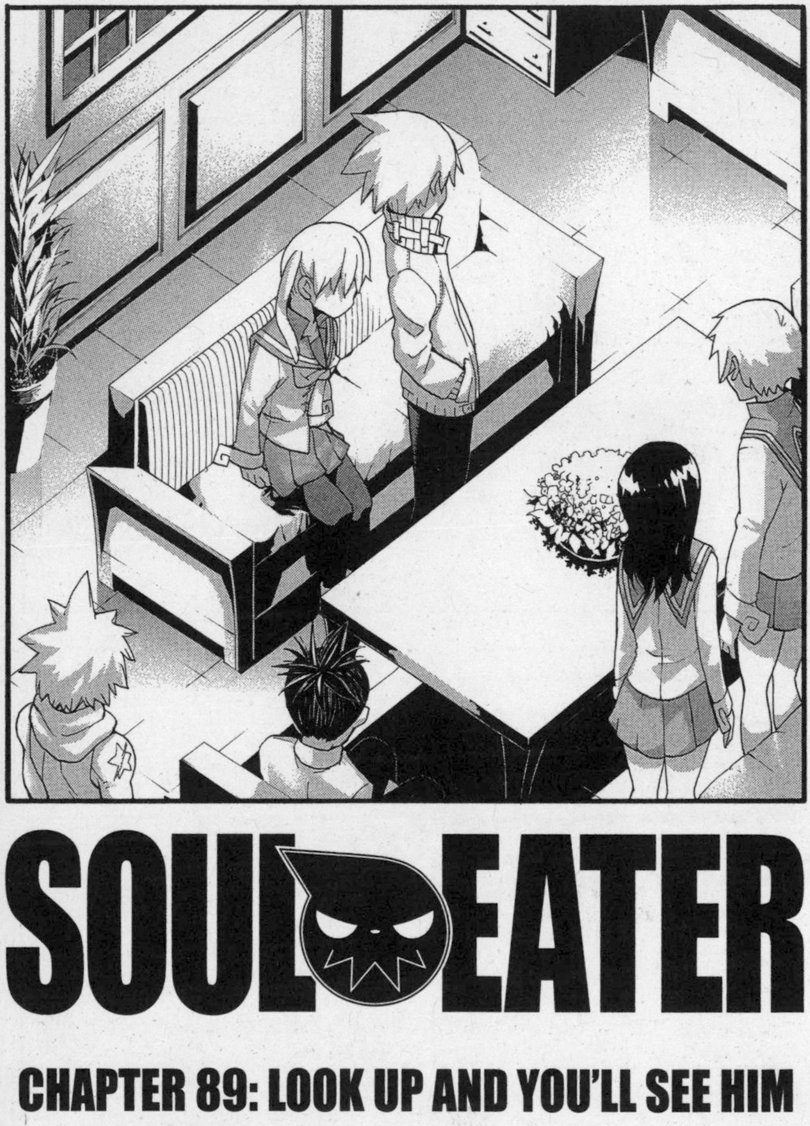

SOUL EATER

CHAPTER 89: LOOK UP AND YOU'LL SEE HIM

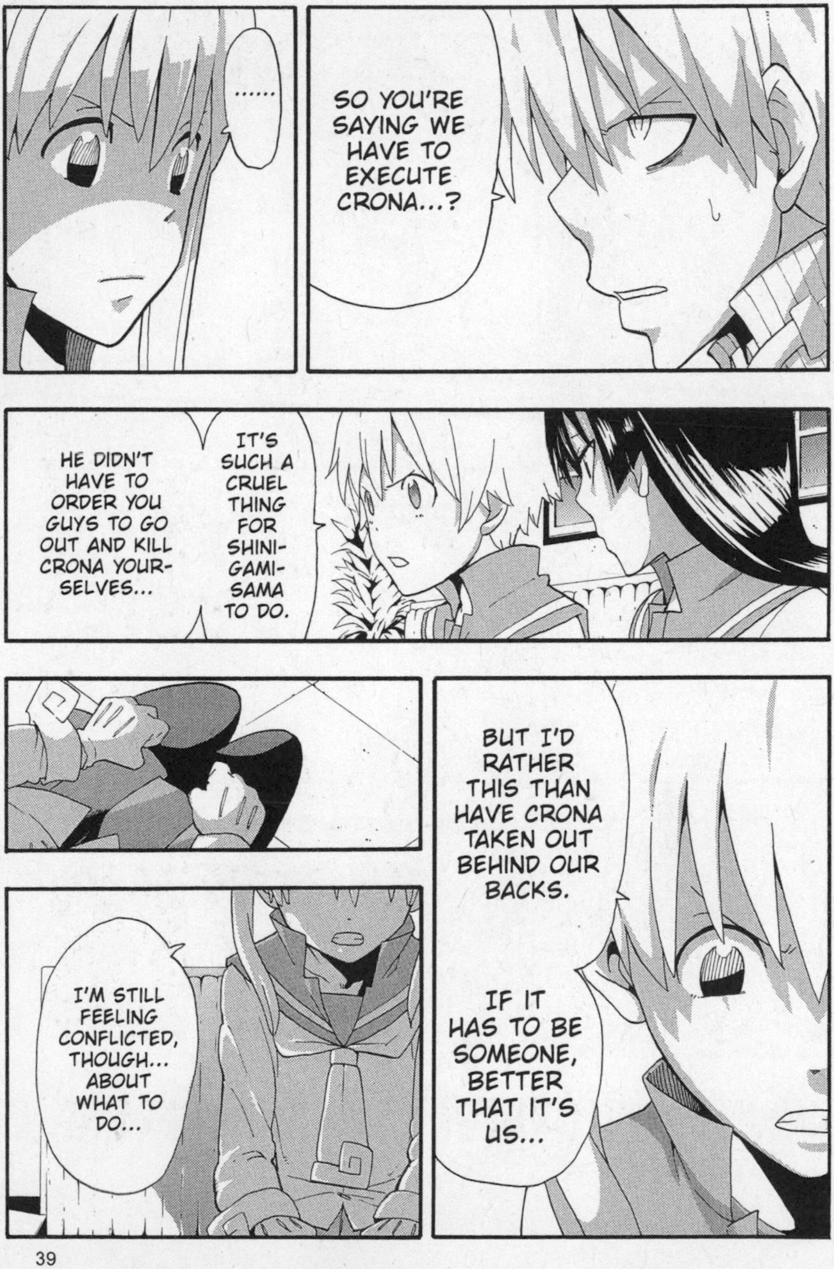
SO YOU'RE SAYING WE HAVE TO EXECUTE CRONA...?
......
IT'S SUCH A CRUEL THING FOR SHINIGAMI-SAMA TO DO.
HE DIDN'T HAVE TO ORDER YOU GUYS TO GO OUT AND KILL CRONA YOURSELVES...
BUT I'D RATHER THIS THAN HAVE CRONA TAKEN OUT BEHIND OUR BACKS.
IF IT HAS TO BE SOMEONE, BETTER THAT IT'S US...
I'M STILL FEELING CONFLICTED, THOUGH... ABOUT WHAT TO DO...

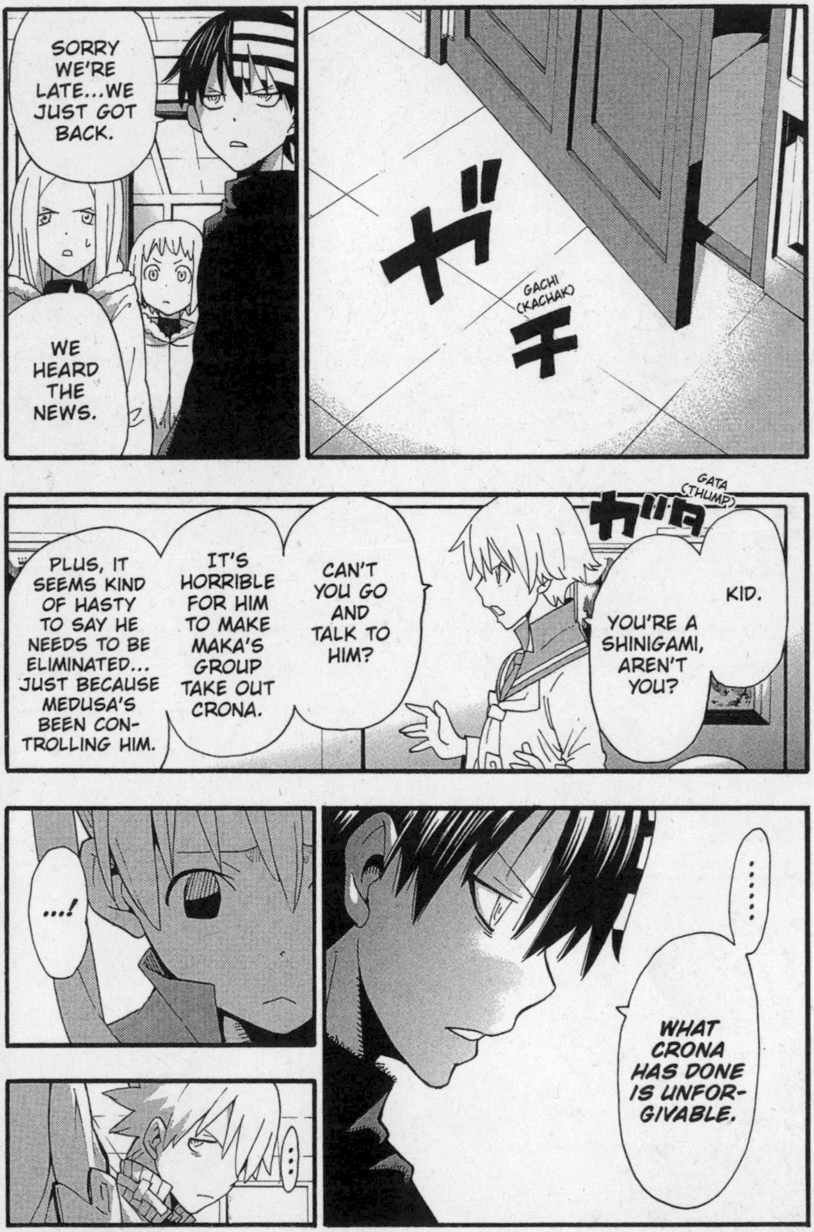
ガチ
GACHI (KACHAK)
SORRY WE'RE LATE...WE JUST GOT BACK.
WE HEARD THE NEWS.
ガタ
GATA (THUMP)
KID.
YOU'RE A SHINIGAMI, AREN'T YOU?
CAN'T YOU GO AND TALK TO HIM?
IT'S HORRIBLE FOR HIM TO MAKE MAKA'S GROUP TAKE OUT CRONA.
PLUS, IT SEEMS KIND OF HASTY TO SAY HE NEEDS TO BE ELIMINATED... JUST BECAUSE MEDUSA'S BEEN CONTROLLING HIM.
......
WHAT CRONA HAS DONE IS UNFORGIVABLE.
...!
...

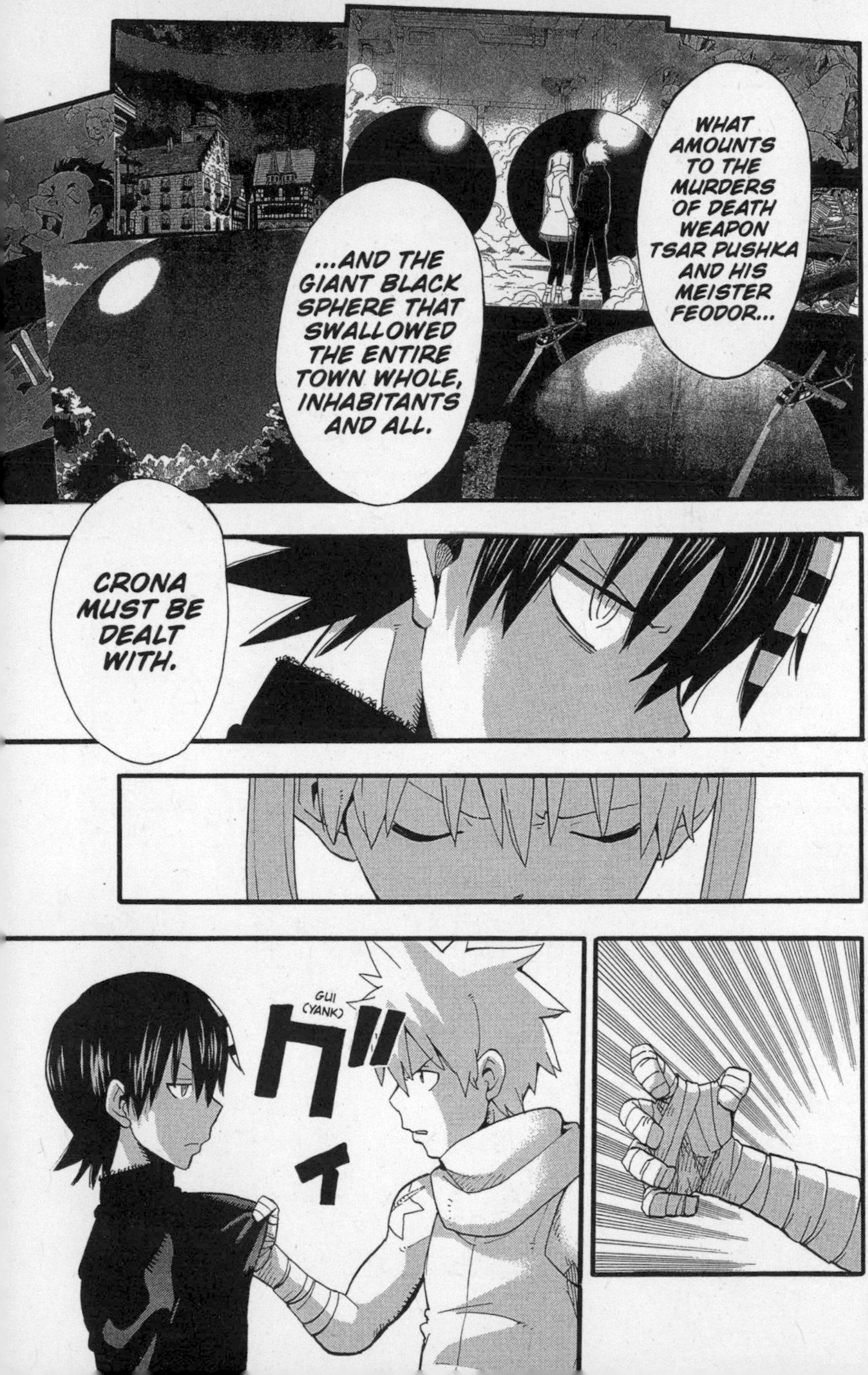
WHAT AMOUNTS TO THE MURDERS OF DEATH WEAPON TSAR PUSHKA AND HIS MEISTER FEODOR...
...AND THE GIANT BLACK SPHERE THAT SWALLOWED THE ENTIRE TOWN WHOLE, INHABITANTS AND ALL.
CRONA MUST BE DEALT WITH.
GUI (YANK)

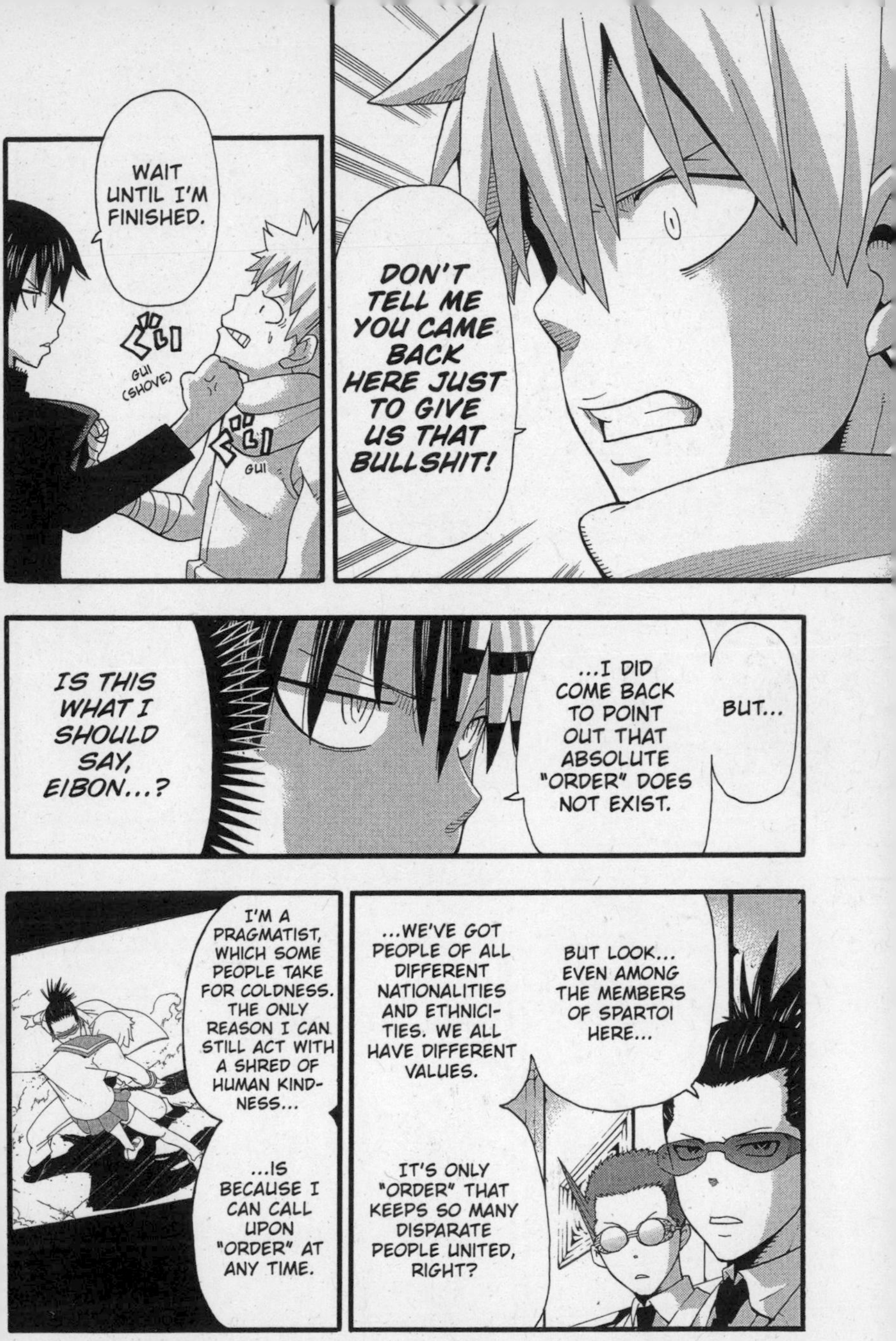
DON'T TELL ME YOU CAME BACK HERE JUST TO GIVE US THAT BULLSHIT!
WAIT UNTIL I'M FINISHED.
GUI (SHOVE)
GUI
BUT...
...I DID COME BACK TO POINT OUT THAT ABSOLUTE "ORDER" DOES NOT EXIST.
IS THIS WHAT I SHOULD SAY, EIBON...?
BUT LOOK... EVEN AMONG THE MEMBERS OF SPARTOI HERE...
...WE'VE GOT PEOPLE OF ALL DIFFERENT NATIONALITIES AND ETHNICI-TIES. WE ALL HAVE DIFFERENT VALUES.
IT'S ONLY "ORDER" THAT KEEPS SO MANY DISPARATE PEOPLE UNITED, RIGHT?
I'M A PRAGMATIST, WHICH SOME PEOPLE TAKE FOR COLDNESS. THE ONLY REASON I CAN STILL ACT WITH A SHRED OF HUMAN KIND-NESS...
...IS BECAUSE I CAN CALL UPON "ORDER" AT ANY TIME.

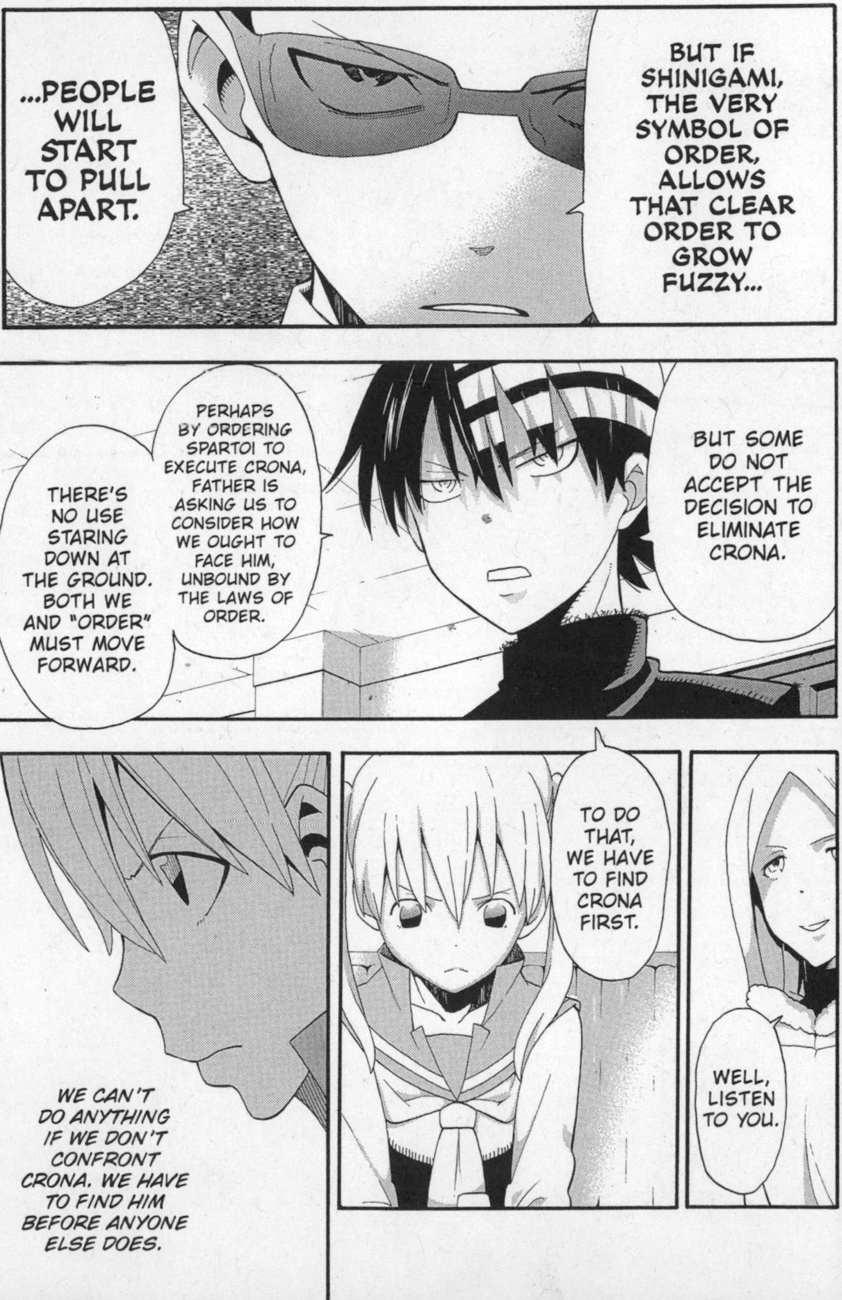
BUT IF SHINIGAMI, THE VERY SYMBOL OF ORDER, ALLOWS THAT CLEAR ORDER TO GROW FUZZY...
...PEOPLE WILL START TO PULL APART.
BUT SOME DO NOT ACCEPT THE DECISION TO ELIMINATE CRONA.
PERHAPS BY ORDERING SPARTOI TO EXECUTE CRONA, FATHER IS ASKING US TO CONSIDER HOW WE OUGHT TO FACE HIM, UNBOUND BY THE LAWS OF ORDER.
THERE'S NO USE STARING DOWN AT THE GROUND. BOTH WE AND "ORDER" MUST MOVE FORWARD.
WELL, LISTEN TO YOU.
TO DO THAT, WE HAVE TO FIND CRONA FIRST.
WE CAN'T DO ANYTHING IF WE DON'T CONFRONT CRONA. WE HAVE TO FIND HIM BEFORE ANYONE ELSE DOES.

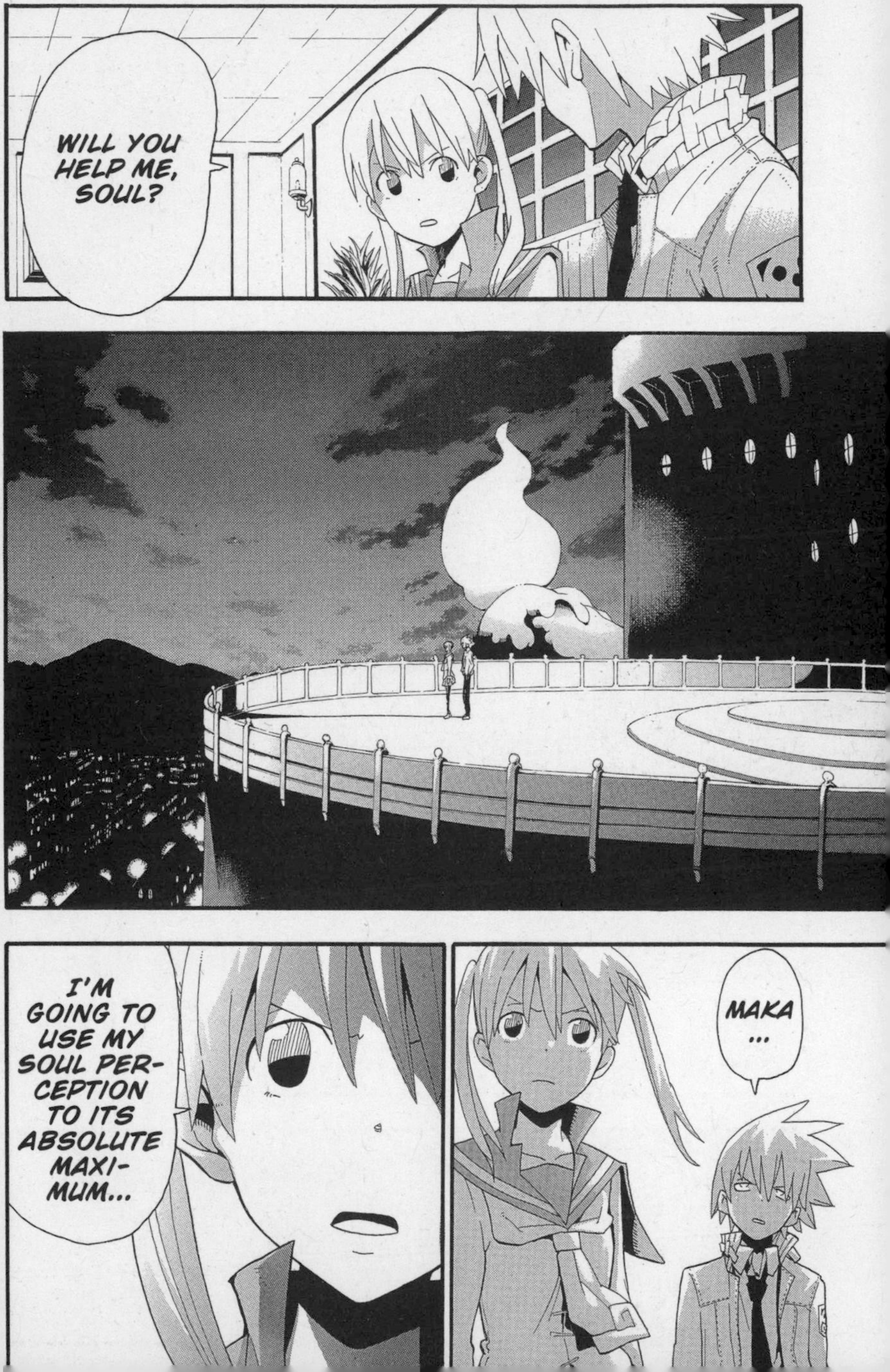
WILL YOU HELP ME, SOUL?
MAKA ...
I'M GOING TO USE MY SOUL PER-CEPTION TO ITS ABSOLUTE MAXI-MUM...

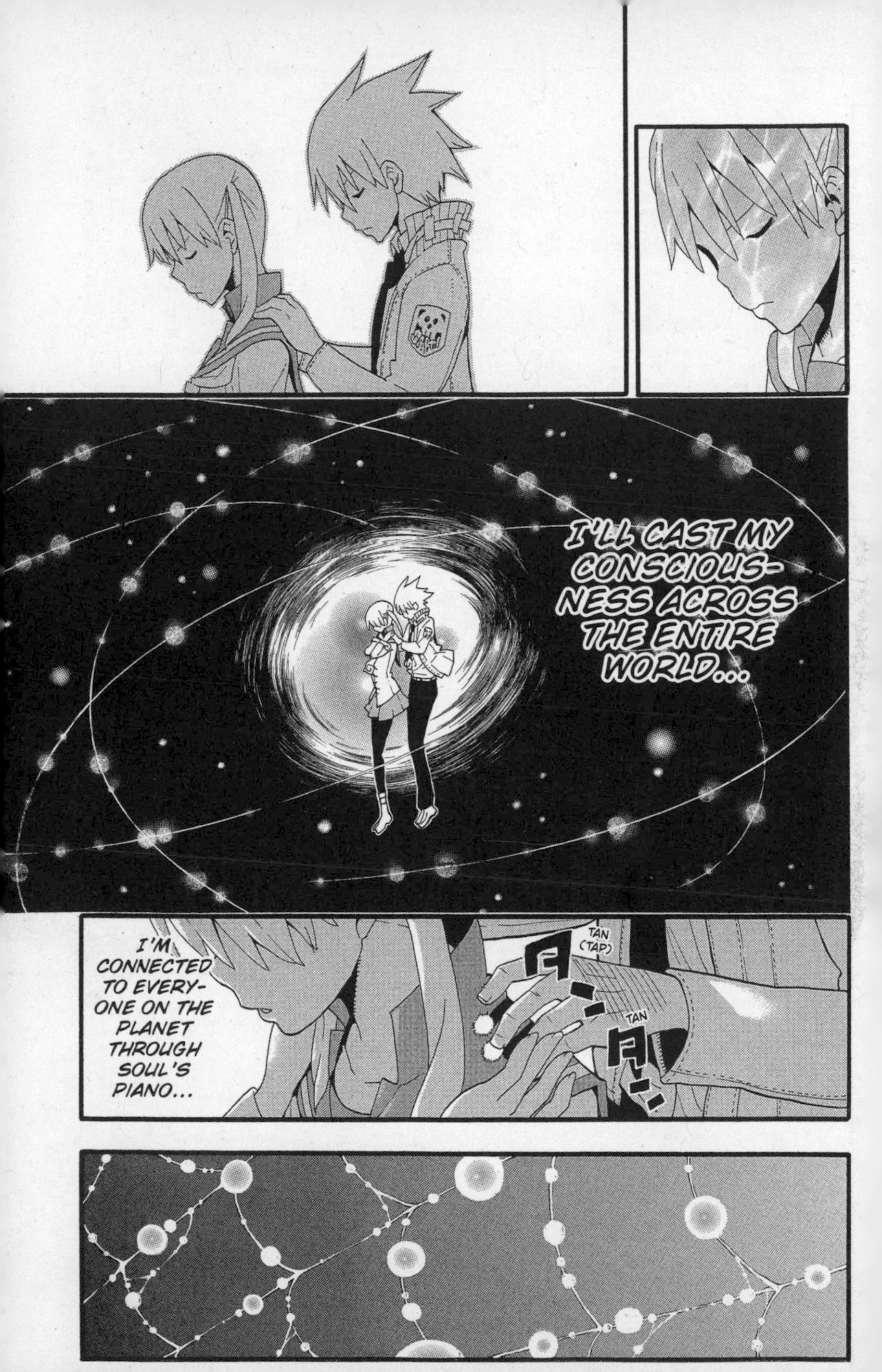
I'LL CAST MY CONSCIOUS-NESS ACROSS THE ENTIRE WORLD...
TAN (TAP)
TAN
I'M CONNECTED TO EVERY-ONE ON THE PLANET THROUGH SOUL'S PIANO...

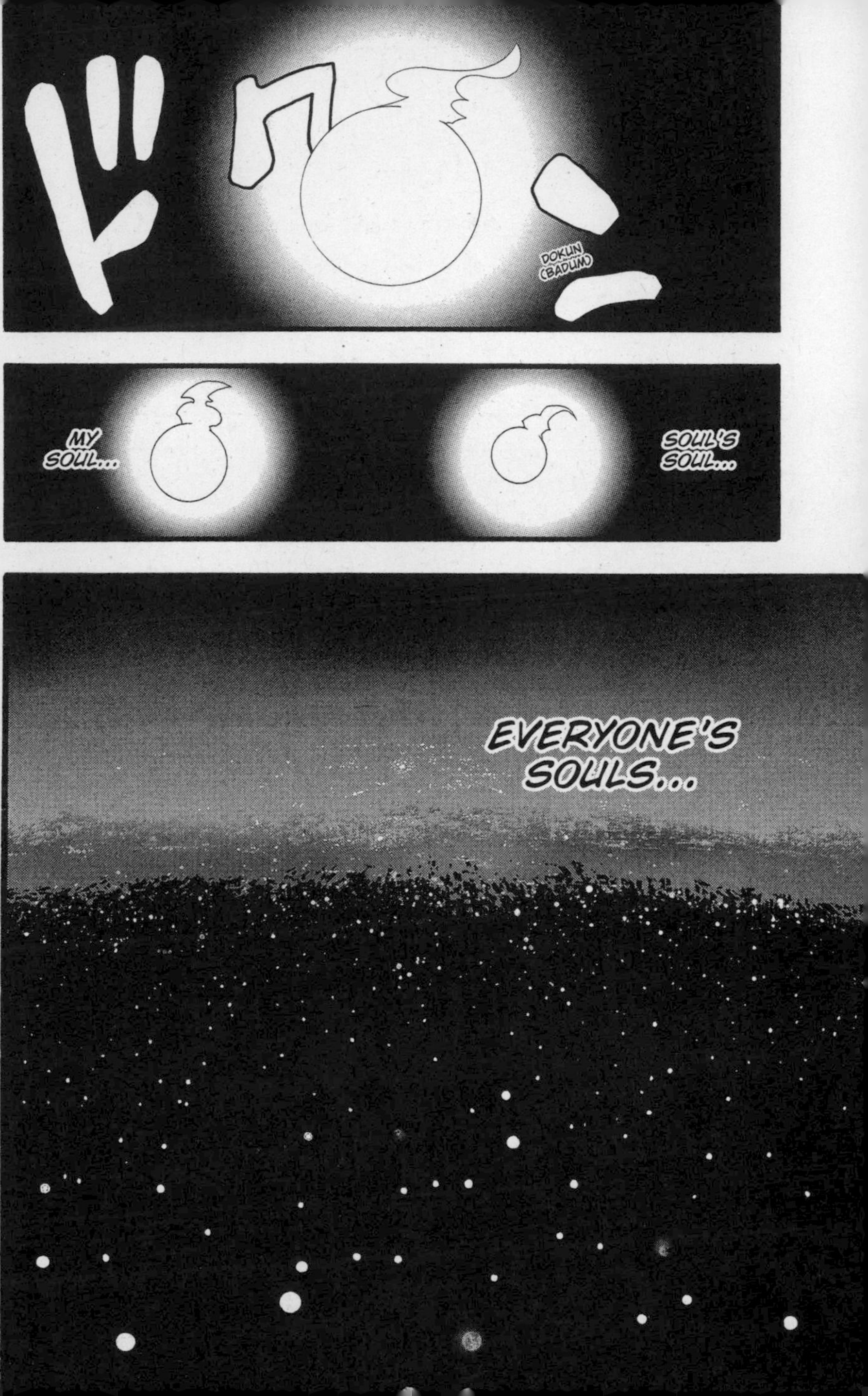
DOKUN
(BADUM)
SOUL'S
SOUL...
MY
SOUL...
EVERYONE'S
SOULS...

CRONA...

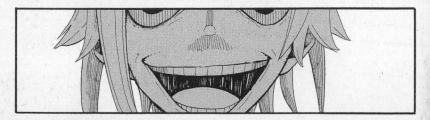

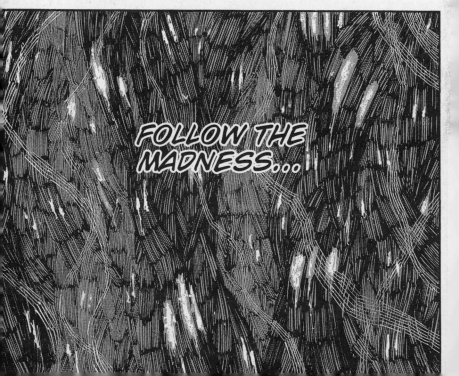

FOLLOW THE MADNESS...

I'LL SEARCH THE ENTIRE WORLD...

HERE?

HERE?

HERE?

HERE?

HERE?

HERE?

HERE?

HERE?

HERE?

HERE?

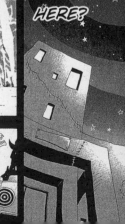

...TO FIND YOU.

HERE?

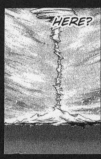

HERE?

HERE?

HERE?

HERE?

HERE?

HERE?

HER

HERE?

HERE?

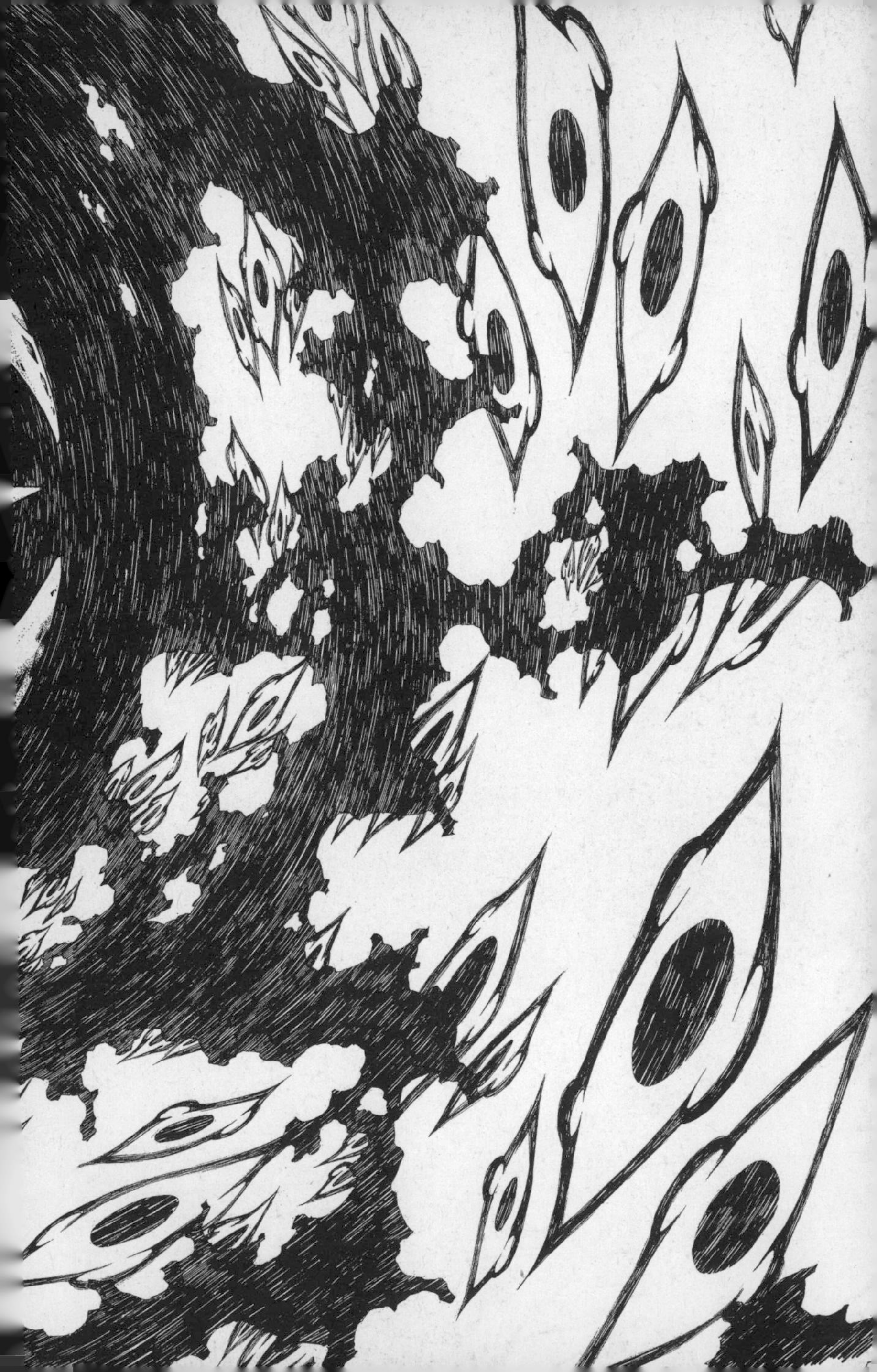

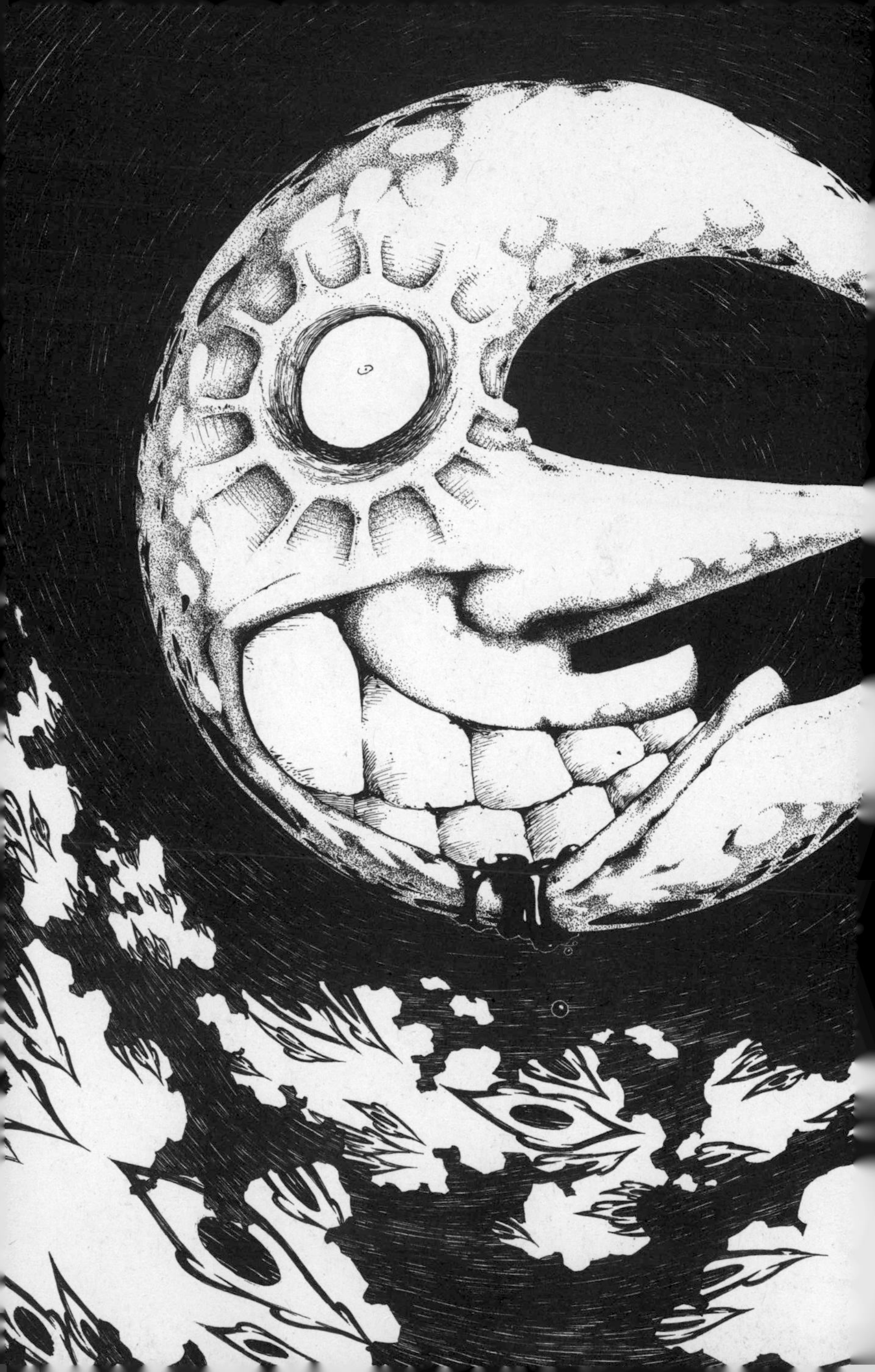

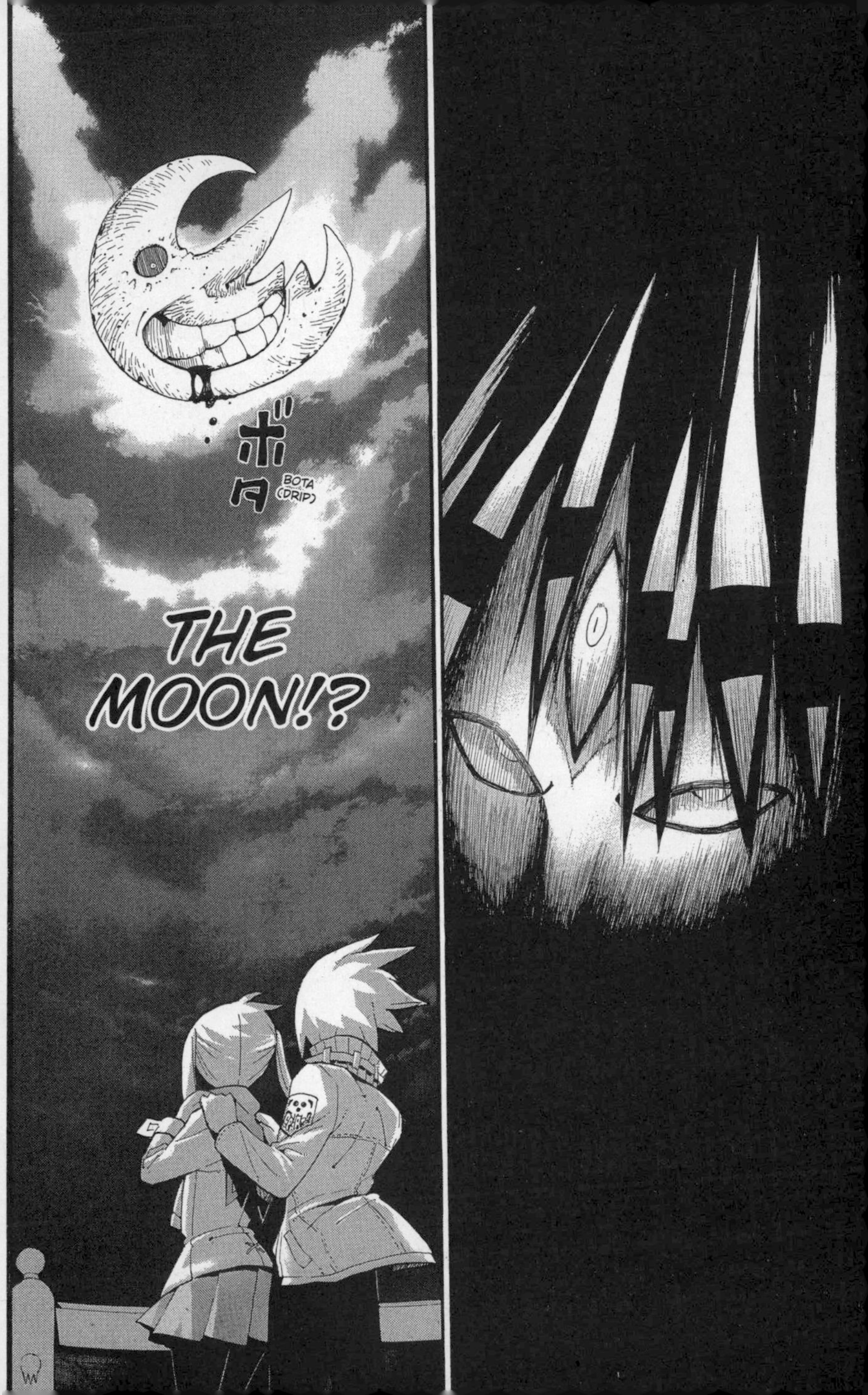
ボタ
BOTA (DRIP)
THE MOON!?

YOU FIND HIM?

WHAT'S UP, MAKA?

I FOUND HIM...

ビ゠チャ
BICHA
(SPLAT)

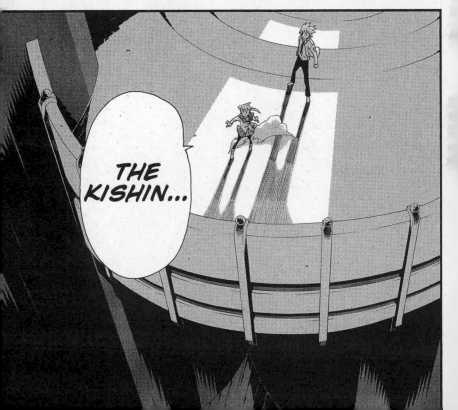

THE KISHIN...

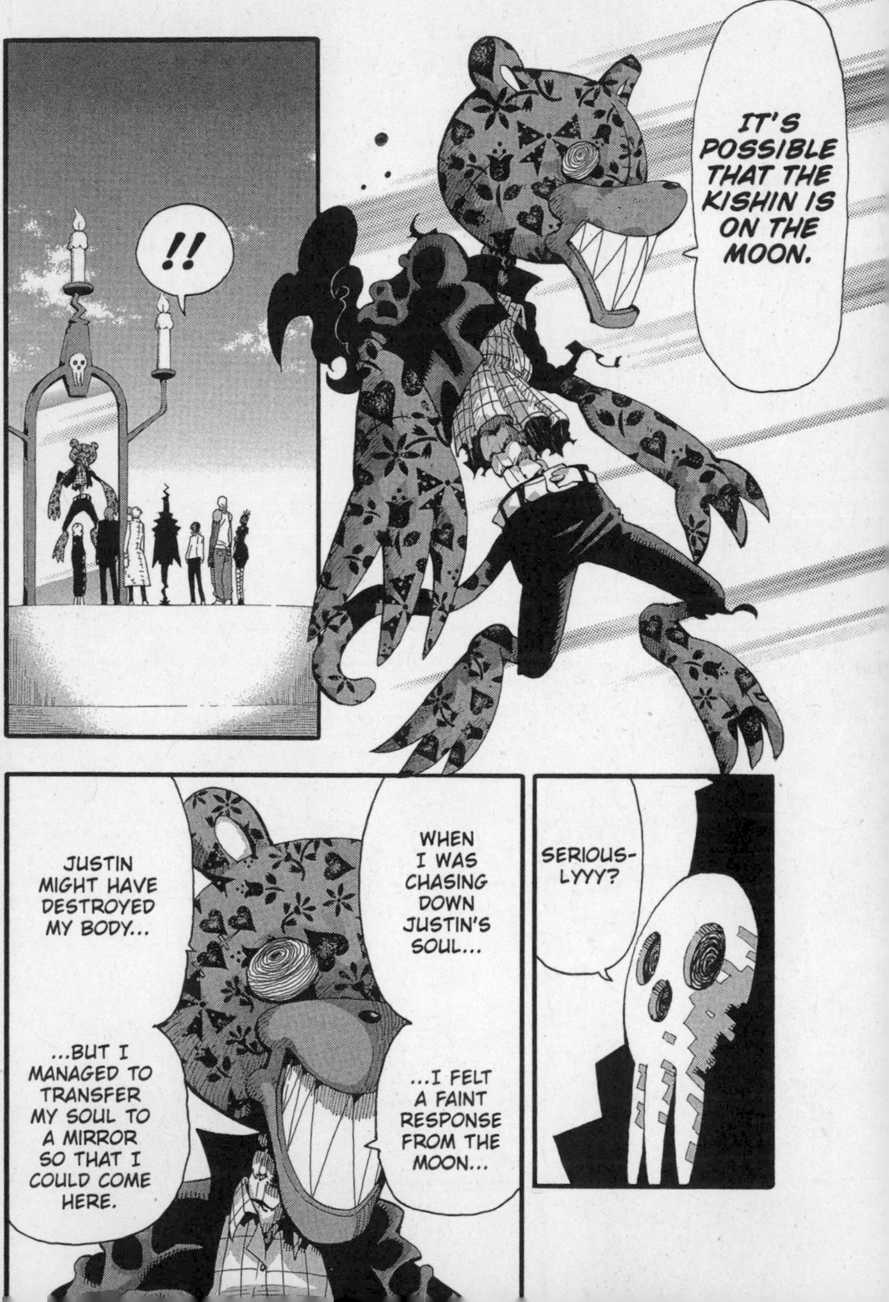
IT'S POSSIBLE THAT THE KISHIN IS ON THE MOON.
!!
SERIOUS-LYYY?
WHEN I WAS CHASING DOWN JUSTIN'S SOUL...
...I FELT A FAINT RESPONSE FROM THE MOON...
JUSTIN MIGHT HAVE DESTROYED MY BODY...
...BUT I MANAGED TO TRANSFER MY SOUL TO A MIRROR SO THAT I COULD COME HERE.

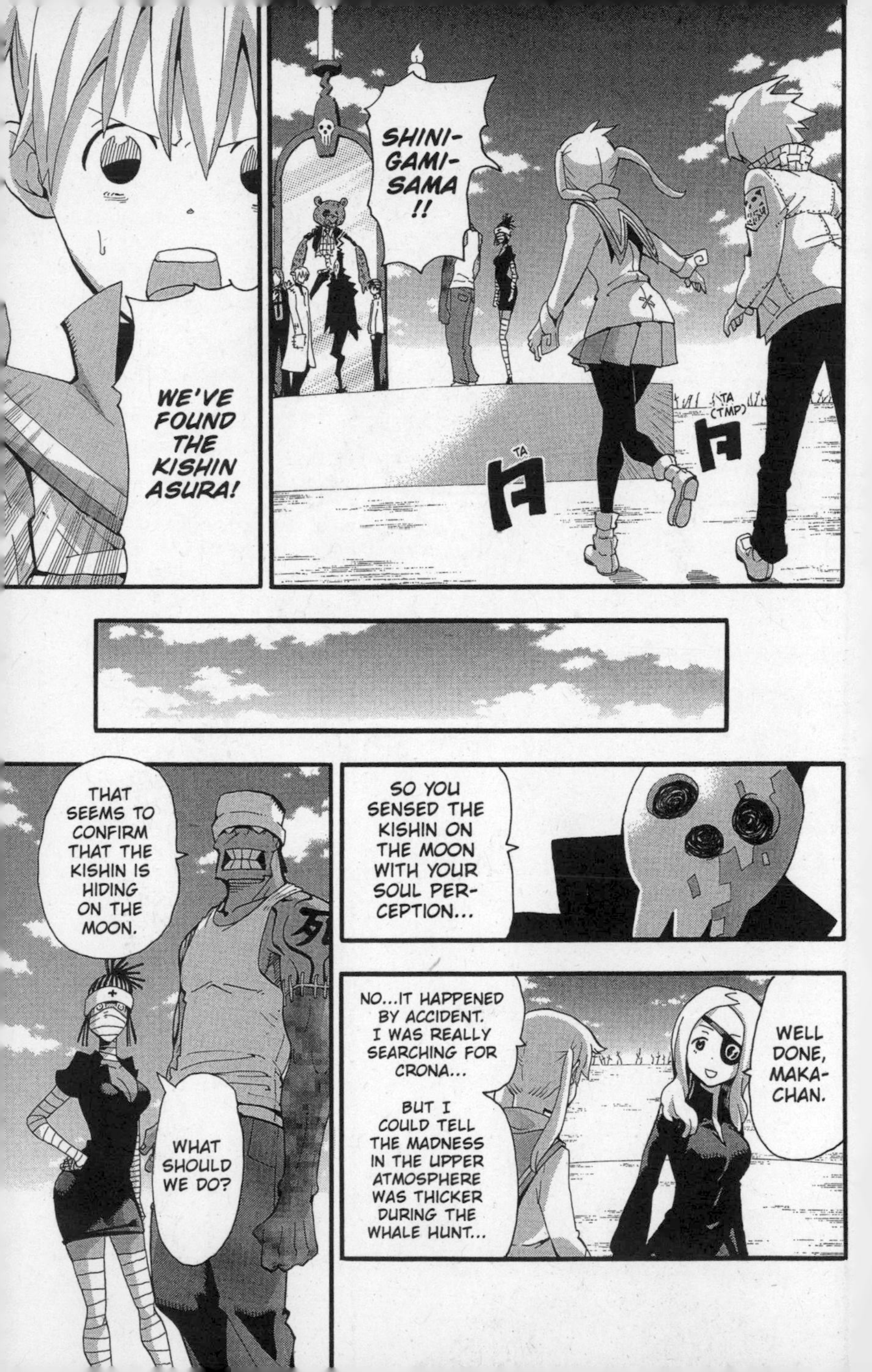
SHINI-GAMI-SAMA!!
TA (TMP)
TA
WE'VE FOUND THE KISHIN ASURA!
SO YOU SENSED THE KISHIN ON THE MOON WITH YOUR SOUL PERCEPTION...
WELL DONE, MAKA-CHAN.
NO...IT HAPPENED BY ACCIDENT. I WAS REALLY SEARCHING FOR CRONA...
BUT I COULD TELL THE MADNESS IN THE UPPER ATMOSPHERE WAS THICKER DURING THE WHALE HUNT...
THAT SEEMS TO CONFIRM THAT THE KISHIN IS HIDING ON THE MOON.
WHAT SHOULD WE DO?

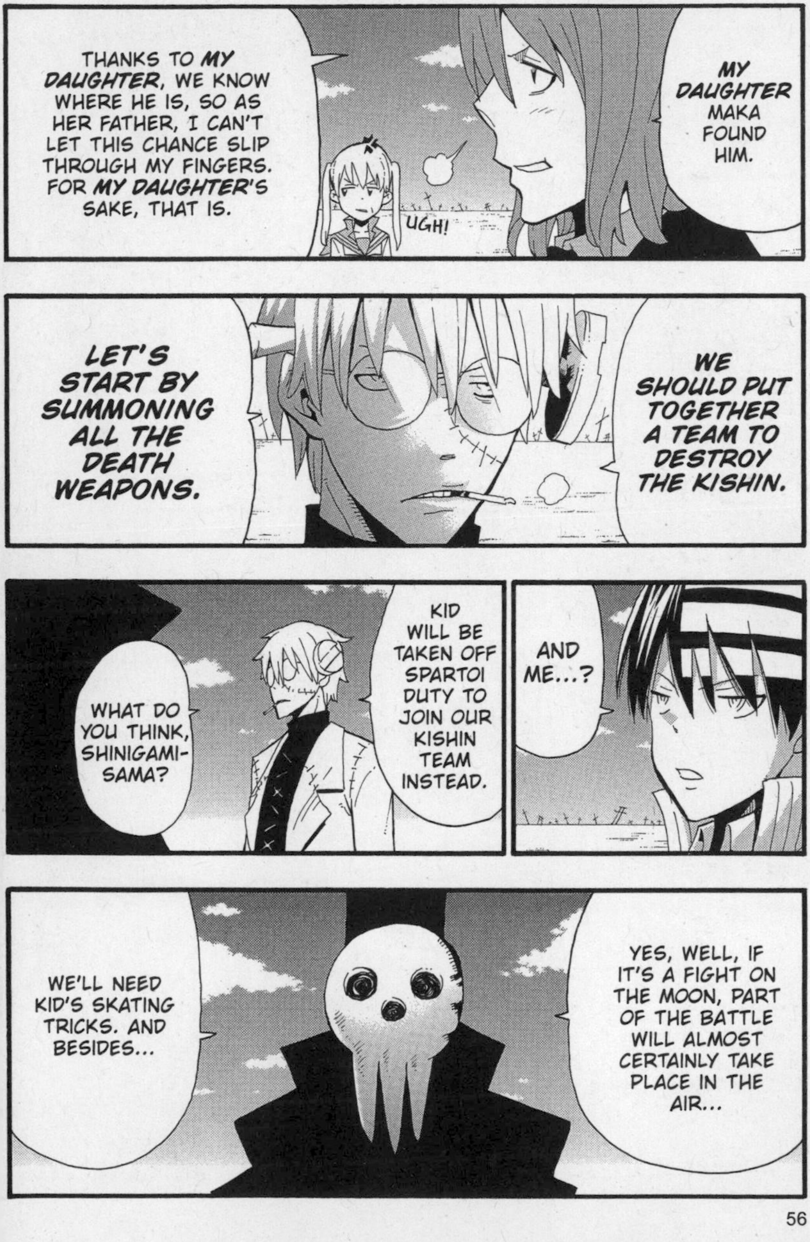
MY DAUGHTER MAKA FOUND HIM.
UGH!
THANKS TO MY DAUGHTER, WE KNOW WHERE HE IS, SO AS HER FATHER, I CAN'T LET THIS CHANCE SLIP THROUGH MY FINGERS. FOR MY DAUGHTER'S SAKE, THAT IS.
WE SHOULD PUT TOGETHER A TEAM TO DESTROY THE KISHIN.
LET'S START BY SUMMONING ALL THE DEATH WEAPONS.
AND ME...?
KID WILL BE TAKEN OFF SPARTOI DUTY TO JOIN OUR KISHIN TEAM INSTEAD.
WHAT DO YOU THINK, SHINIGAMI-SAMA?
YES, WELL, IF IT'S A FIGHT ON THE MOON, PART OF THE BATTLE WILL ALMOST CERTAINLY TAKE PLACE IN THE AIR...
WE'LL NEED KID'S SKATING TRICKS. AND BESIDES...

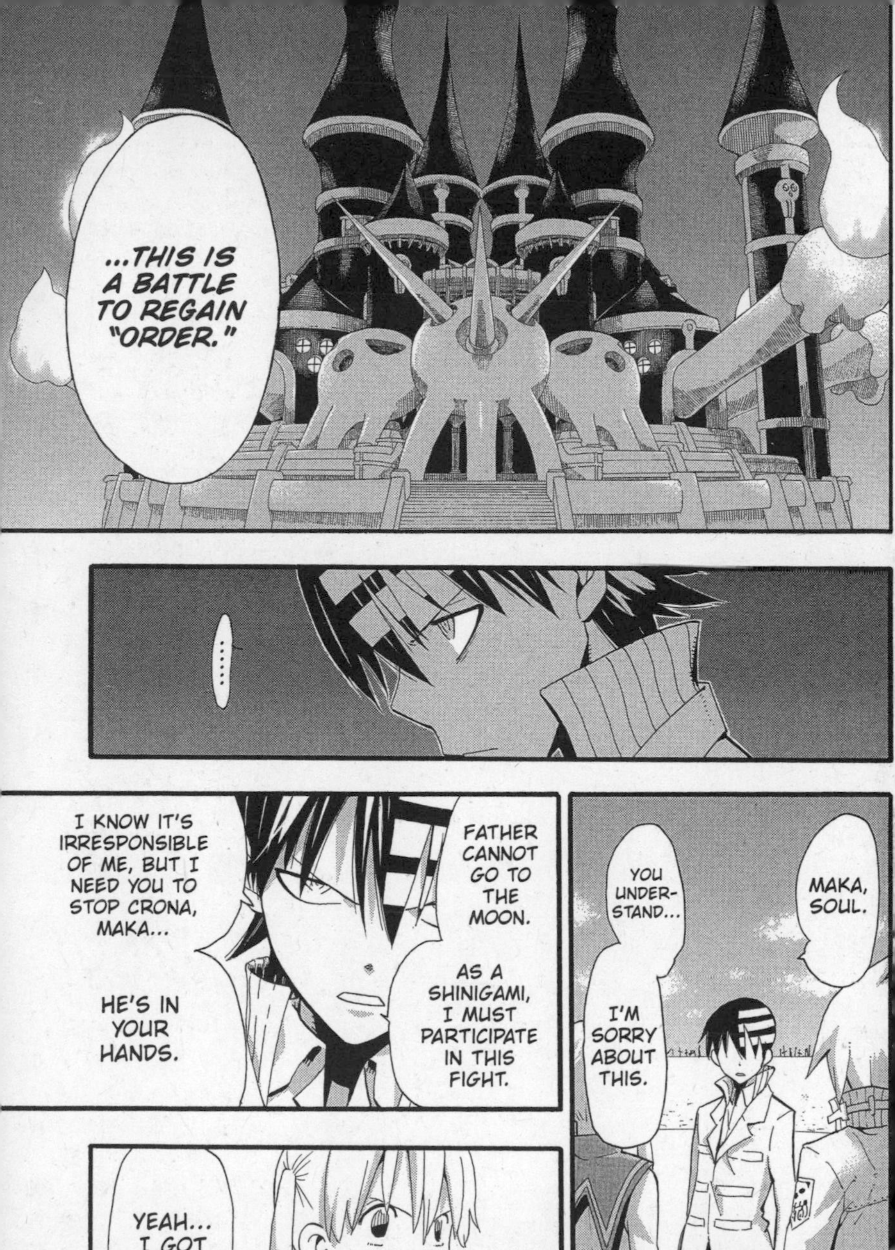
...THIS IS A BATTLE TO REGAIN "ORDER."
......
MAKA, SOUL.
YOU UNDER-STAND...
I'M SORRY ABOUT THIS.
FATHER CANNOT GO TO THE MOON.
AS A SHINIGAMI, I MUST PARTICIPATE IN THIS FIGHT.
I KNOW IT'S IRRESPONSIBLE OF ME, BUT I NEED YOU TO STOP CRONA, MAKA...
HE'S IN YOUR HANDS.
YEAH... I GOT IT.

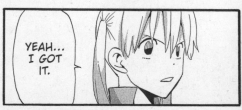

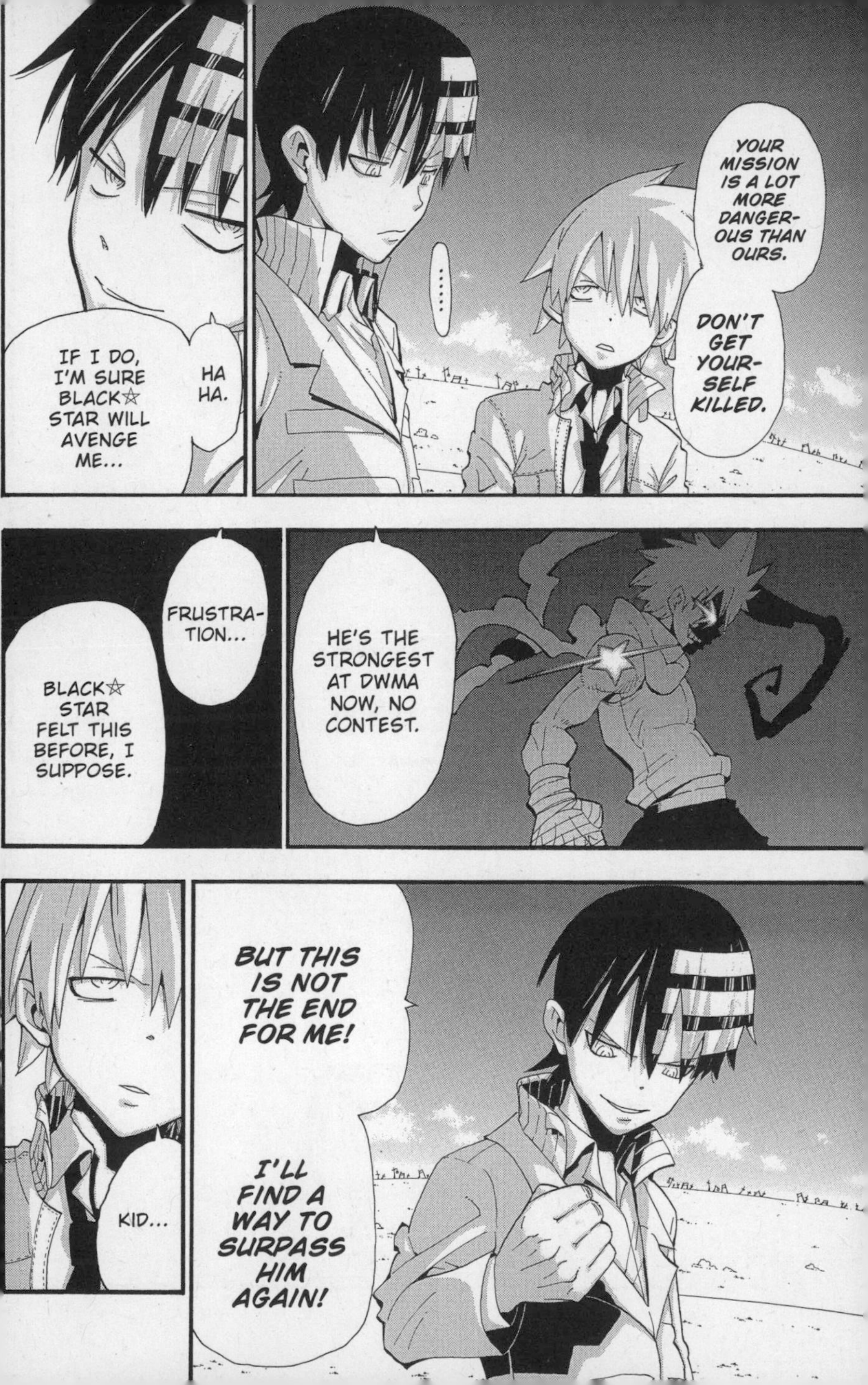
YOUR MISSION IS A LOT MORE DANGER-OUS THAN OURS.
DON'T GET YOURSELF KILLED.
......
HA HA.
IF I DO, I'M SURE BLACK☆STAR WILL AVENGE ME...
HE'S THE STRONGEST AT DWMA NOW, NO CONTEST.
FRUSTRATION...
BLACK☆STAR FELT THIS BEFORE, I SUPPOSE.
BUT THIS IS NOT THE END FOR ME!
I'LL FIND A WAY TO SURPASS HIM AGAIN!
KID...

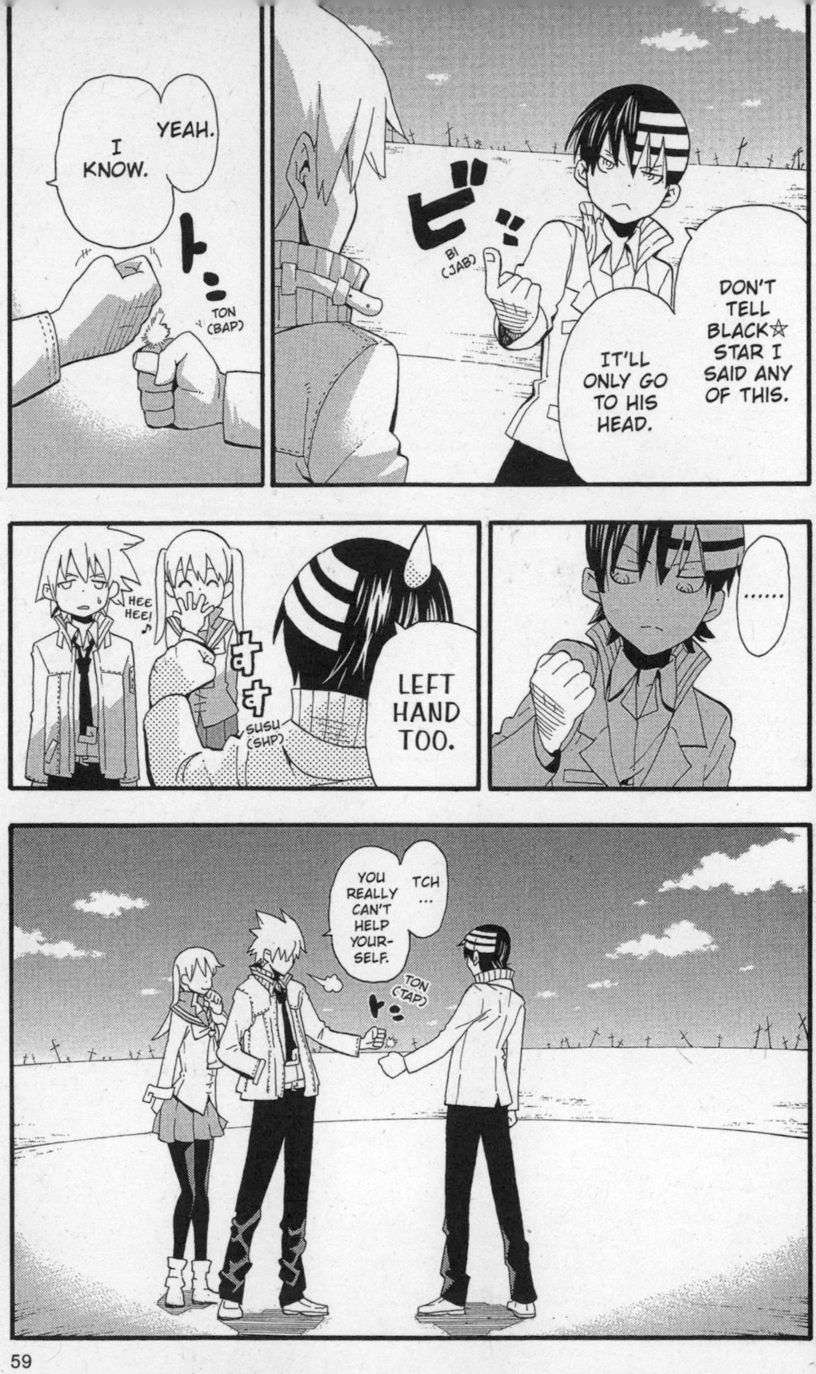
ビッ
BI (JAB)
DON'T TELL BLACK☆STAR I SAID ANY OF THIS.
IT'LL ONLY GO TO HIS HEAD.
YEAH. I KNOW.
トン
TON (BAP)
......
LEFT HAND TOO.
すす
SUSU (SHP)
HEE HEE! ♪
TCH ...
YOU REALLY CAN'T HELP YOUR-SELF.
トン
TON (TAP)

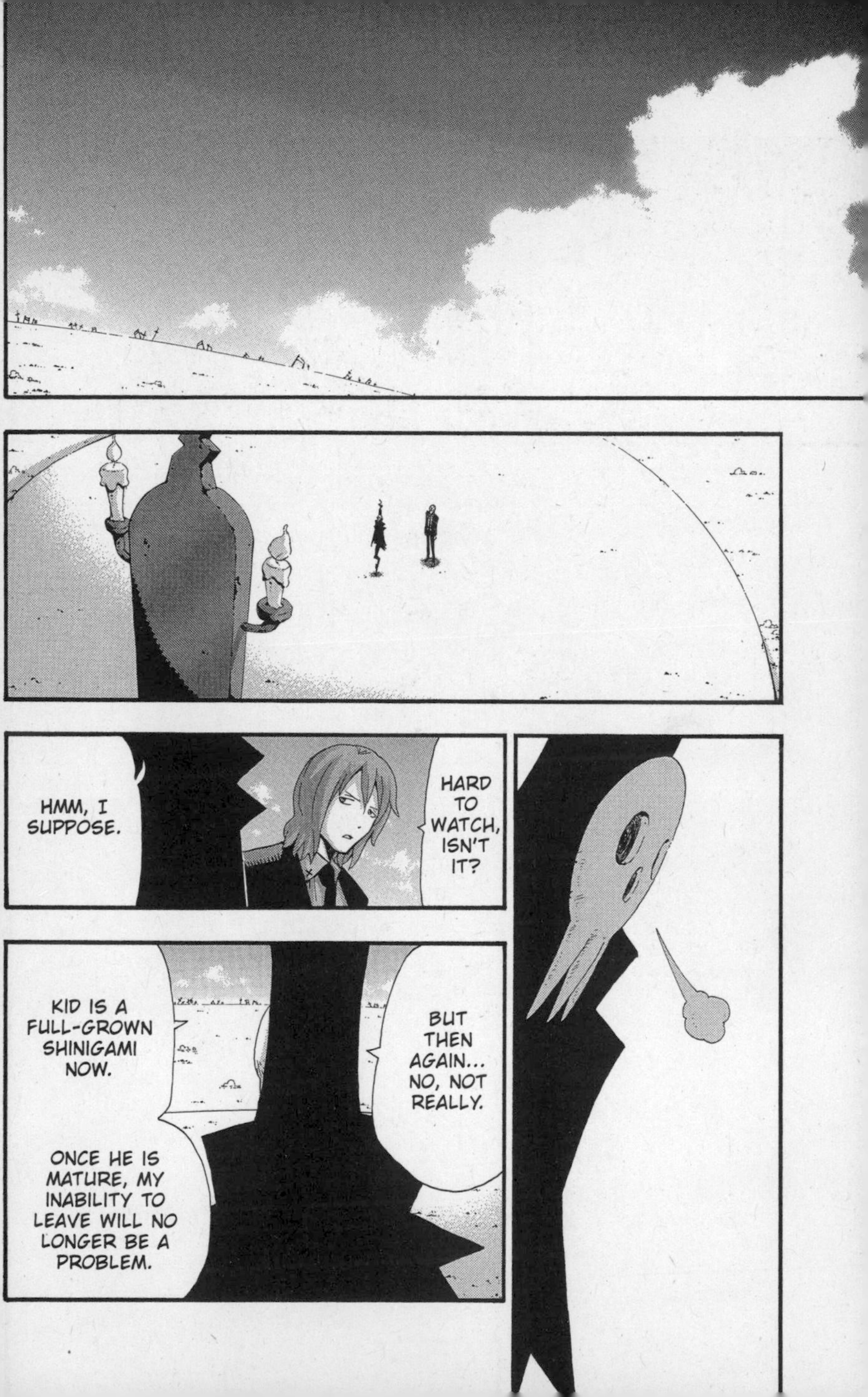
HARD TO WATCH, ISN'T IT?
HMM, I SUPPOSE.
BUT THEN AGAIN... NO, NOT REALLY.
KID IS A FULL-GROWN SHINIGAMI NOW.
ONCE HE IS MATURE, MY INABILITY TO LEAVE WILL NO LONGER BE A PROBLEM.

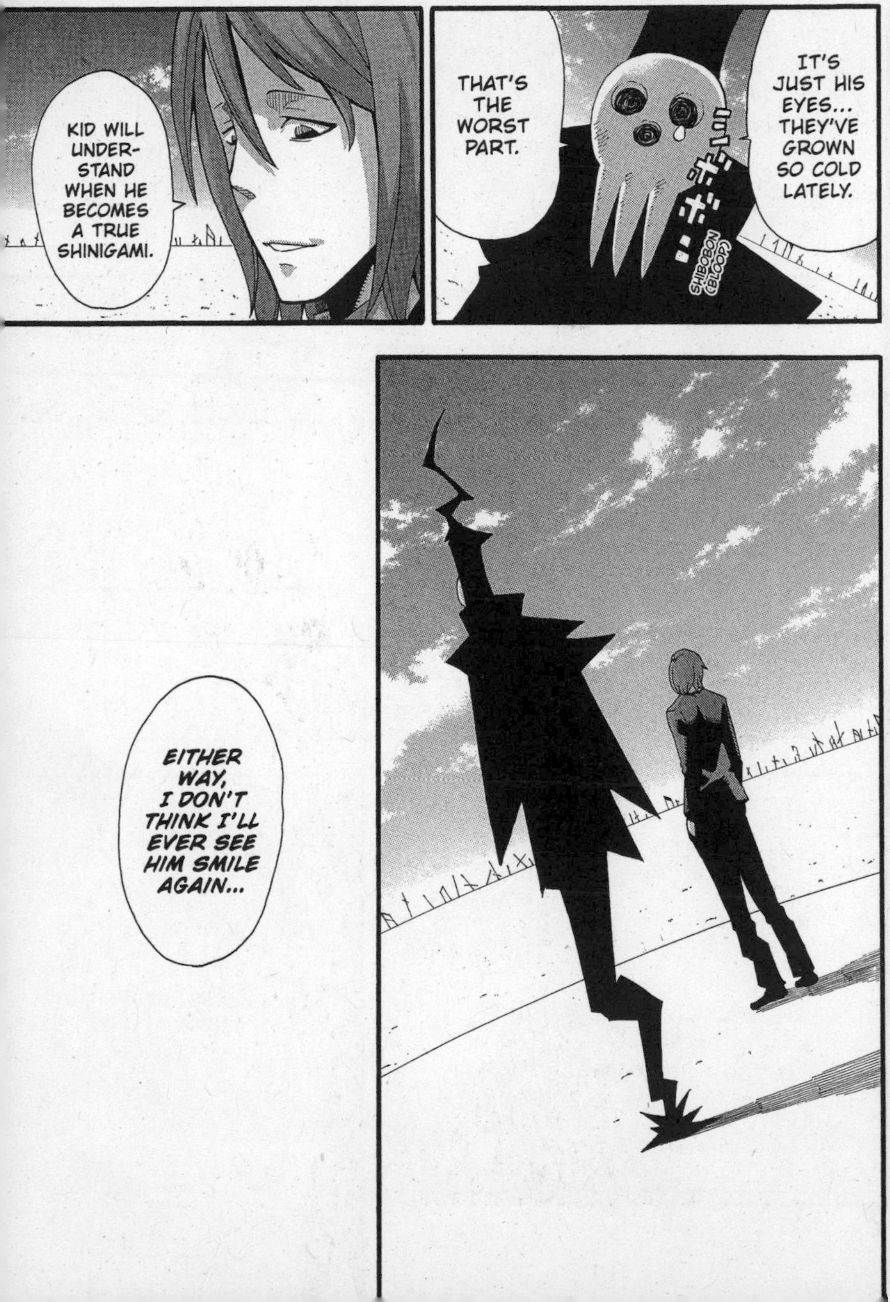
IT'S JUST HIS EYES... THEY'VE GROWN SO COLD LATELY.
THAT'S THE WORST PART.
SHIBOBON (BLOOP)
KID WILL UNDER-STAND WHEN HE BECOMES A TRUE SHINIGAMI.
EITHER WAY, I DON'T THINK I'LL EVER SEE HIM SMILE AGAIN...

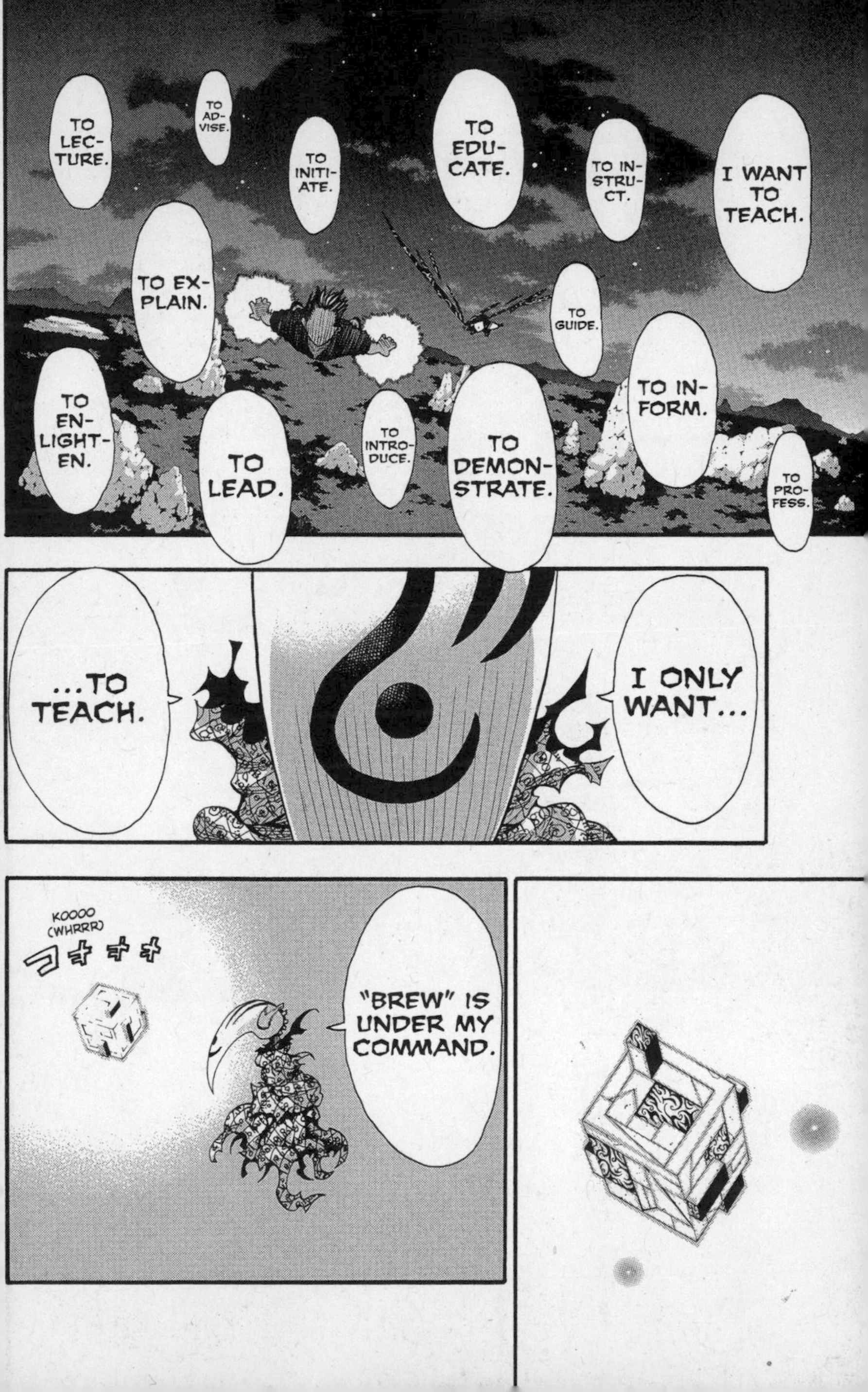
I WANT TO TEACH.
TO INSTRUCT.
TO EDUCATE.
TO INITIATE.
TO ADVISE.
TO LECTURE.
TO GUIDE.
TO EXPLAIN.
TO INFORM.
TO PROFESS.
TO DEMONSTRATE.
TO INTRODUCE.
TO LEAD.
TO ENLIGHTEN.
I ONLY WANT...
...TO TEACH.
"BREW" IS UNDER MY COMMAND.
KOOOO (WHRRR)
コォォォ

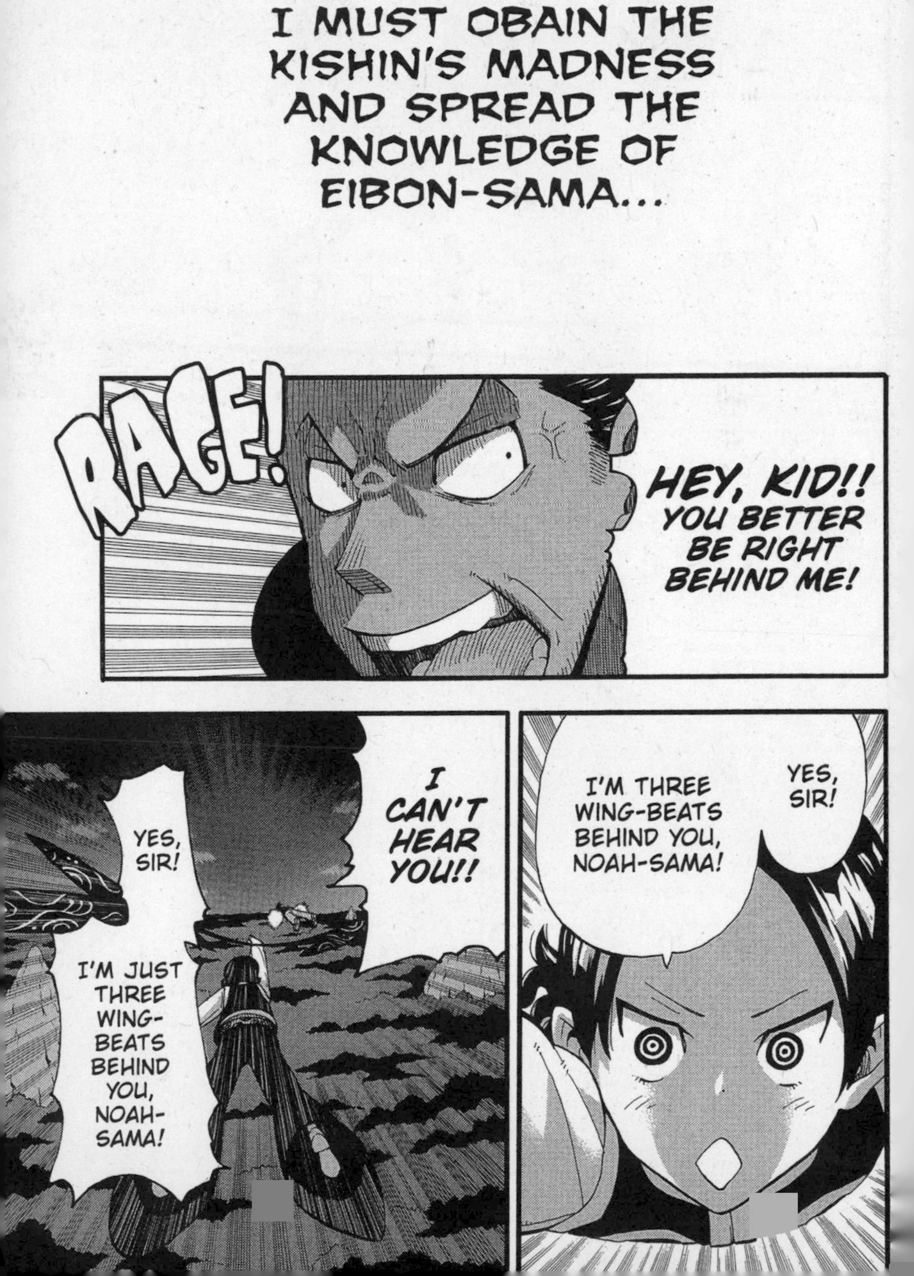
I MUST OBAIN THE KISHIN'S MADNESS AND SPREAD THE KNOWLEDGE OF EIBON-SAMA...
HEY, KID!! YOU BETTER BE RIGHT BEHIND ME!
RAGE!
YES, SIR!
I'M THREE WING-BEATS BEHIND YOU, NOAH-SAMA!
I CAN'T HEAR YOU!!
YES, SIR!
I'M JUST THREE WING-BEATS BEHIND YOU, NOAH-SAMA!

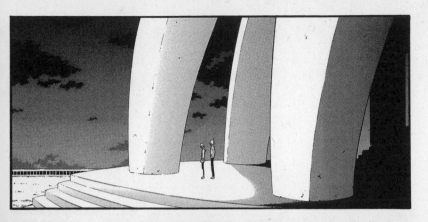

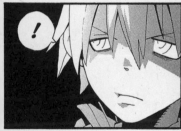

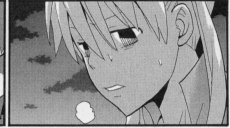

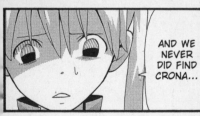

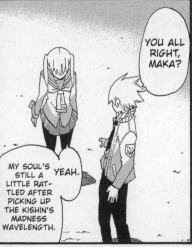

!
YOU ALL RIGHT, MAKA?
YEAH.
MY SOUL'S STILL A LITTLE RAT-TLED AFTER PICKING UP THE KISHIN'S MADNESS WAVELENGTH.
AND WE NEVER DID FIND CRONA...
I THINK WE SHOULD CALL IT QUITS FOR TODAY.

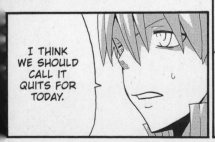

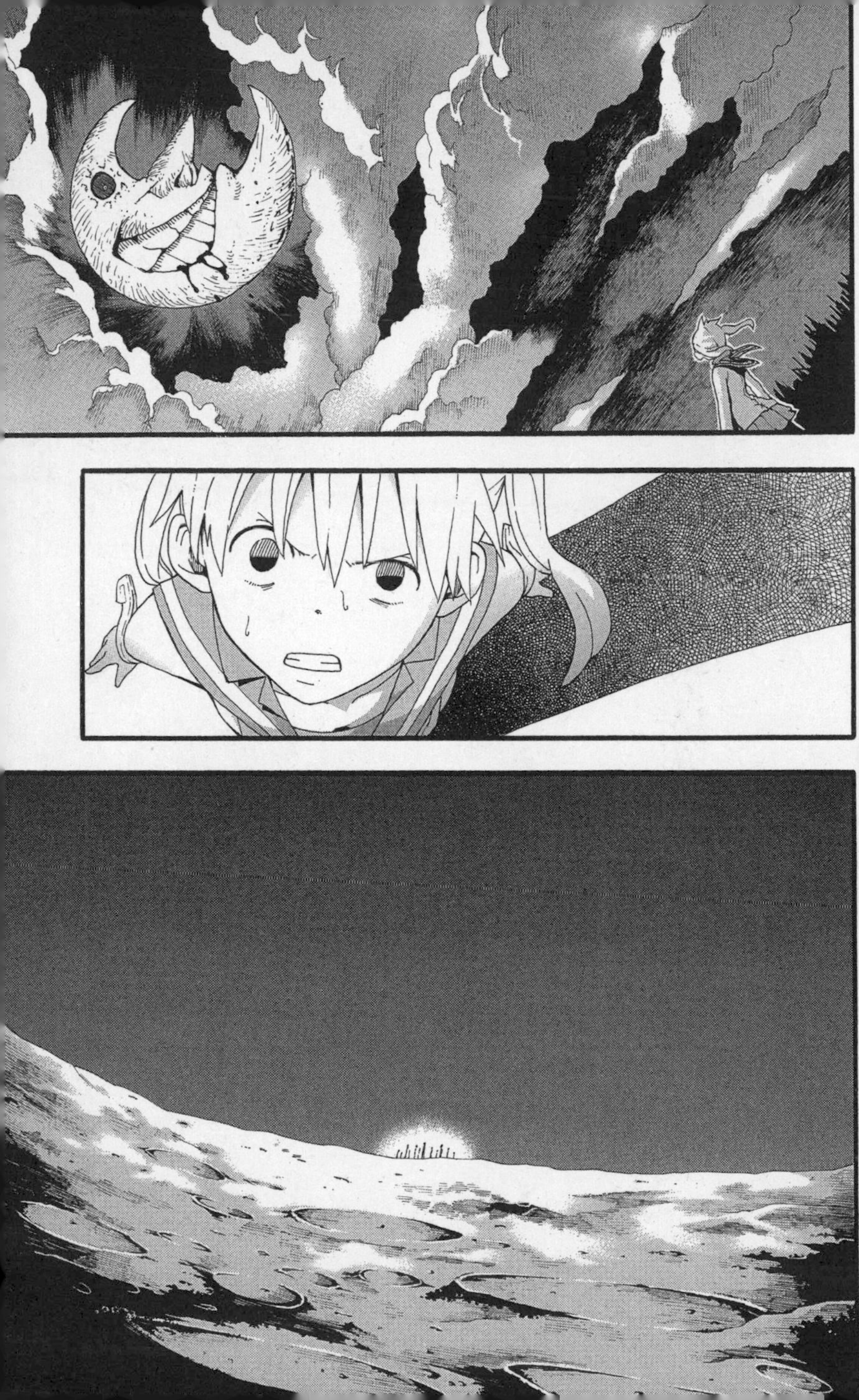

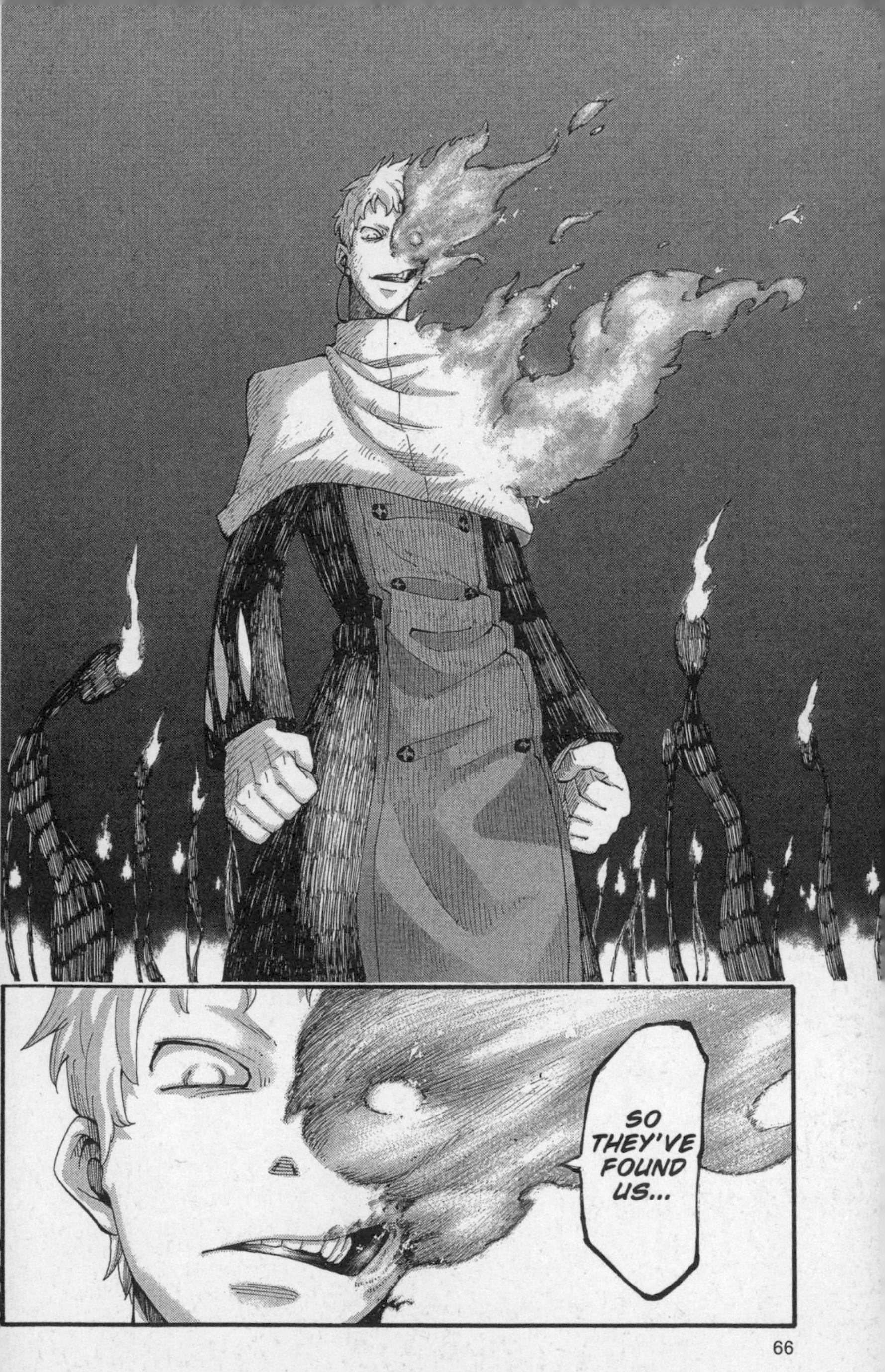
SO THEY'VE FOUND US...

SOUL EATER

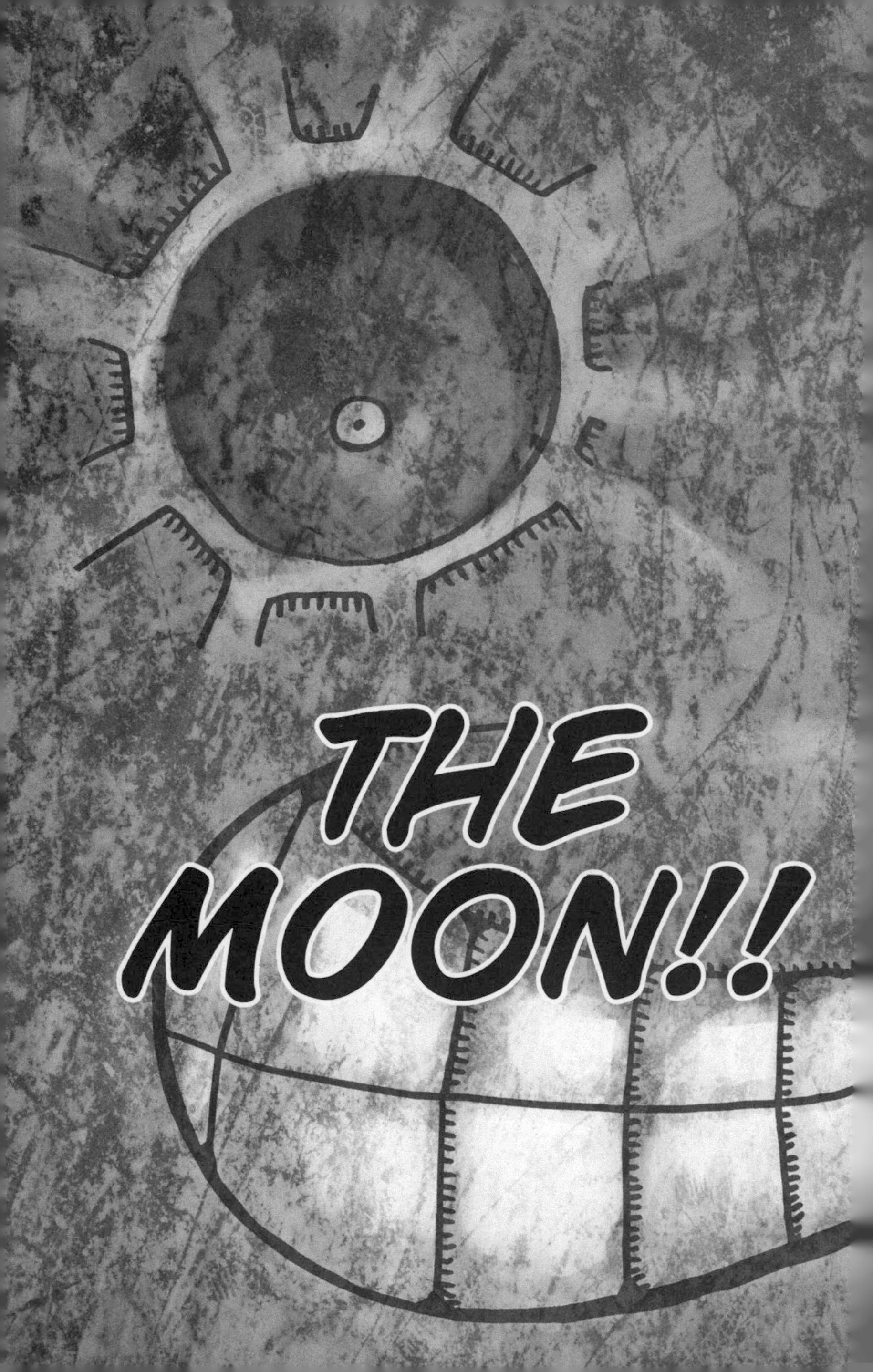
THE MOON!!

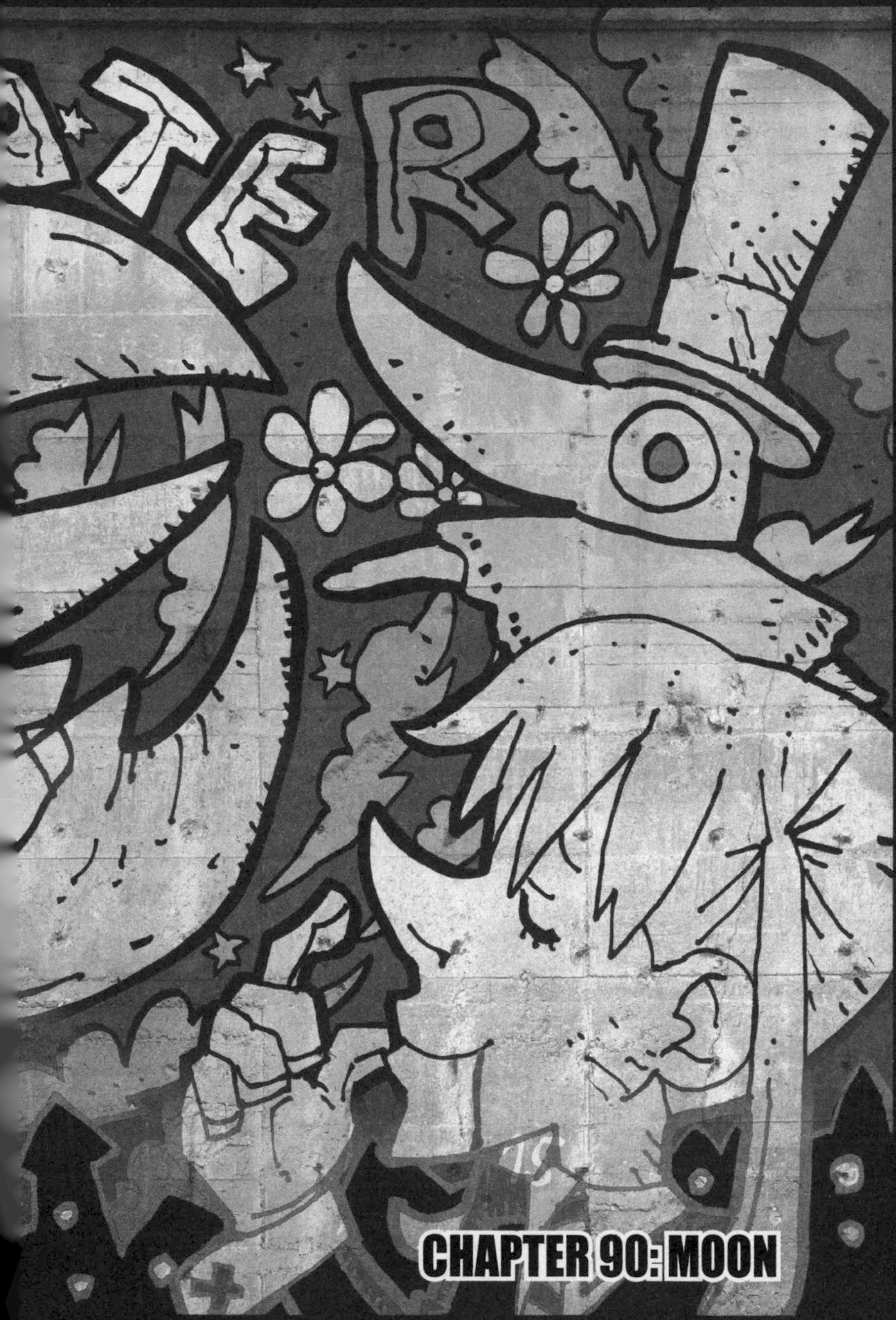

CHAPTER 90: MOON

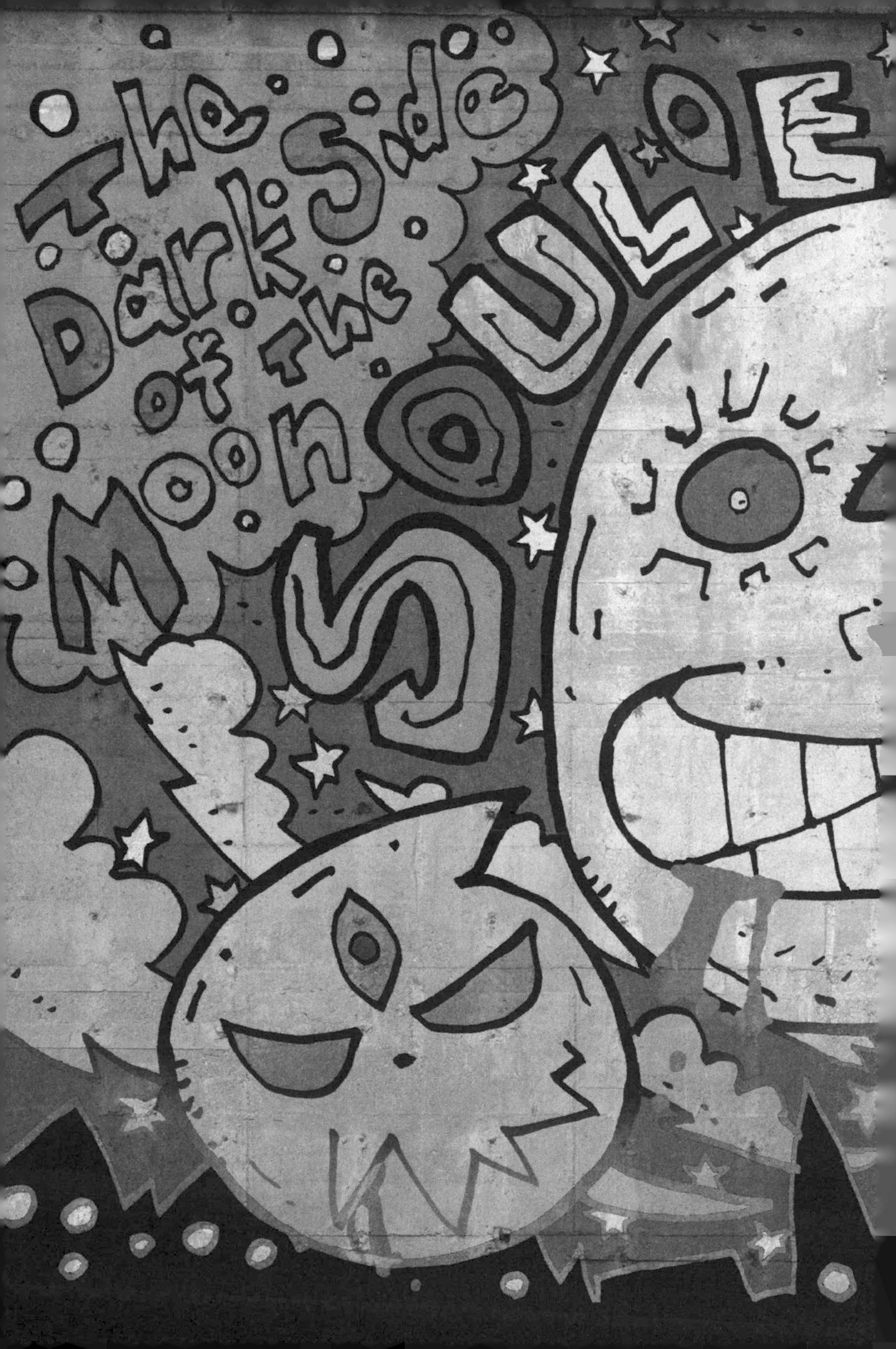
The Dark Side
of the
Moon
SOUL

SOUL EATER

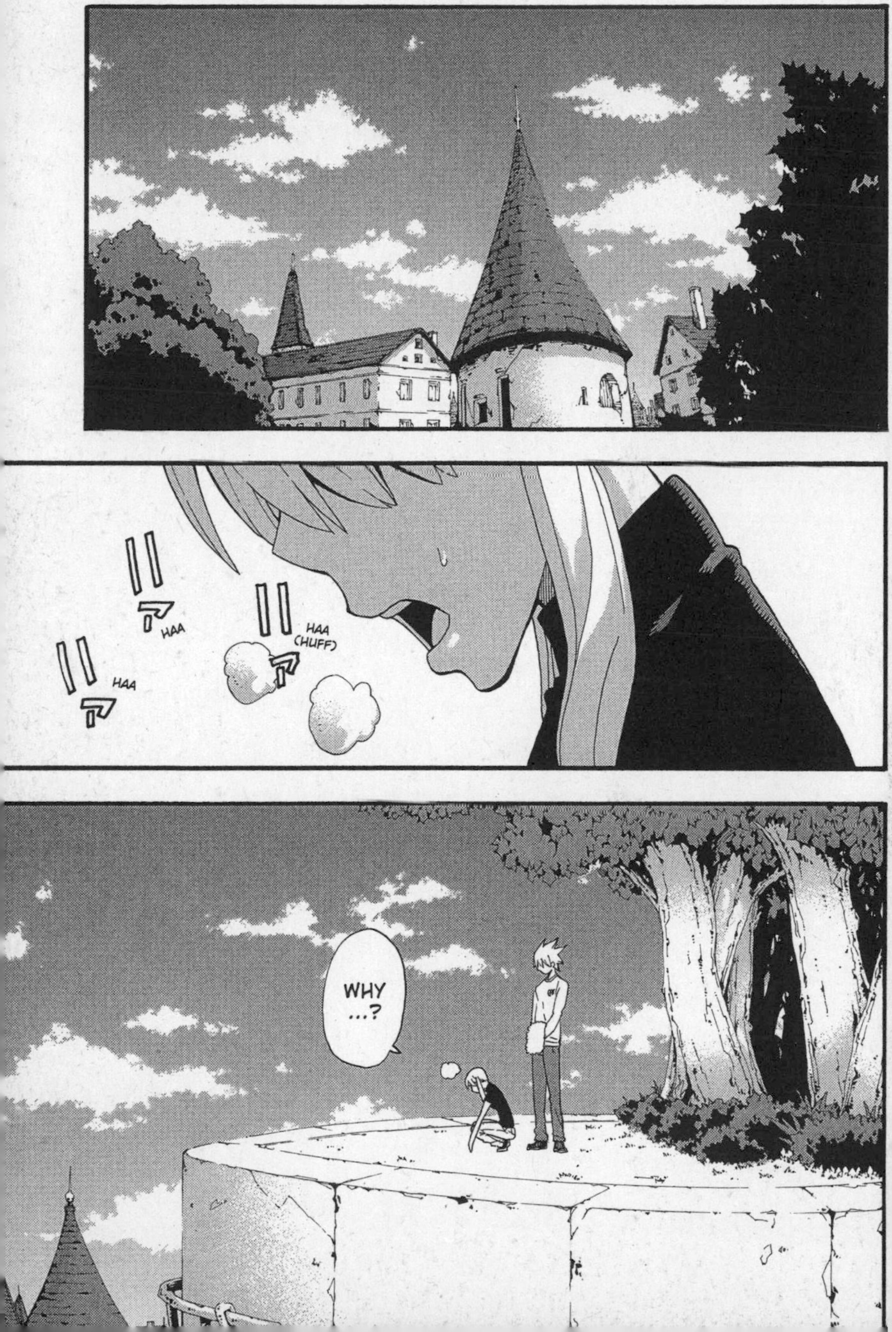
HAA (HUFF)
HAA
HAA
WHY ...?

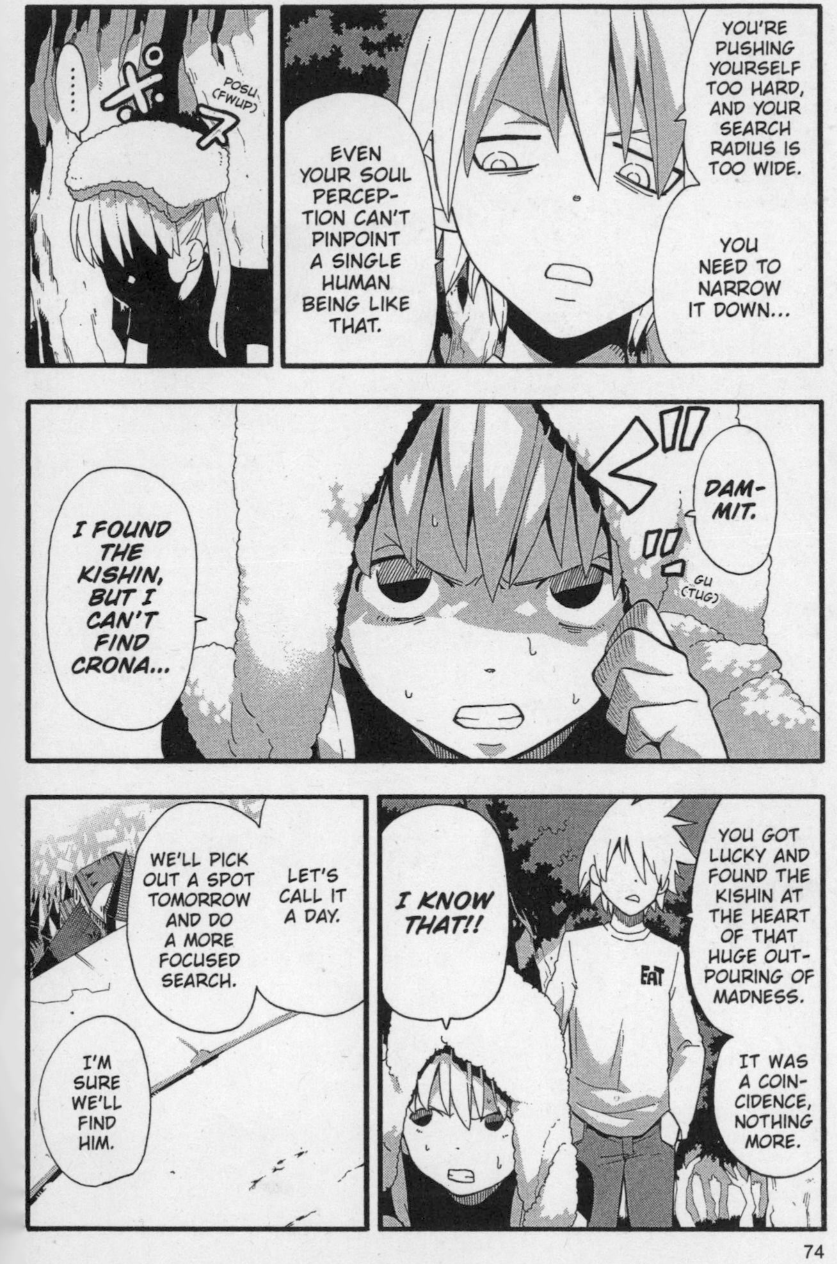
YOU'RE PUSHING YOURSELF TOO HARD, AND YOUR SEARCH RADIUS IS TOO WIDE.
YOU NEED TO NARROW IT DOWN...
EVEN YOUR SOUL PERCEPTION CAN'T PINPOINT A SINGLE HUMAN BEING LIKE THAT.
POSU (FWUP)
......
DAMMIT.
GU (TUG)
I FOUND THE KISHIN, BUT I CAN'T FIND CRONA...
YOU GOT LUCKY AND FOUND THE KISHIN AT THE HEART OF THAT HUGE OUTPOURING OF MADNESS.
IT WAS A COINCIDENCE, NOTHING MORE.
EAT
I KNOW THAT!!
LET'S CALL IT A DAY.
WE'LL PICK OUT A SPOT TOMORROW AND DO A MORE FOCUSED SEARCH.
I'M SURE WE'LL FIND HIM.

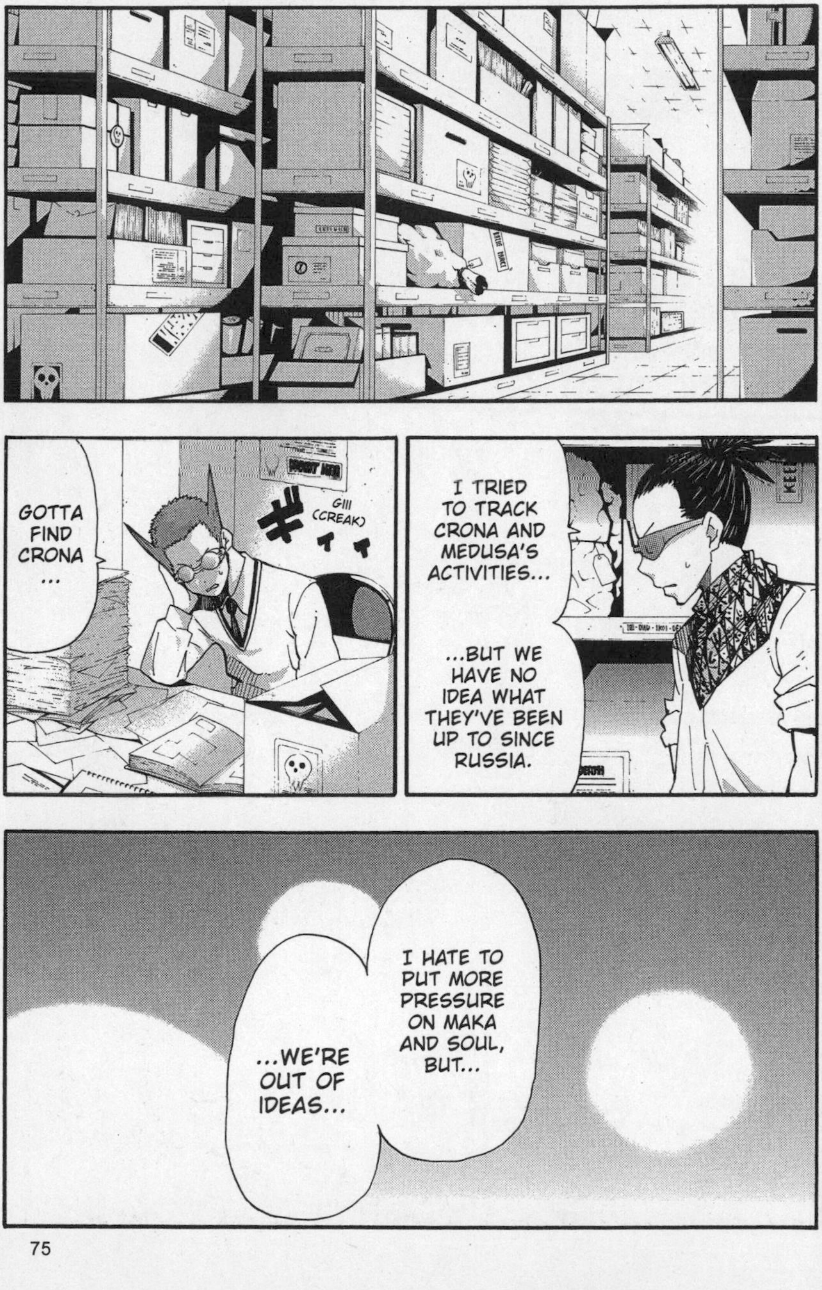
I TRIED TO TRACK CRONA AND MEDUSA'S ACTIVITIES...
...BUT WE HAVE NO IDEA WHAT THEY'VE BEEN UP TO SINCE RUSSIA.
GOTTA FIND CRONA ...
GIII (CREAK)
I HATE TO PUT MORE PRESSURE ON MAKA AND SOUL, BUT...
...WE'RE OUT OF IDEAS...

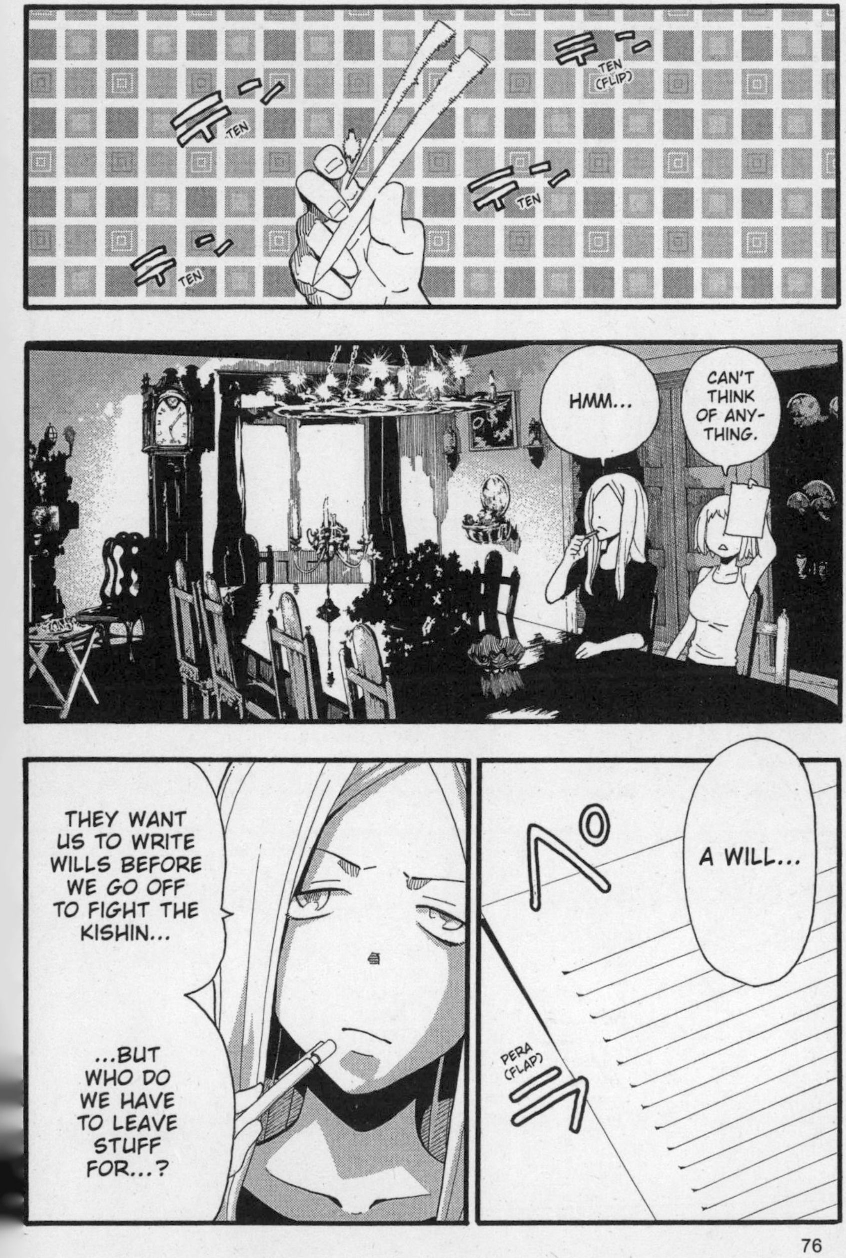
TEN (FLIP)
TEN
TEN
TEN
CAN'T THINK OF ANY-THING.
HMM...
A WILL...
PERA (FLAP)
THEY WANT US TO WRITE WILLS BEFORE WE GO OFF TO FIGHT THE KISHIN...
...BUT WHO DO WE HAVE TO LEAVE STUFF FOR...?

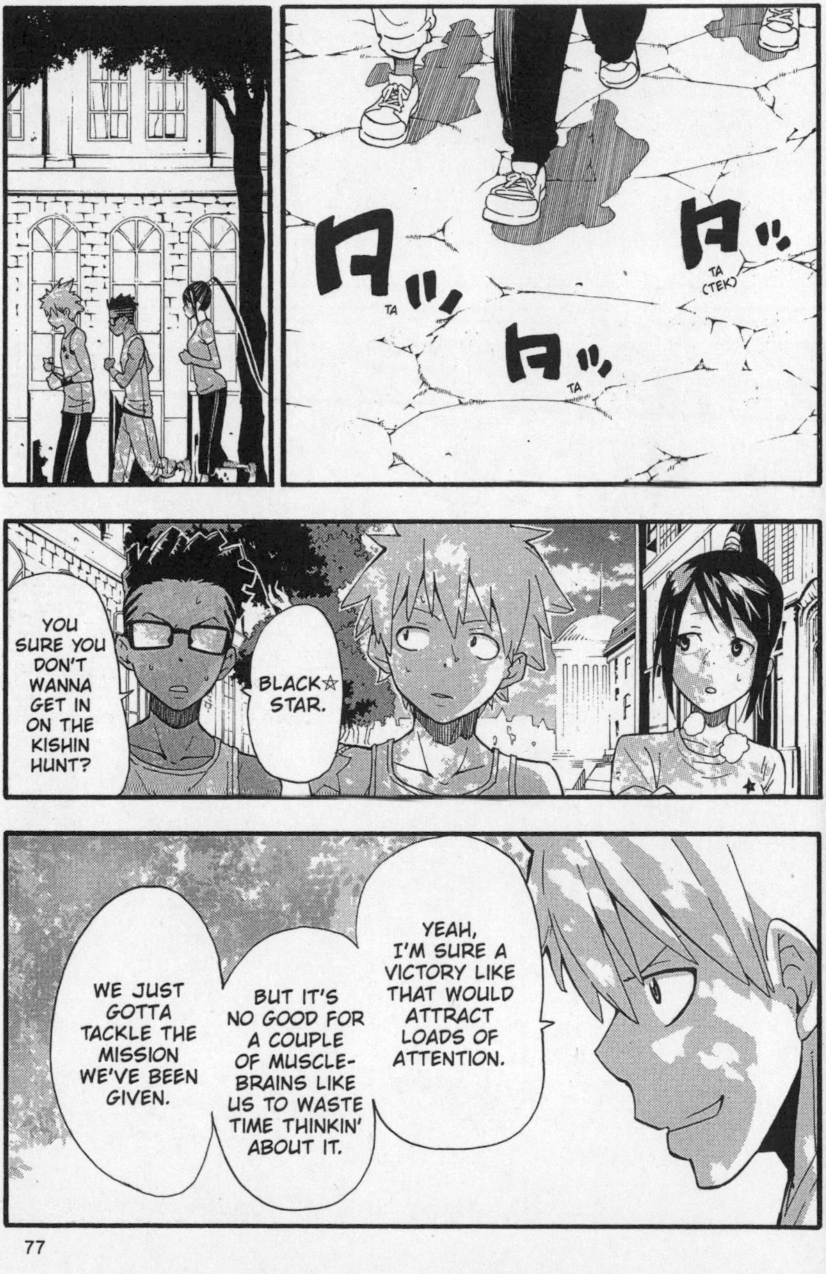
TA (TEK)
TA
TA
BLACK☆ STAR.
YOU SURE YOU DON'T WANNA GET IN ON THE KISHIN HUNT?
YEAH, I'M SURE A VICTORY LIKE THAT WOULD ATTRACT LOADS OF ATTENTION.
BUT IT'S NO GOOD FOR A COUPLE OF MUSCLE-BRAINS LIKE US TO WASTE TIME THINKIN' ABOUT IT.
WE JUST GOTTA TACKLE THE MISSION WE'VE BEEN GIVEN.

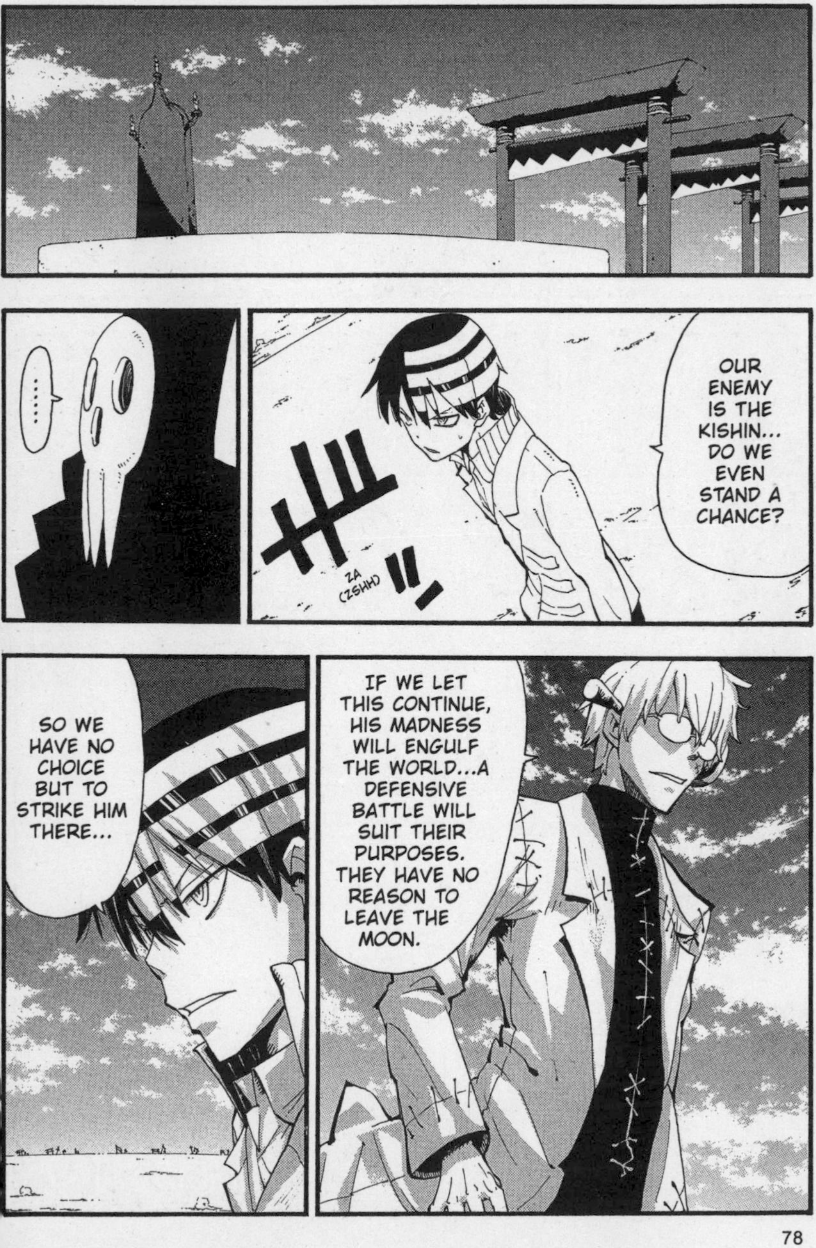
OUR ENEMY IS THE KISHIN... DO WE EVEN STAND A CHANCE?
ZA (ZSHH)
......
IF WE LET THIS CONTINUE, HIS MADNESS WILL ENGULF THE WORLD...A DEFENSIVE BATTLE WILL SUIT THEIR PURPOSES. THEY HAVE NO REASON TO LEAVE THE MOON.
SO WE HAVE NO CHOICE BUT TO STRIKE HIM THERE...

SHINIGAMI-SAMA IS TIED DOWN TO DEATH CITY...KID'S AWAKENING IS CRUCIAL TO OUR VICTORY...

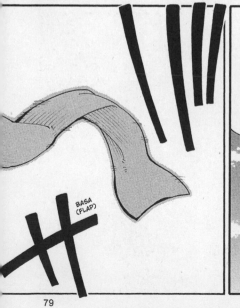

BASA
(FLAP)

WE'VE GOT THE DEATH WEAPONS FROM EAST ASIA, WEST ASIA, AND AFRICA.

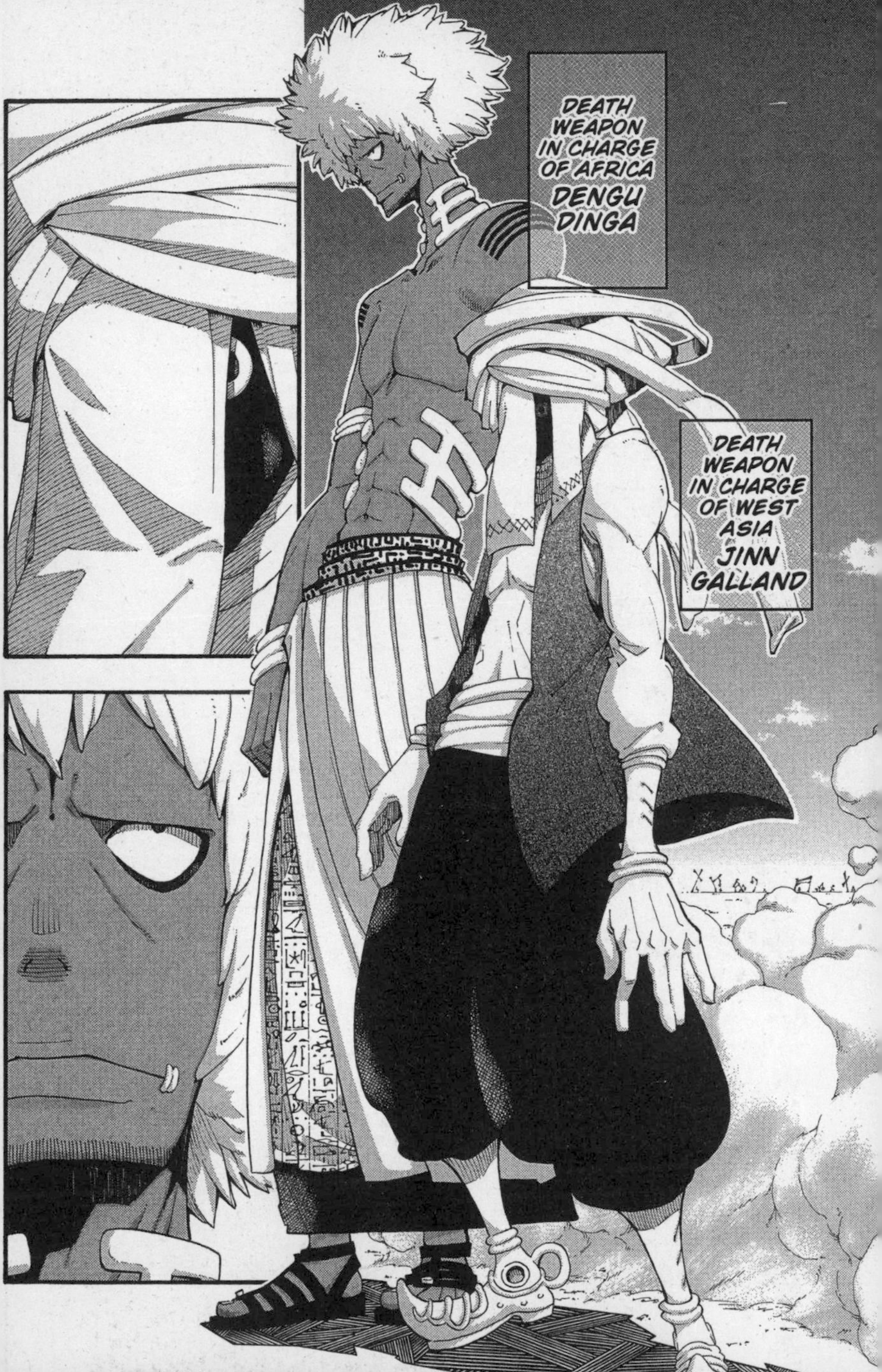
DEATH WEAPON IN CHARGE OF AFRICA DENGU DINGA
DEATH WEAPON IN CHARGE OF WEST ASIA JINN GALLAND

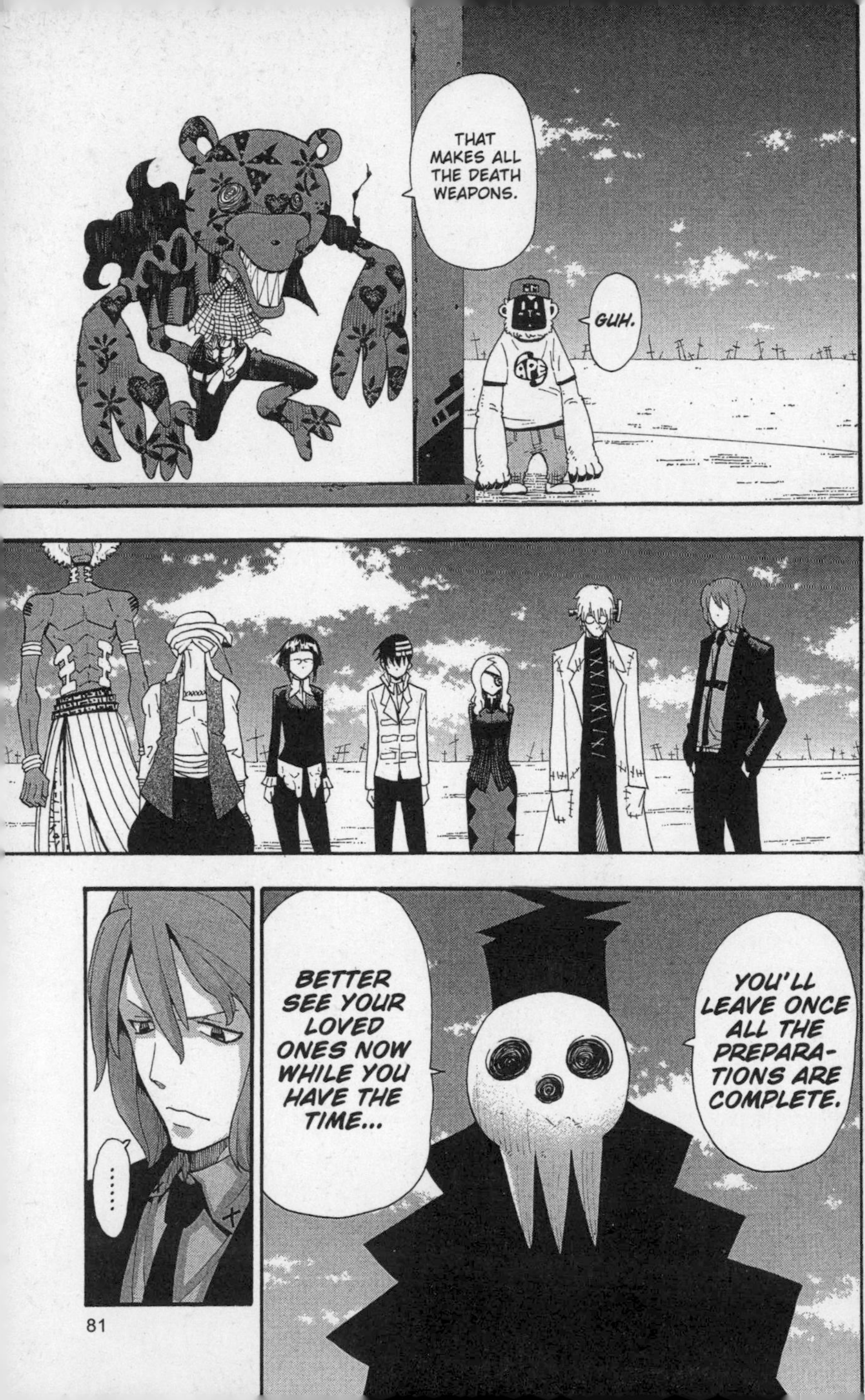
THAT MAKES ALL THE DEATH WEAPONS.
GUH.
YOU'LL LEAVE ONCE ALL THE PREPARA-TIONS ARE COMPLETE.
BETTER SEE YOUR LOVED ONES NOW WHILE YOU HAVE THE TIME...
......

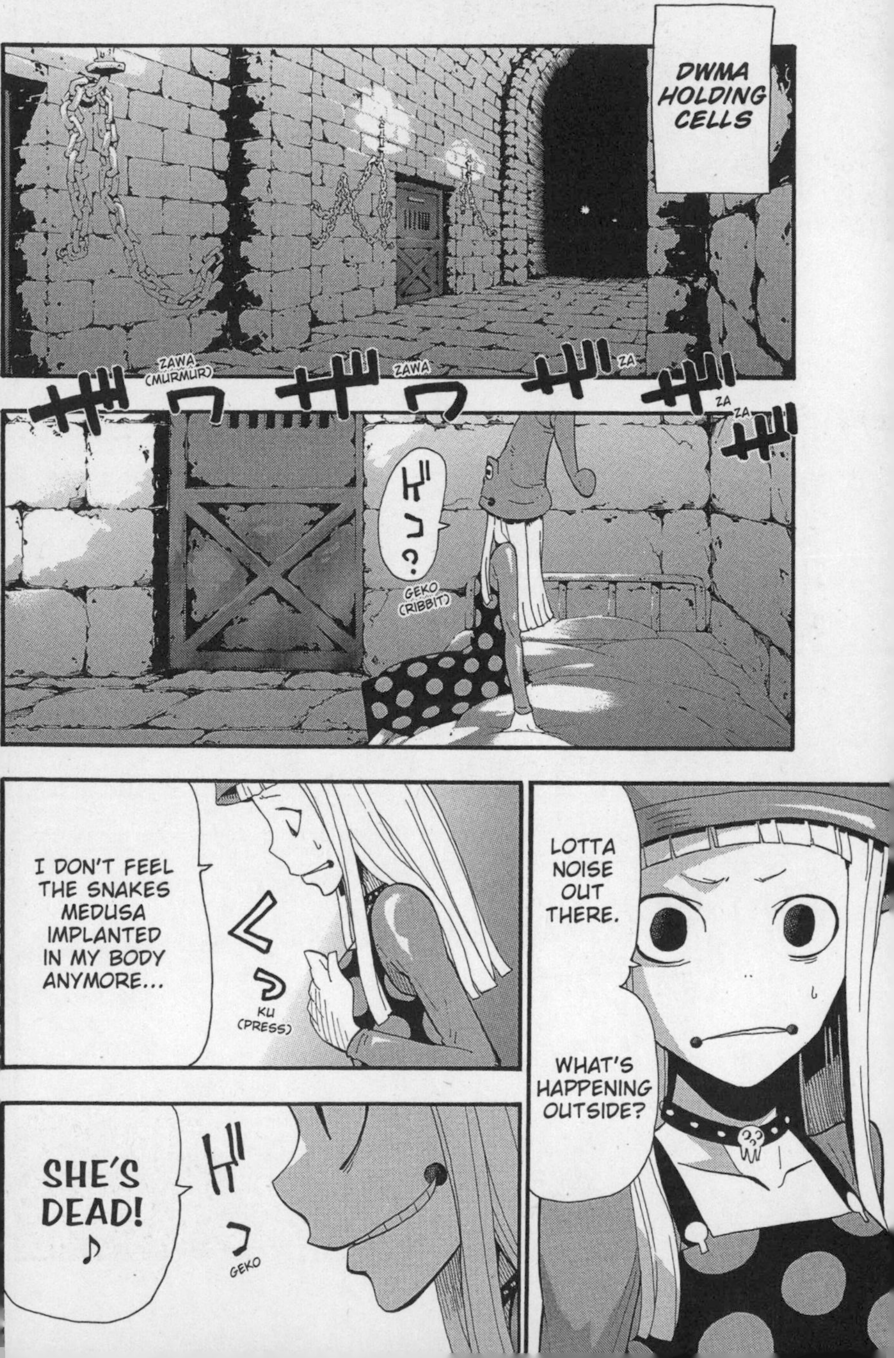
DWMA HOLDING CELLS
ZAWA (MURMUR)
ZAWA
ZA
ZA
ZA
GEKO (RIBBIT)
LOTTA NOISE OUT THERE.
WHAT'S HAPPENING OUTSIDE?
I DON'T FEEL THE SNAKES MEDUSA IMPLANTED IN MY BODY ANYMORE...
KU (PRESS)
SHE'S DEAD! ♪
GEKO

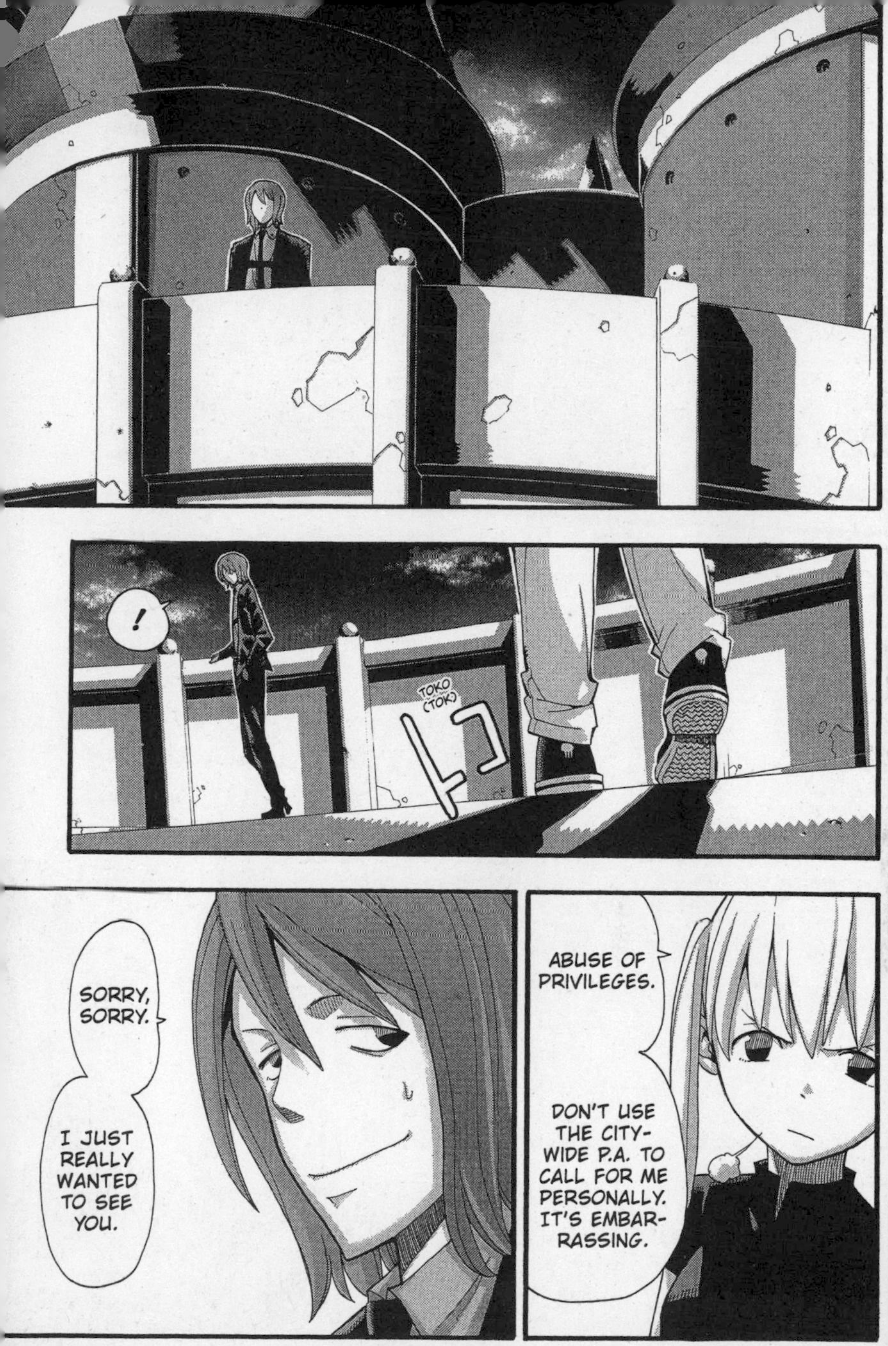
TOKO (TOK)
!
ABUSE OF PRIVILEGES.
DON'T USE THE CITY-WIDE P.A. TO CALL FOR ME PERSONALLY. IT'S EMBARRASSING.
SORRY, SORRY.
I JUST REALLY WANTED TO SEE YOU.

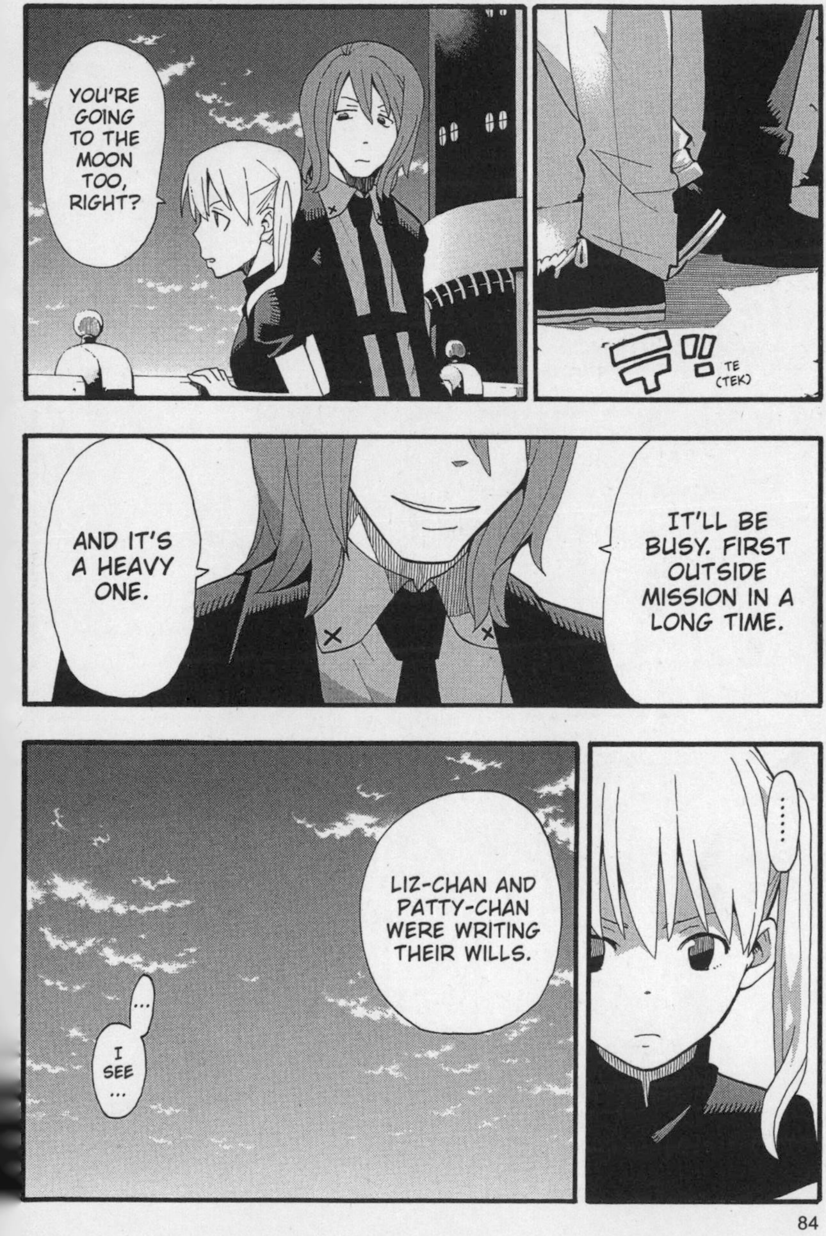
TE (TEK)
YOU'RE GOING TO THE MOON TOO, RIGHT?
IT'LL BE BUSY. FIRST OUTSIDE MISSION IN A LONG TIME.
AND IT'S A HEAVY ONE.
......
LIZ-CHAN AND PATTY-CHAN WERE WRITING THEIR WILLS.
... I SEE ...

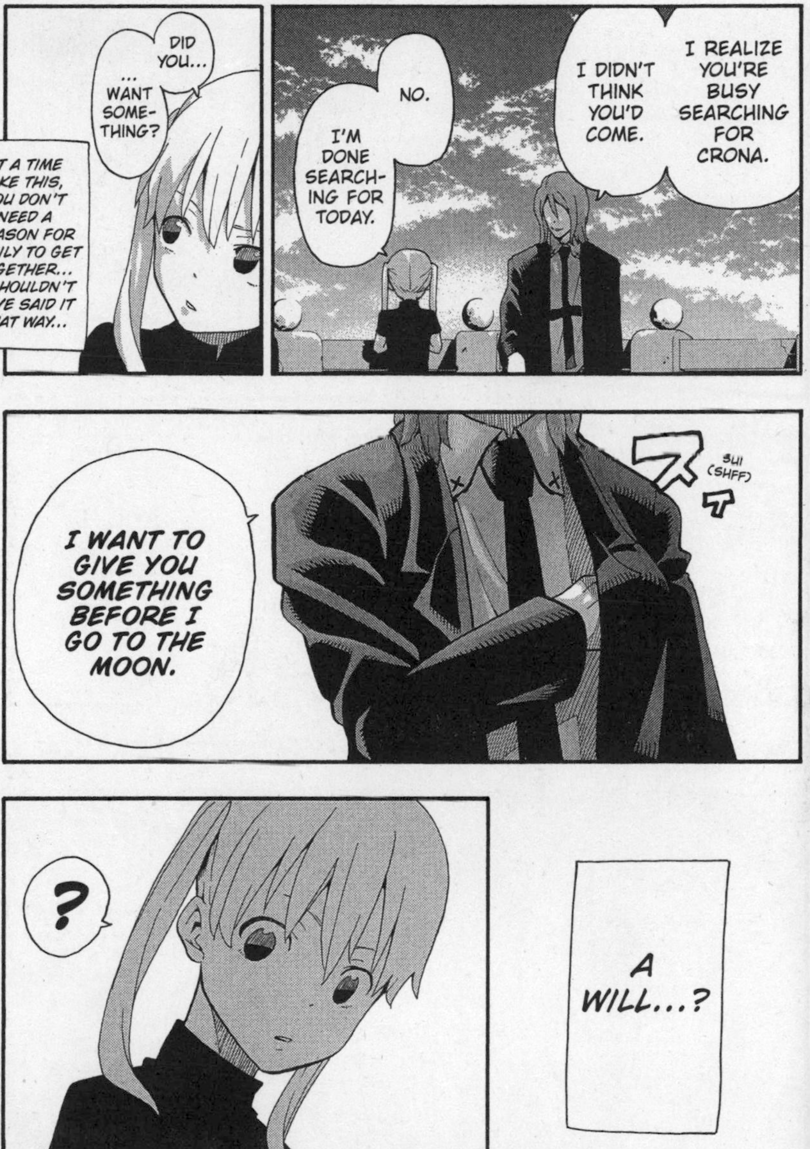
I REALIZE YOU'RE BUSY SEARCHING FOR CRONA.
I DIDN'T THINK YOU'D COME.
NO.
I'M DONE SEARCHING FOR TODAY.
DID YOU...
...WANT SOMETHING?
AT A TIME LIKE THIS, YOU DON'T NEED A REASON FOR FAMILY TO GET TOGETHER... I SHOULDN'T HAVE SAID IT THAT WAY...
SUI (SHFF)
I WANT TO GIVE YOU SOMETHING BEFORE I GO TO THE MOON.
A WILL...?
?

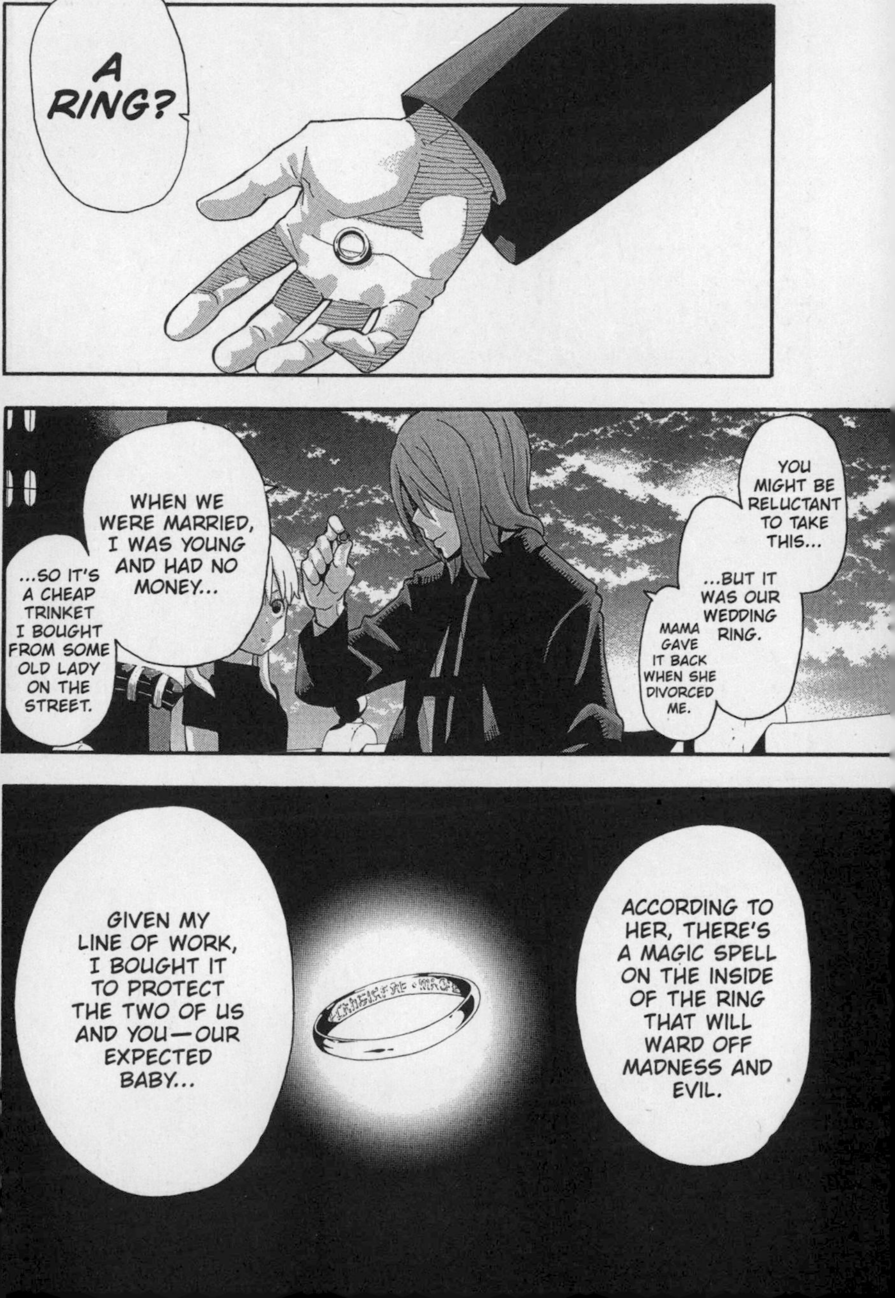
A RING?
YOU MIGHT BE RELUCTANT TO TAKE THIS...
...BUT IT WAS OUR WEDDING RING.
MAMA GAVE IT BACK WHEN SHE DIVORCED ME.
WHEN WE WERE MARRIED, I WAS YOUNG AND HAD NO MONEY...
...SO IT'S A CHEAP TRINKET I BOUGHT FROM SOME OLD LADY ON THE STREET.
ACCORDING TO HER, THERE'S A MAGIC SPELL ON THE INSIDE OF THE RING THAT WILL WARD OFF MADNESS AND EVIL.
GIVEN MY LINE OF WORK, I BOUGHT IT TO PROTECT THE TWO OF US AND YOU—OUR EXPECTED BABY...

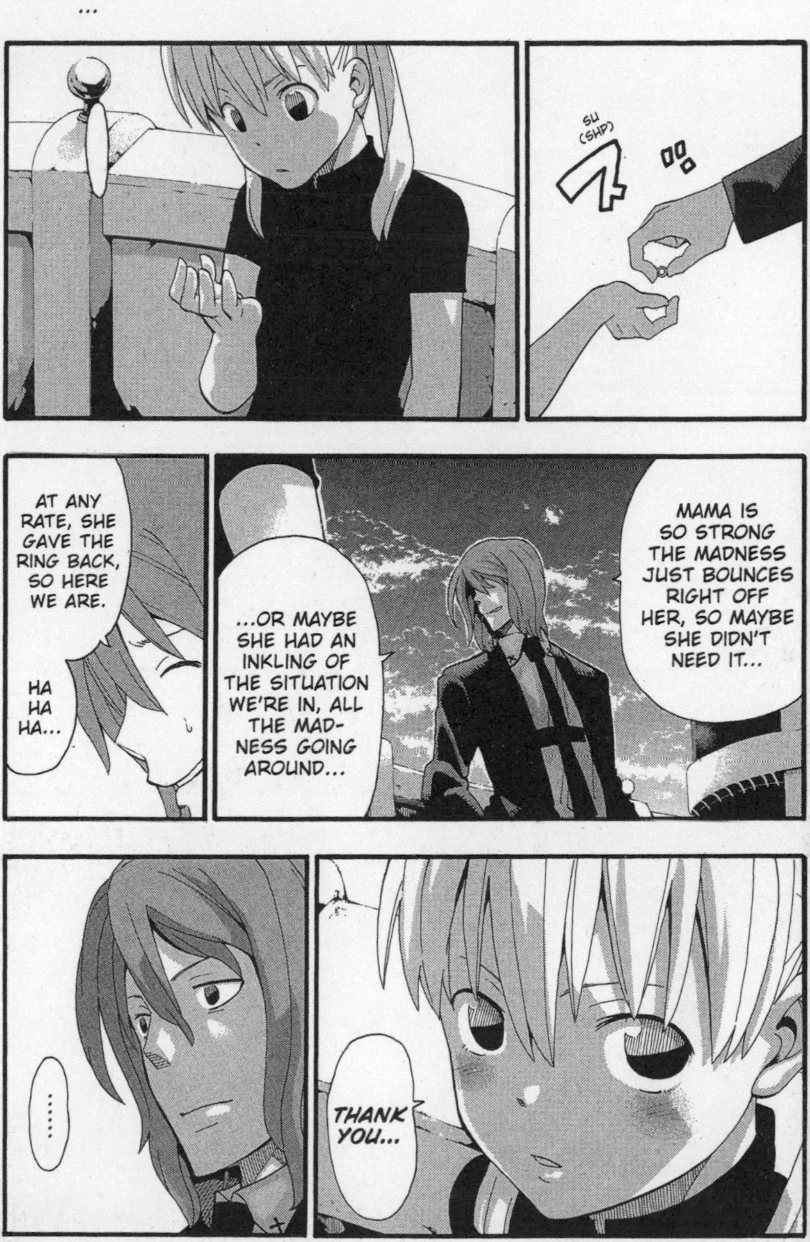
...
SU (SHP)
MAMA IS SO STRONG THE MADNESS JUST BOUNCES RIGHT OFF HER, SO MAYBE SHE DIDN'T NEED IT...
...OR MAYBE SHE HAD AN INKLING OF THE SITUATION WE'RE IN, ALL THE MAD-NESS GOING AROUND...
AT ANY RATE, SHE GAVE THE RING BACK, SO HERE WE ARE.
HA HA HA...
THANK YOU...
......

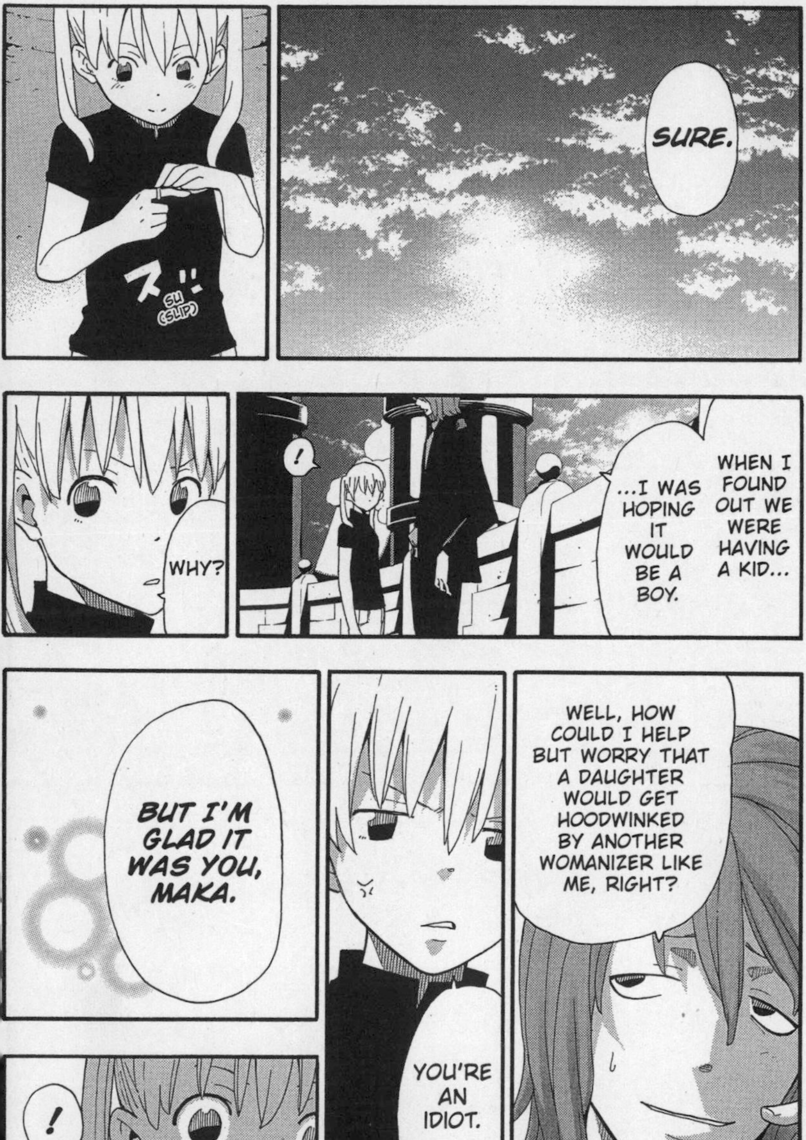
SURE.
ス゛
SU (SLIP)
WHEN I FOUND OUT WE WERE HAVING A KID...
...I WAS HOPING IT WOULD BE A BOY.
!
WHY?
WELL, HOW COULD I HELP BUT WORRY THAT A DAUGHTER WOULD GET HOODWINKED BY ANOTHER WOMANIZER LIKE ME, RIGHT?
YOU'RE AN IDIOT.
BUT I'M GLAD IT WAS YOU, MAKA.
!

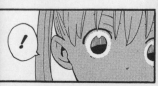

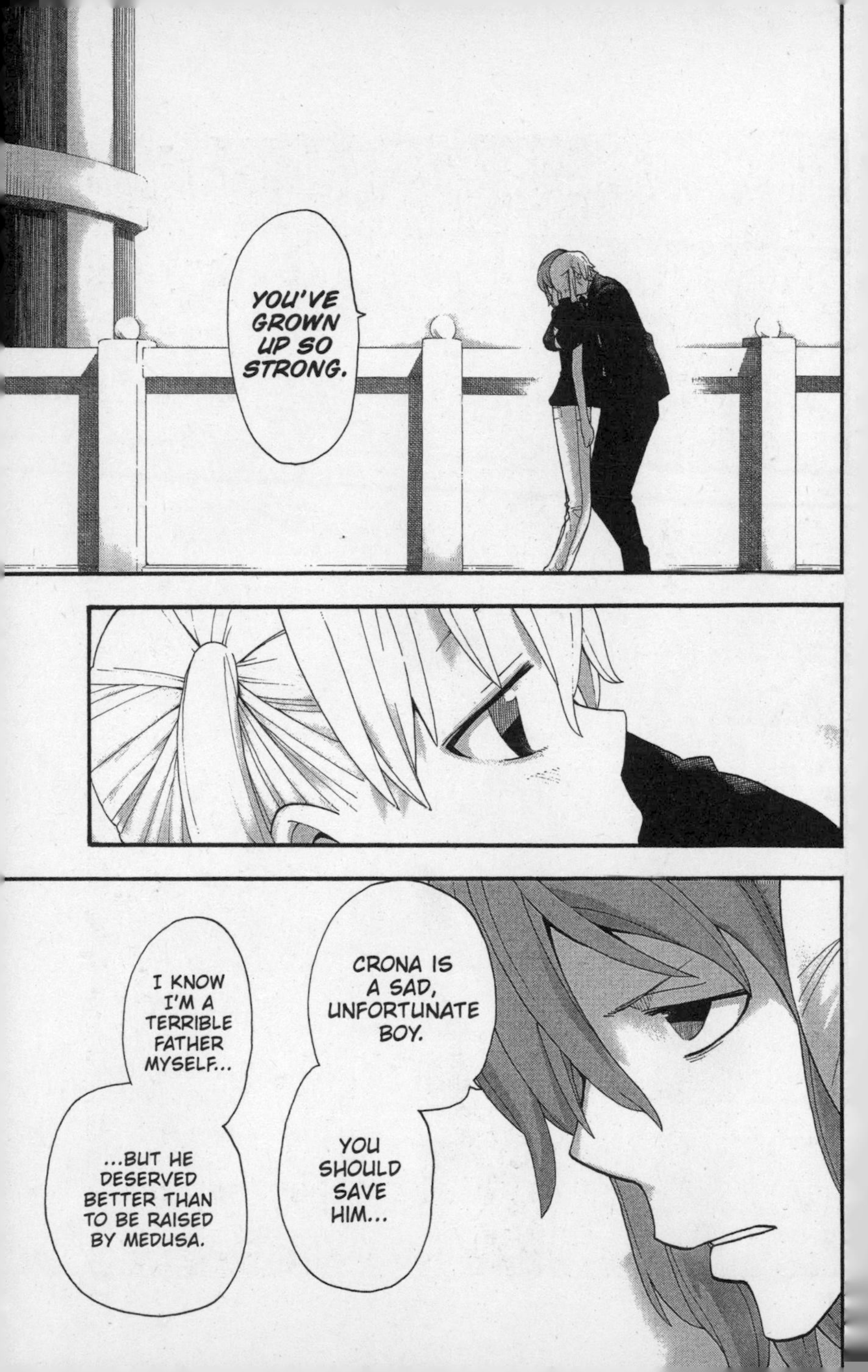
YOU'VE GROWN UP SO STRONG.
CRONA IS A SAD, UNFORTUNATE BOY.
I KNOW I'M A TERRIBLE FATHER MYSELF...
YOU SHOULD SAVE HIM...
...BUT HE DESERVED BETTER THAN TO BE RAISED BY MEDUSA.

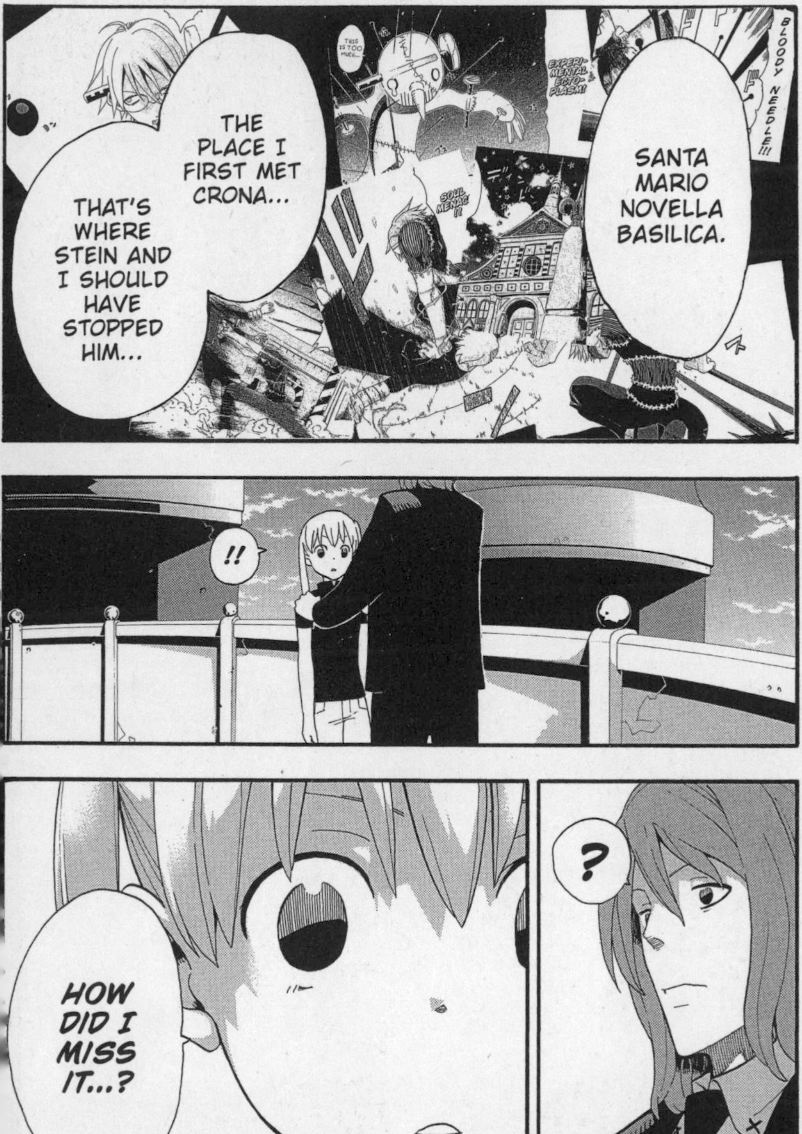

BLOODY NEEDLE!!!
SANTA MARIO NOVELLA BASILICA.
EXPERI-MENTAL ECTO-PLASM!
SOUL MENAC !!
THIS IS TOO MUCH...
THE PLACE I FIRST MET CRONA...
THAT'S WHERE STEIN AND I SHOULD HAVE STOPPED HIM...
!!
?
HOW DID I MISS IT...?

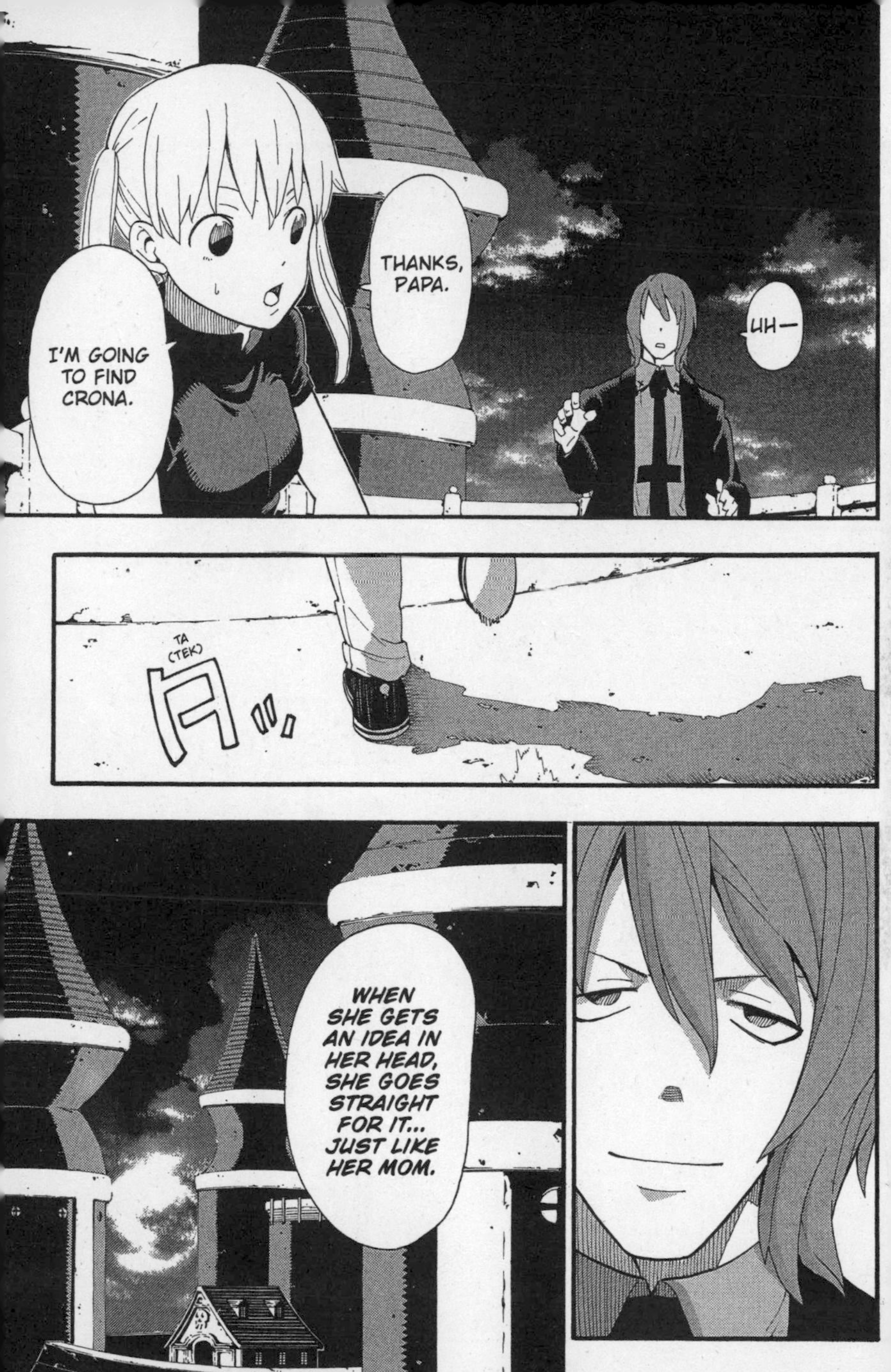
UH—
THANKS, PAPA.
I'M GOING TO FIND CRONA.
TA (TEK)
WHEN SHE GETS AN IDEA IN HER HEAD, SHE GOES STRAIGHT FOR IT... JUST LIKE HER MOM.

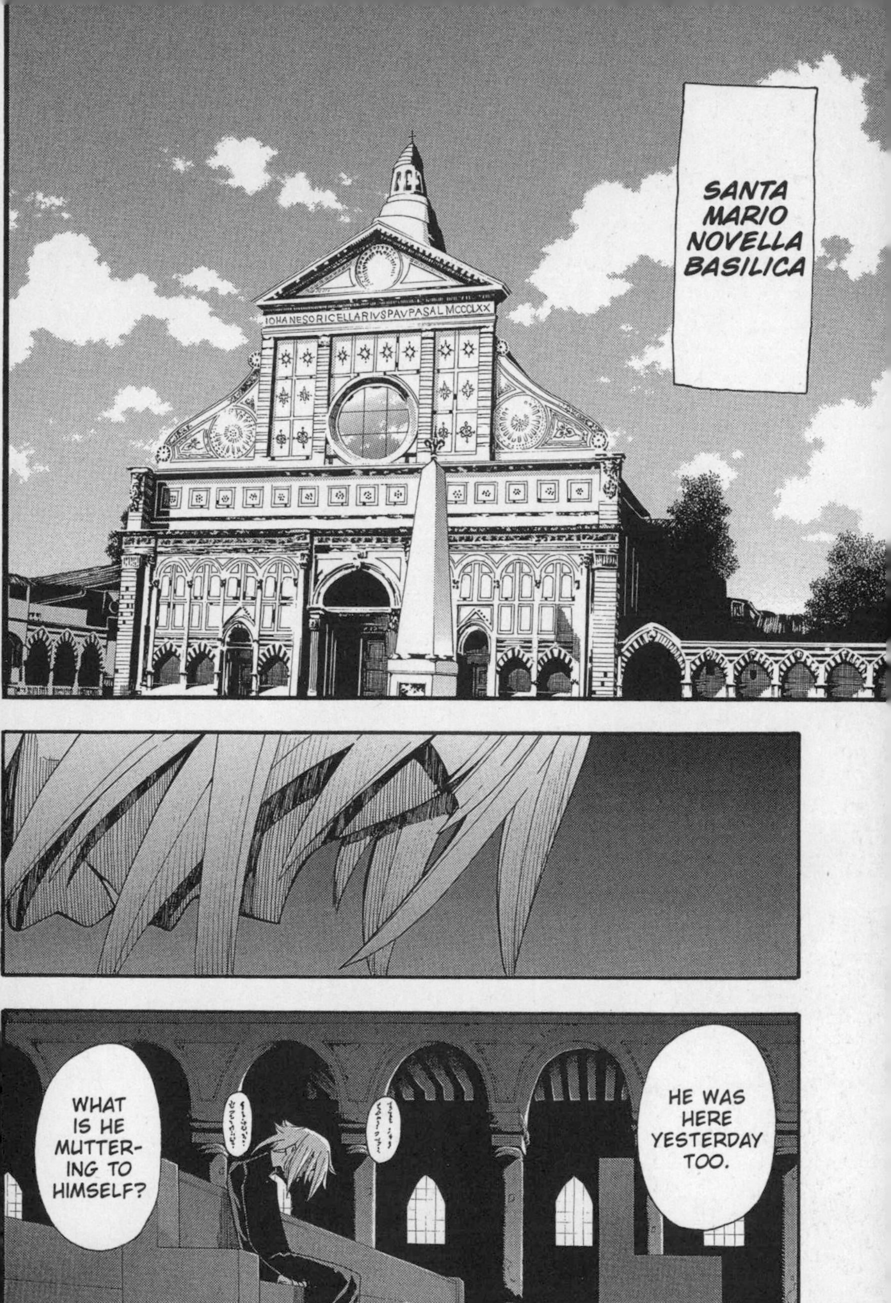
SANTA MARIO NOVELLA BASILICA
IOHANESORICELLARIVSPAVPASAL MCCCLXX
HE WAS HERE YESTERDAY TOO.
WHAT IS HE MUTTERING TO HIMSELF?

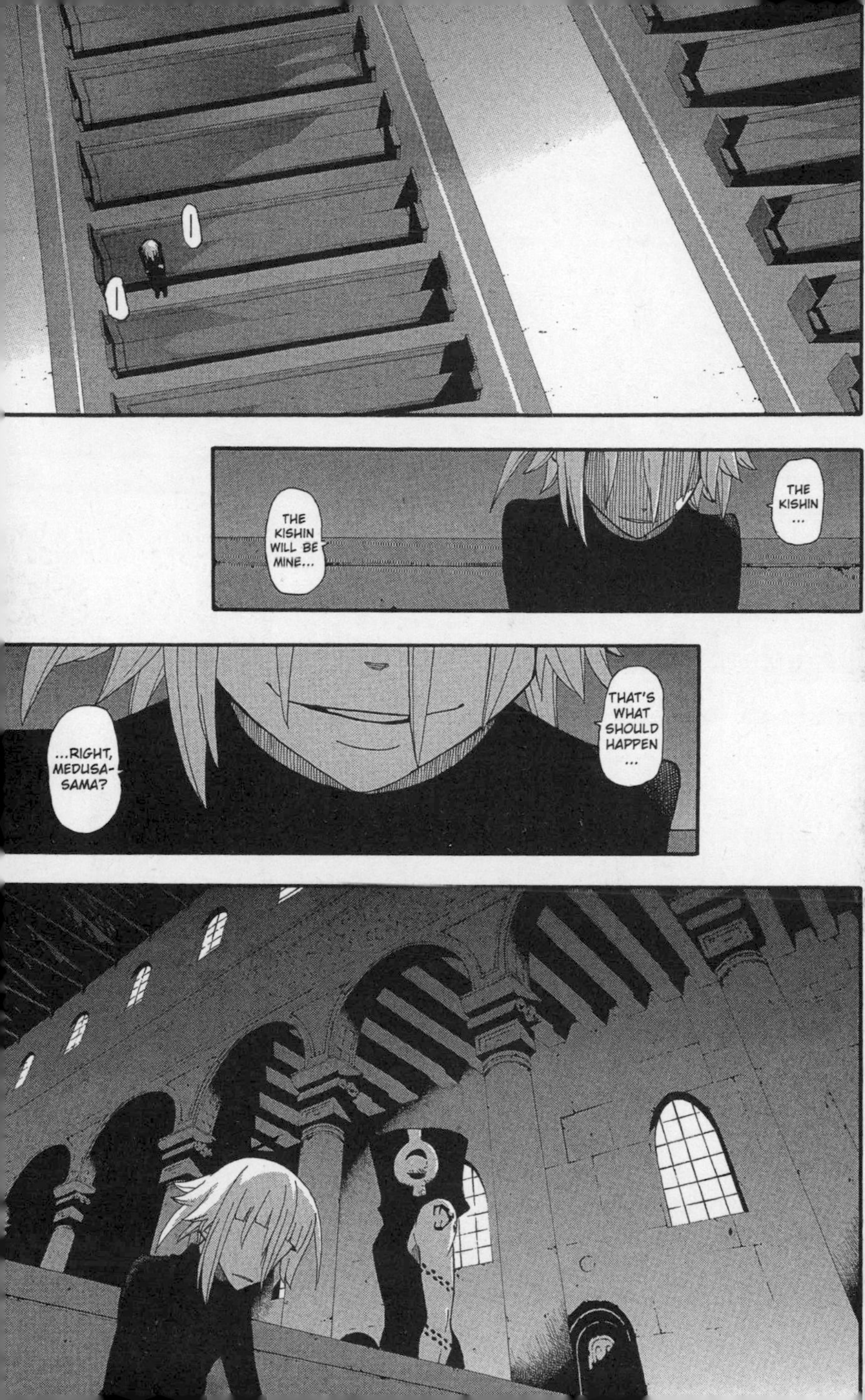
!
!
THE KISHIN ...
THE KISHIN WILL BE MINE...
THAT'S WHAT SHOULD HAPPEN ...
...RIGHT, MEDUSA-SAMA?

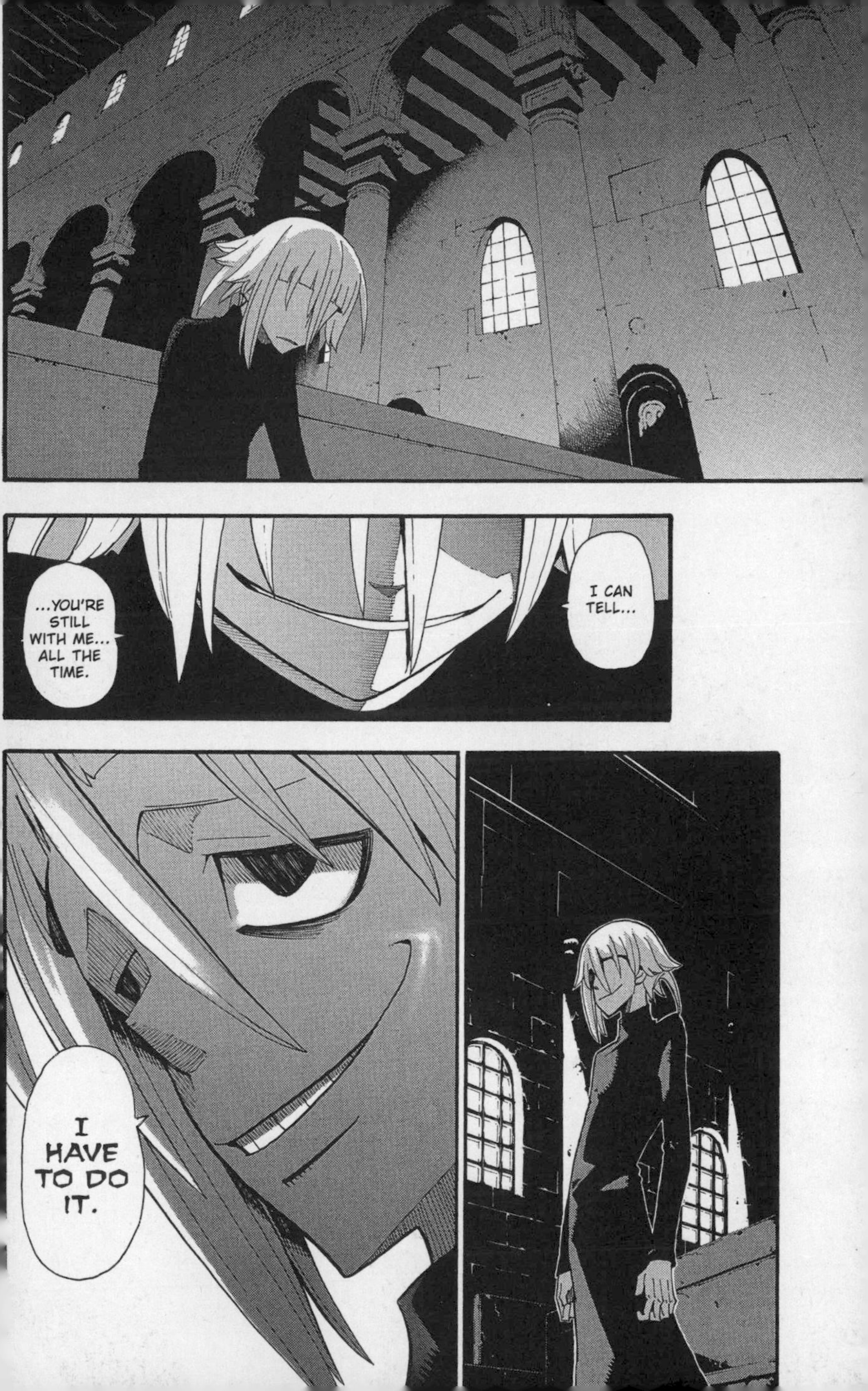
I CAN TELL...
...YOU'RE STILL WITH ME... ALL THE TIME.
I HAVE TO DO IT.

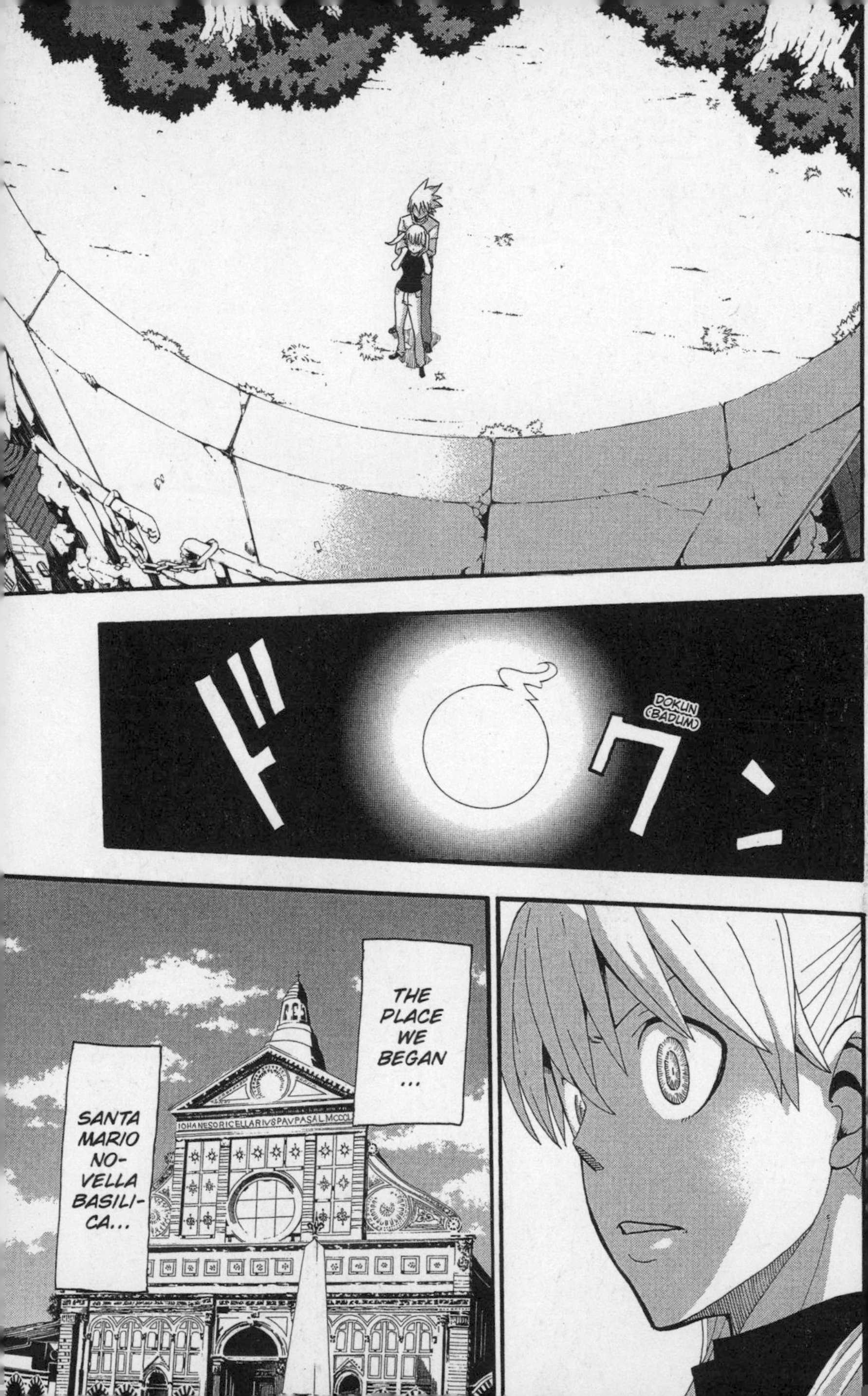
ドクン
DOKUN (BADUM)
THE PLACE WE BEGAN...
SANTA MARIO NO-VELLA BASILI-CA...

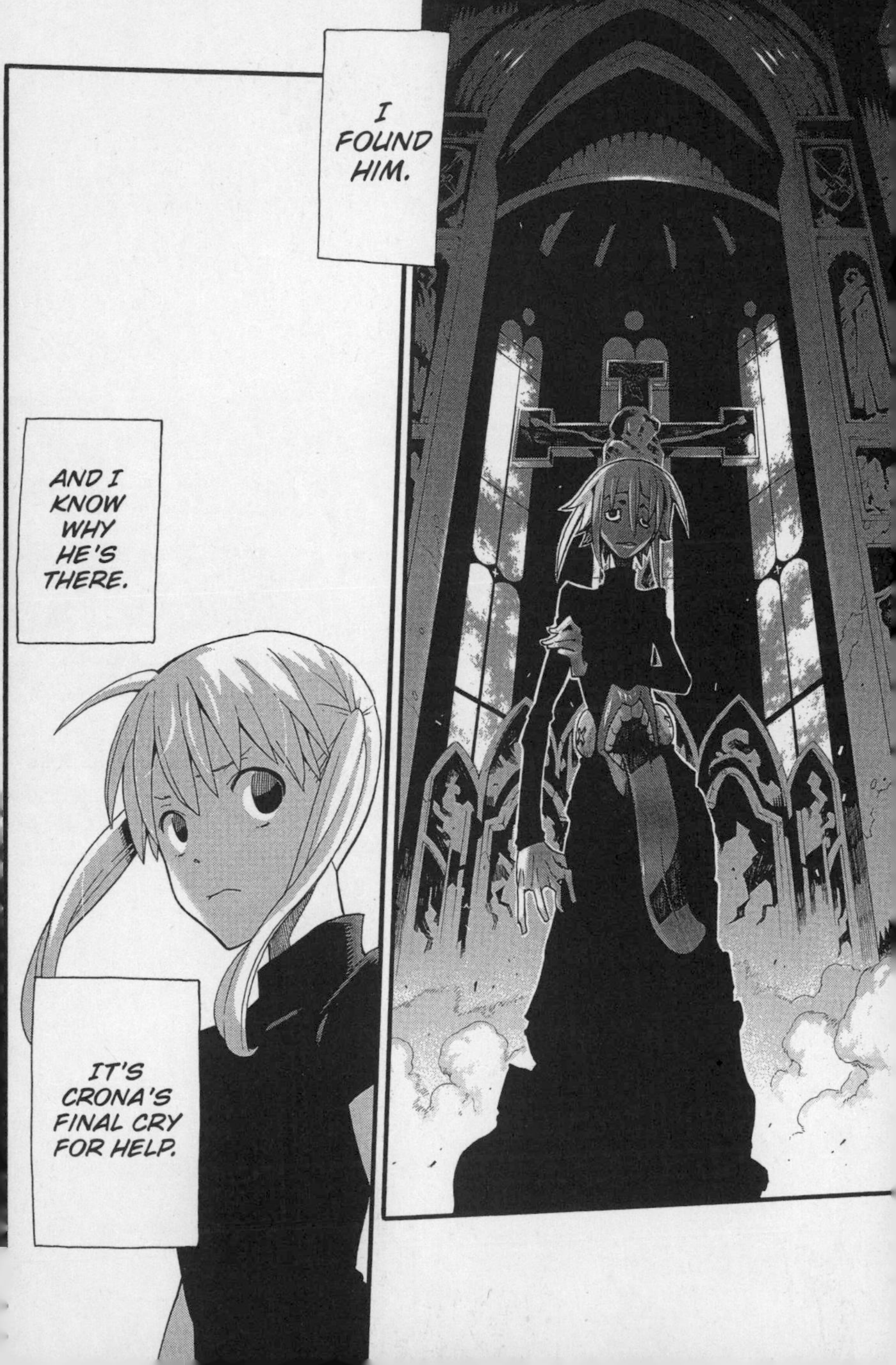
I FOUND HIM.
AND I KNOW WHY HE'S THERE.
IT'S CRONA'S FINAL CRY FOR HELP.

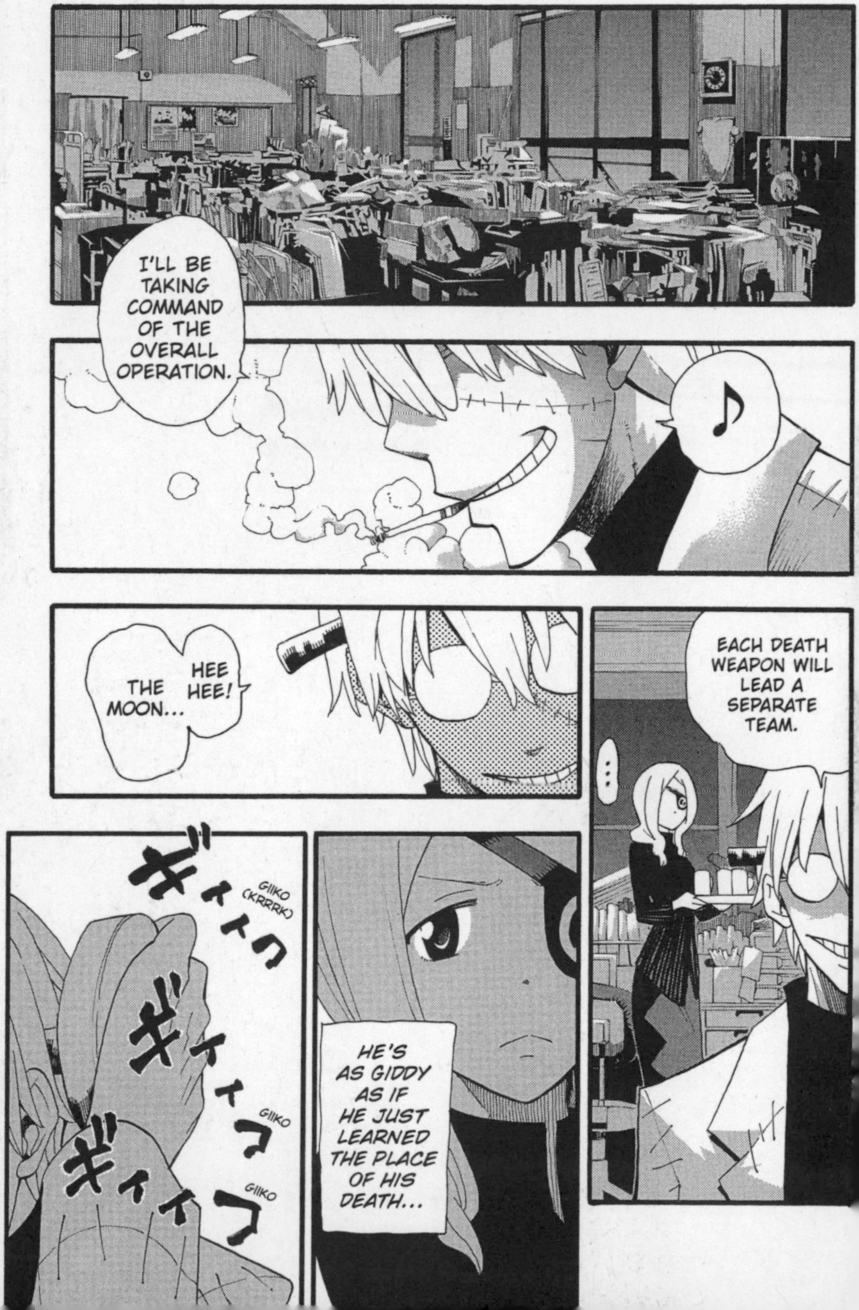
I'LL BE TAKING COMMAND OF THE OVERALL OPERATION.
♪
EACH DEATH WEAPON WILL LEAD A SEPARATE TEAM.
...
THE MOON... HEE HEE!
HE'S AS GIDDY AS IF HE JUST LEARNED THE PLACE OF HIS DEATH...
ギィィク
GIIKO (KRRRK)
ギィィコ
GIIKO
ギィィコ
GIIKO

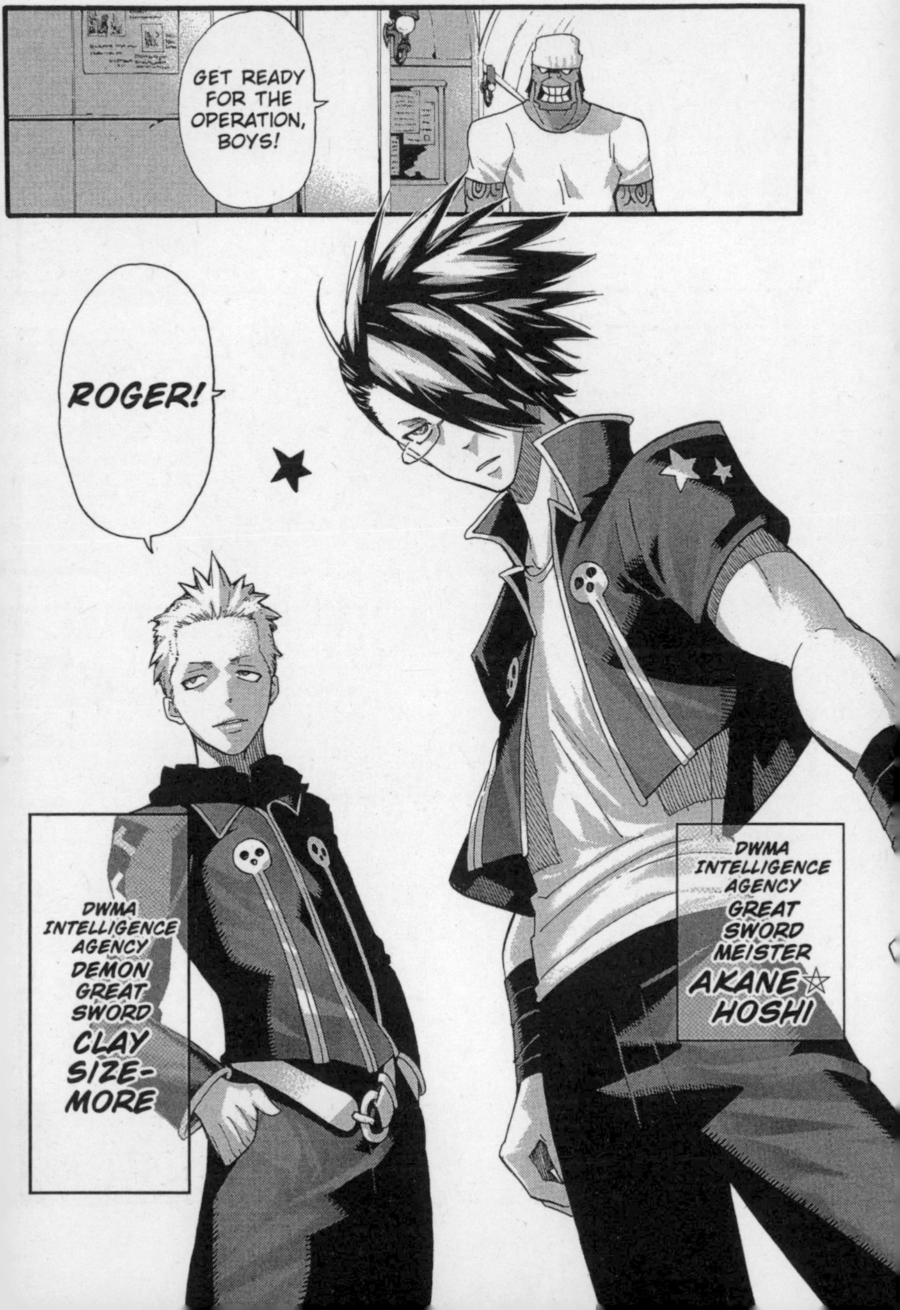
GET READY FOR THE OPERATION, BOYS!
ROGER!
DWMA INTELLIGENCE AGENCY GREAT SWORD MEISTER AKANE☆HOSHI
DWMA INTELLIGENCE AGENCY DEMON GREAT SWORD CLAY SIZE-MORE

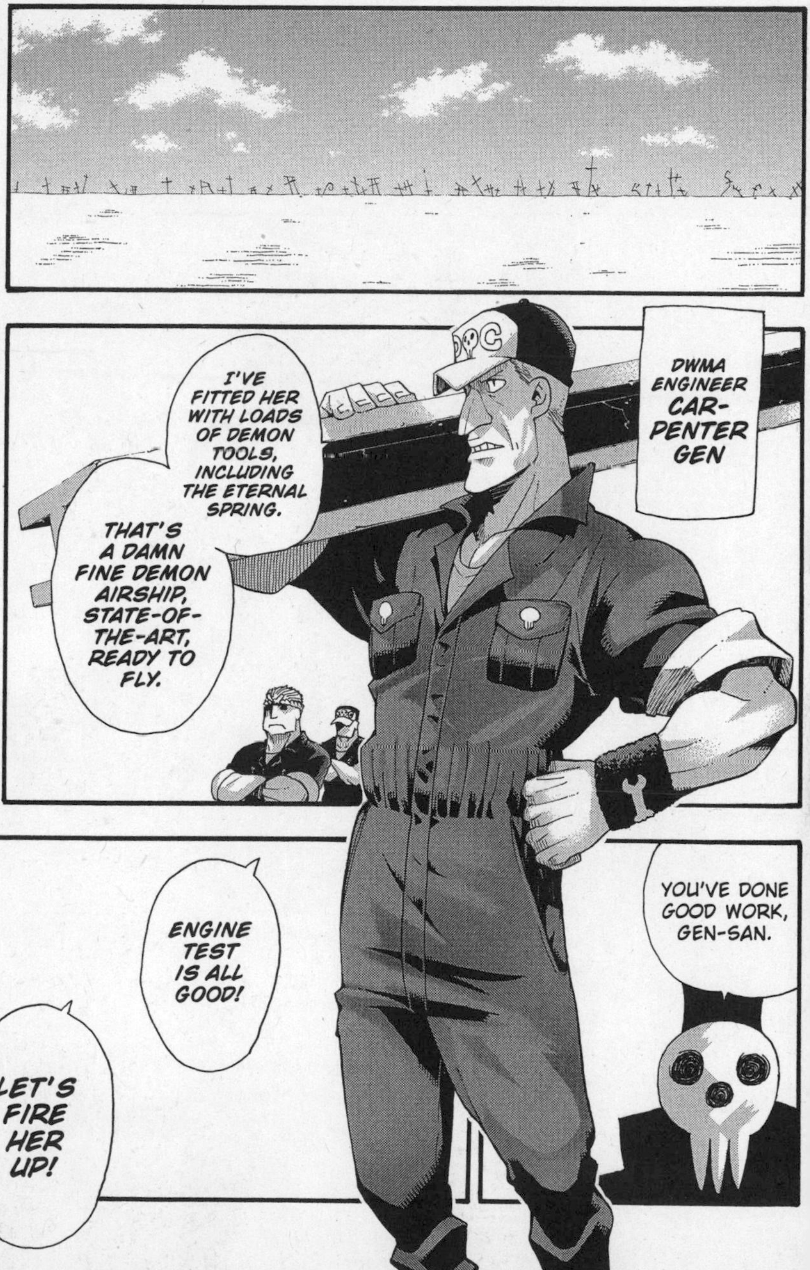
DWMA ENGINEER CARPENTER GEN
I'VE FITTED HER WITH LOADS OF DEMON TOOLS, INCLUDING THE ETERNAL SPRING.
THAT'S A DAMN FINE DEMON AIRSHIP, STATE-OF-THE-ART, READY TO FLY.
YOU'VE DONE GOOD WORK, GEN-SAN.
ENGINE TEST IS ALL GOOD!
LET'S FIRE HER UP!

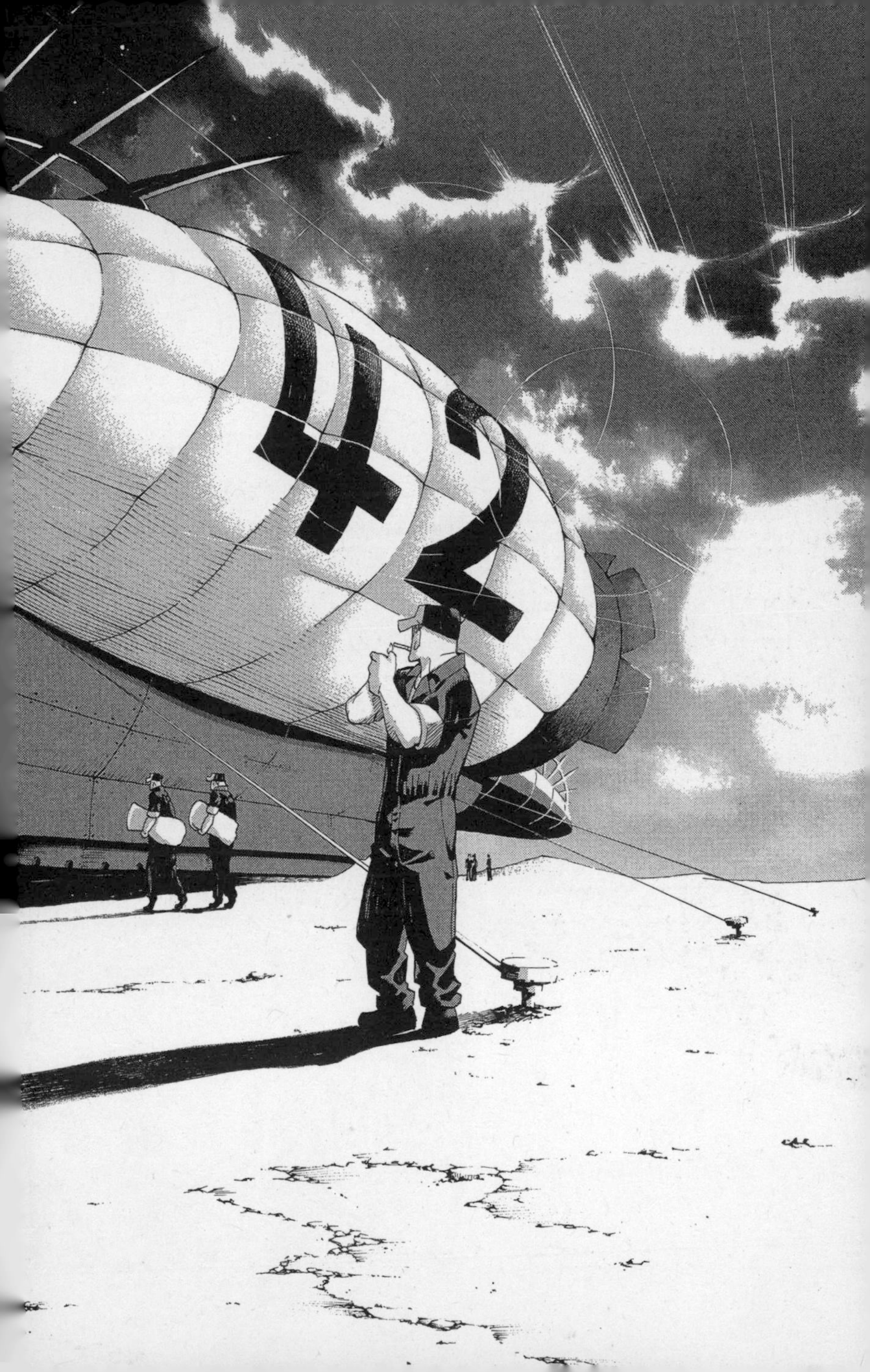

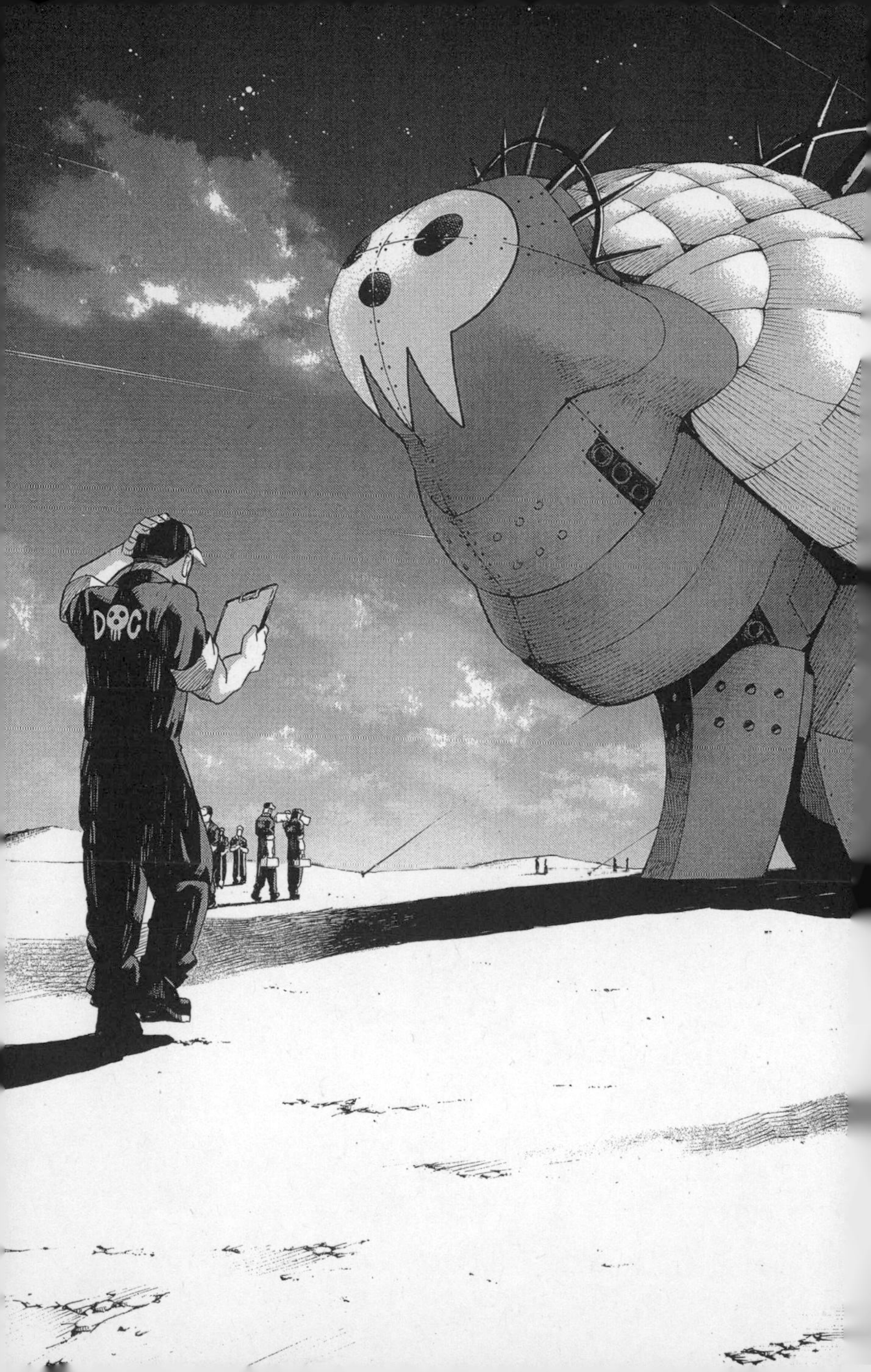

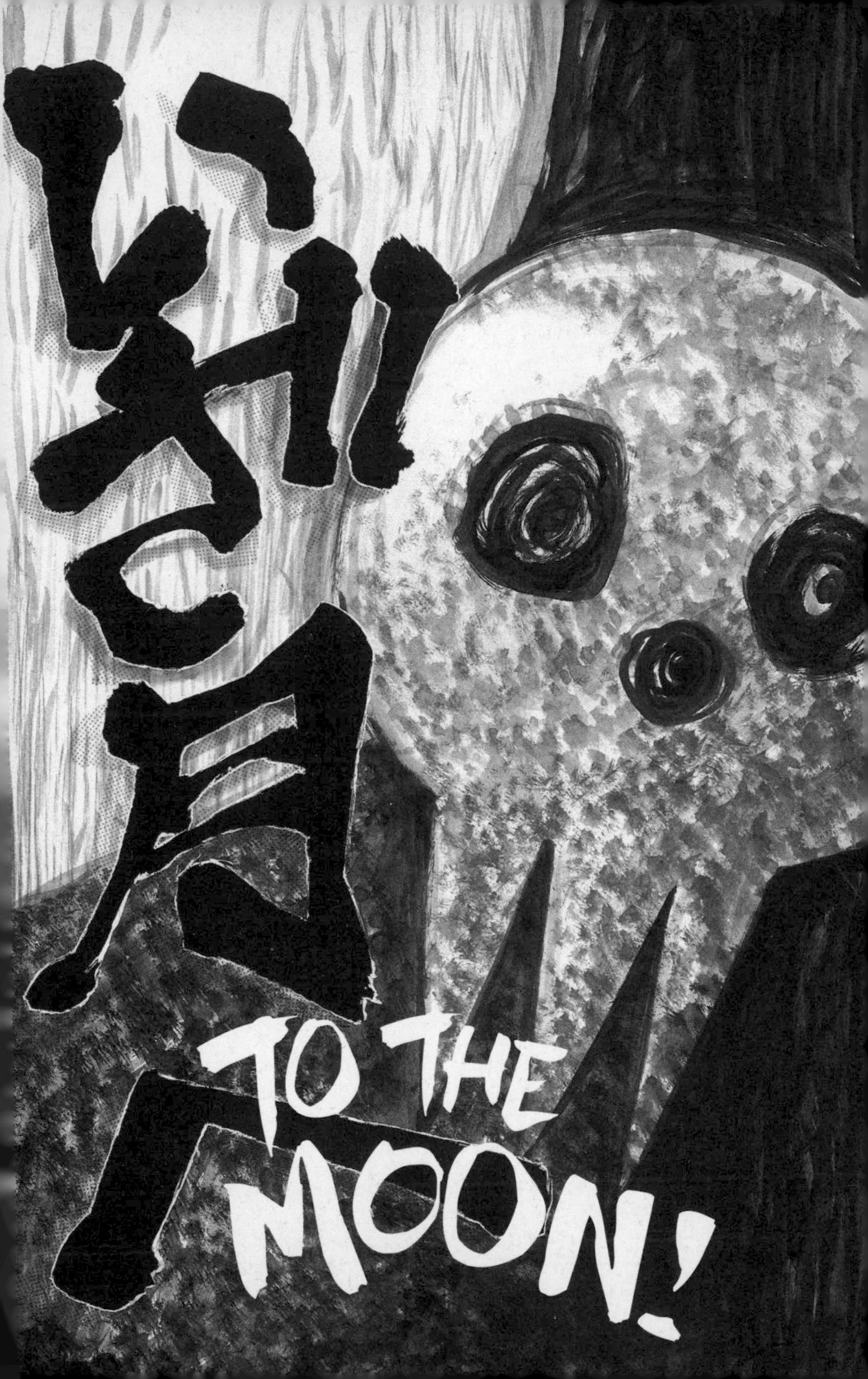
TO THE MOON!

SOUL EATER

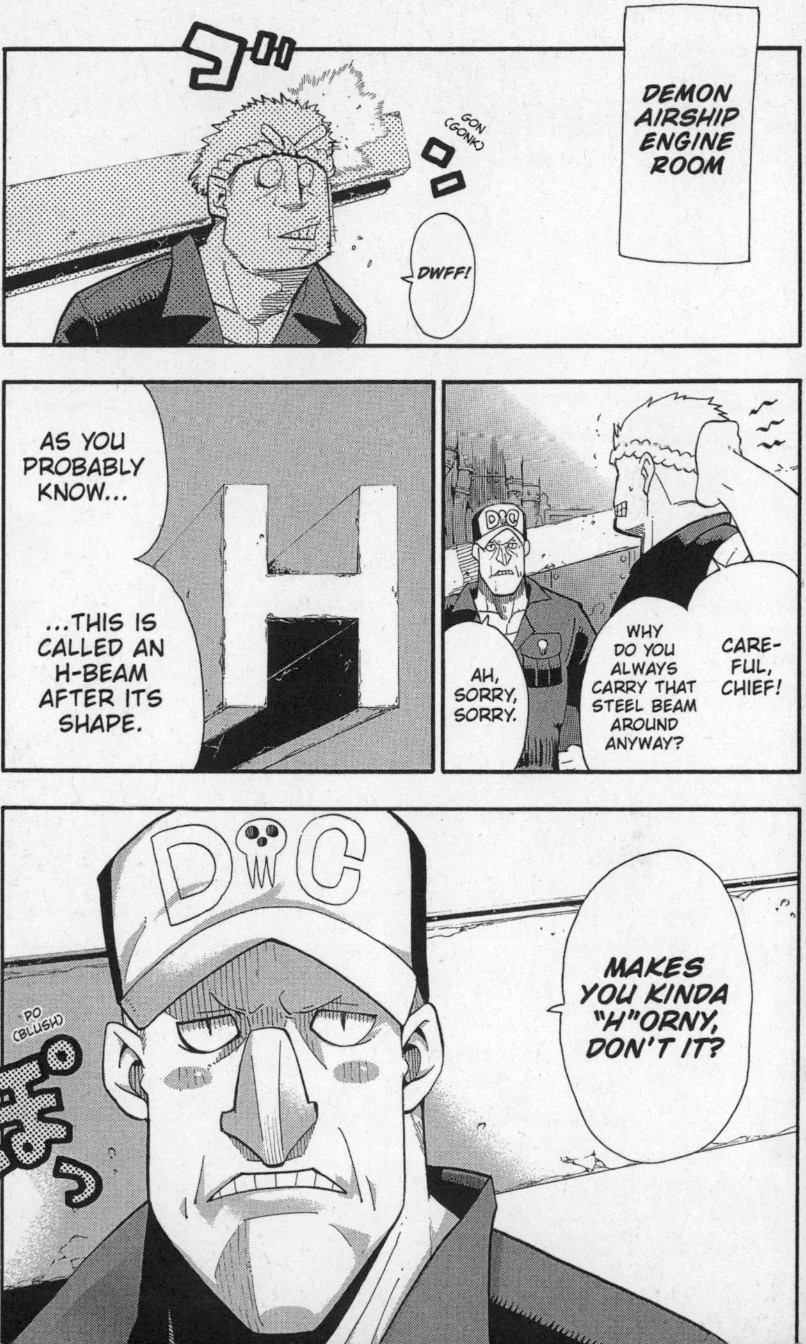
DEMON AIRSHIP ENGINE ROOM
GON (GONK)
DWFF!
CARE-FUL, CHIEF!
WHY DO YOU ALWAYS CARRY THAT STEEL BEAM AROUND ANYWAY?
AH, SORRY, SORRY.
AS YOU PROBABLY KNOW...
...THIS IS CALLED AN H-BEAM AFTER ITS SHAPE.
MAKES YOU KINDA "H"ORNY, DON'T IT?
PO (BLUSH)

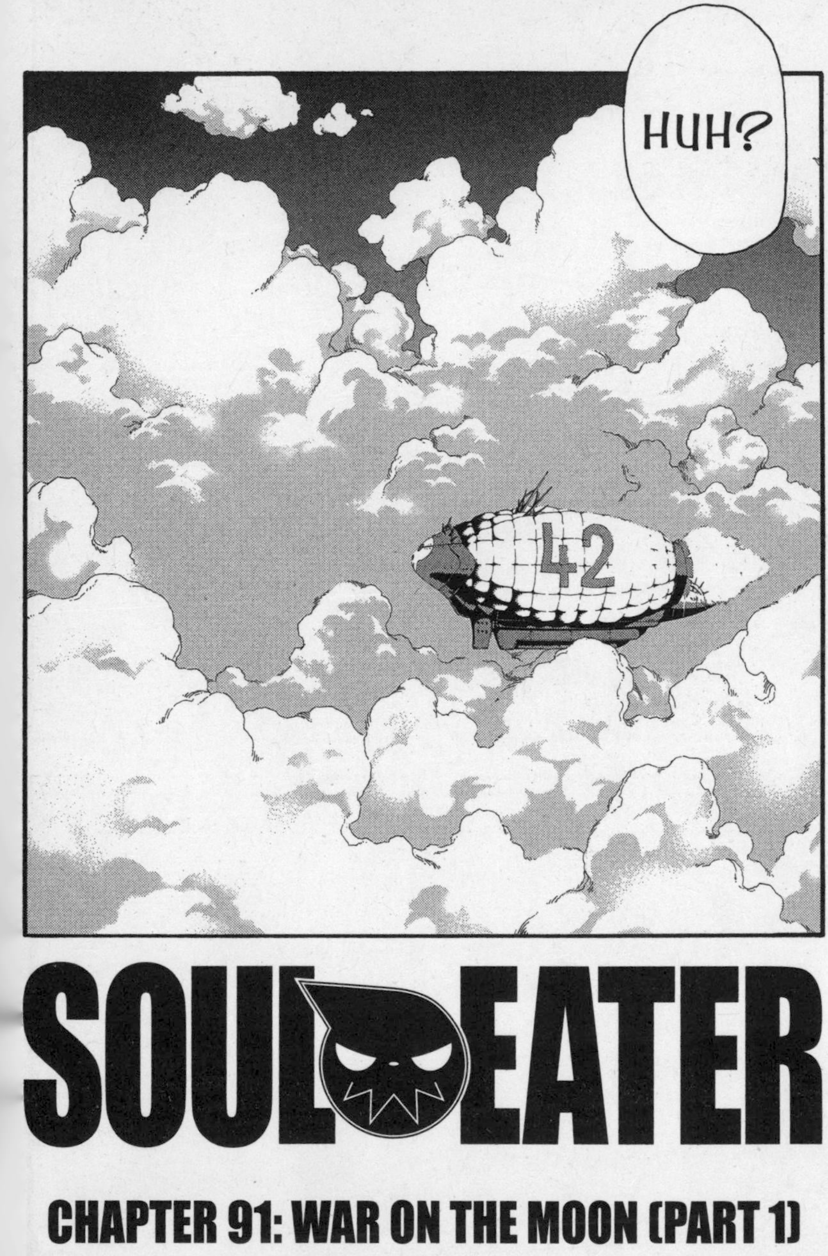
HUH?

SOUL EATER

CHAPTER 91: WAR ON THE MOON (PART 1)

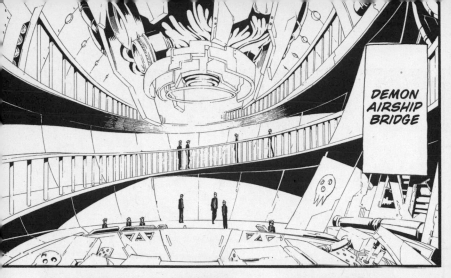

DEMON AIRSHIP BRIDGE

WHAT IS IT?

Bridge, this is Carpenter Gen.

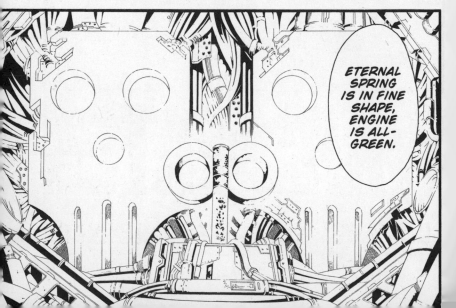

ETERNAL SPRING IS IN FINE SHAPE, ENGINE IS ALL-GREEN.

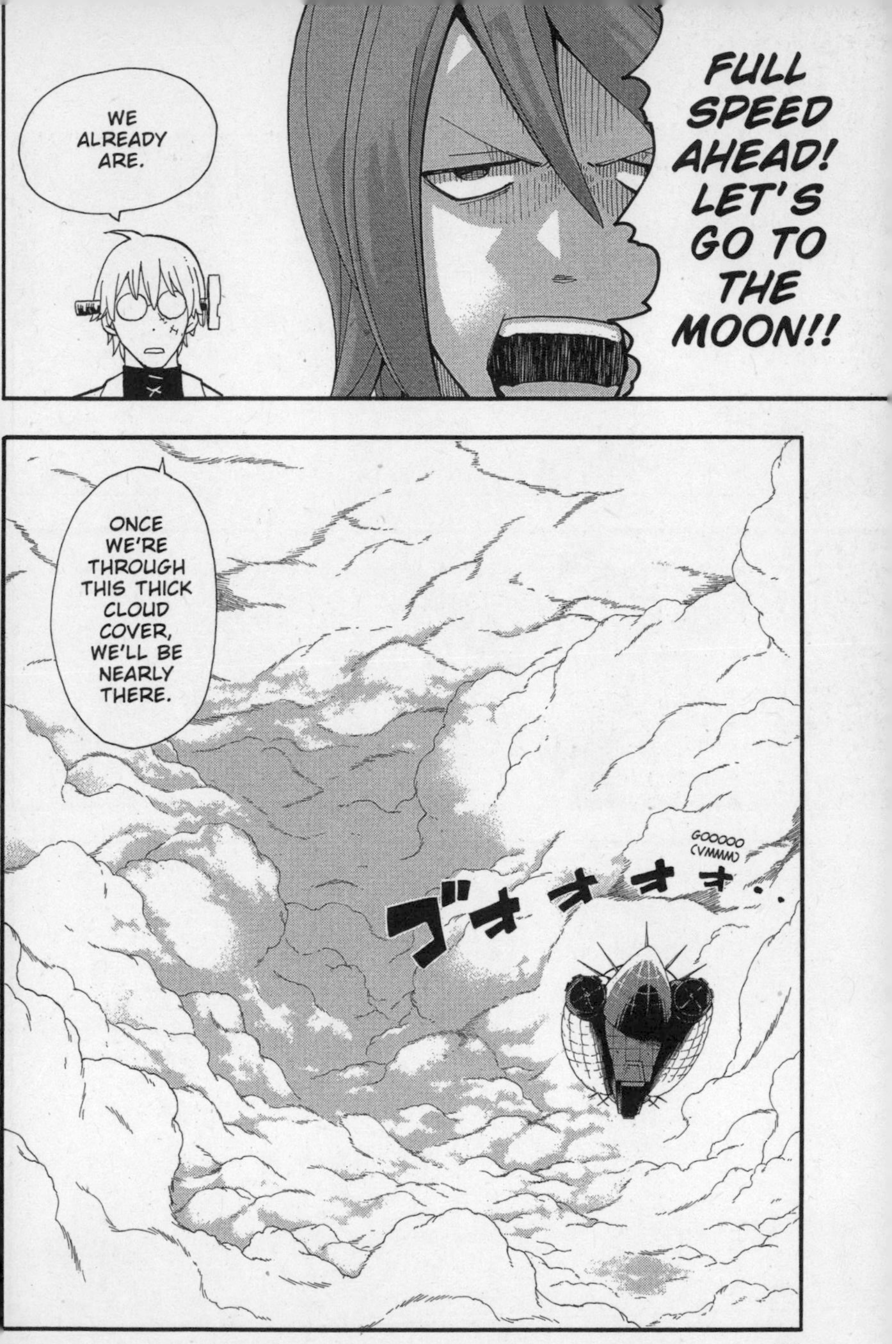
FULL SPEED AHEAD! LET'S GO TO THE MOON!!
WE ALREADY ARE.
ONCE WE'RE THROUGH THIS THICK CLOUD COVER, WE'LL BE NEARLY THERE.
ゴオオオ...
GOOOOO (VMMM)

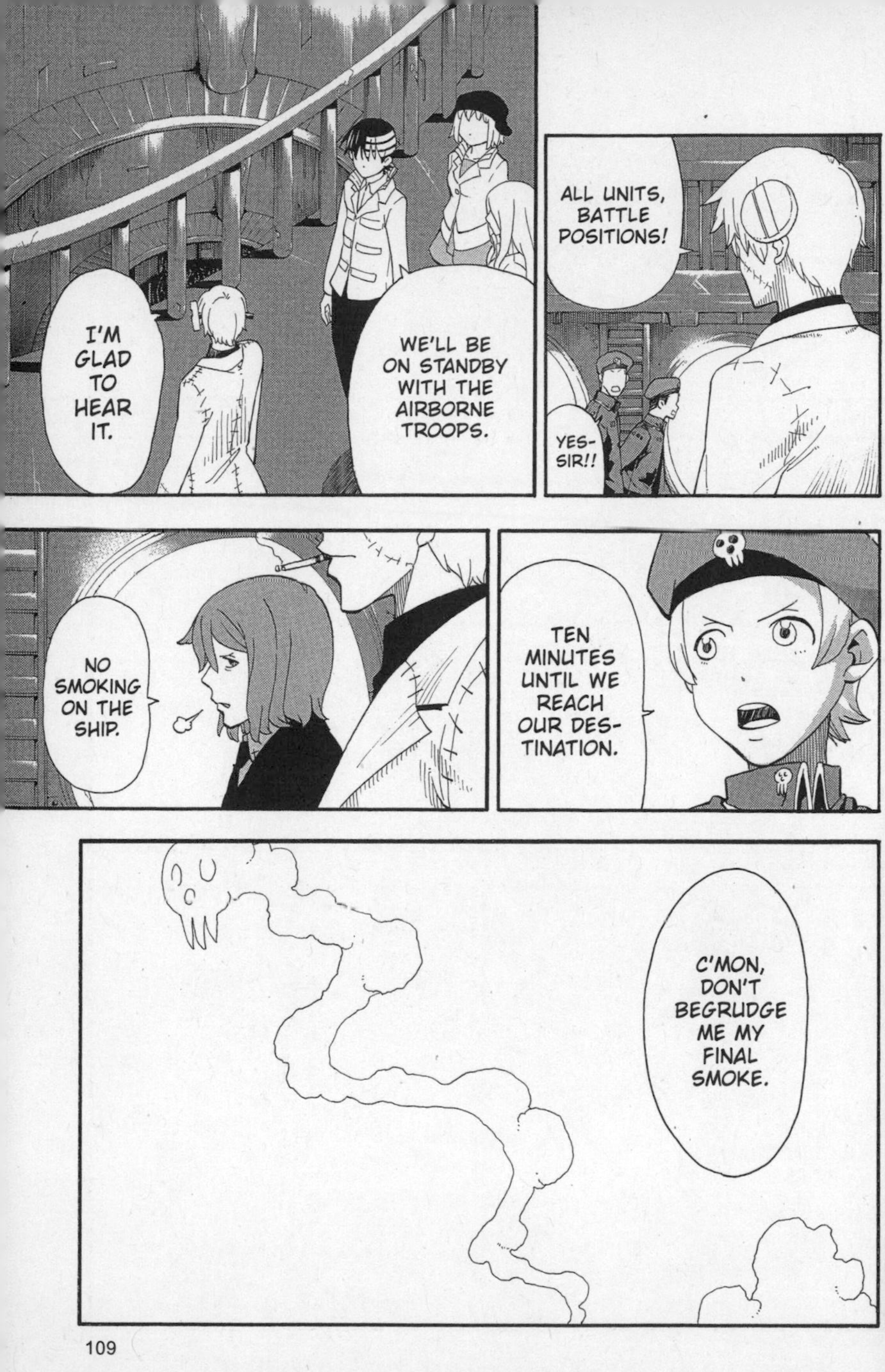
ALL UNITS, BATTLE POSITIONS!
YES-SIR!!
WE'LL BE ON STANDBY WITH THE AIRBORNE TROOPS.
I'M GLAD TO HEAR IT.
TEN MINUTES UNTIL WE REACH OUR DES-TINATION.
NO SMOKING ON THE SHIP.
C'MON, DON'T BEGRUDGE ME MY FINAL SMOKE.

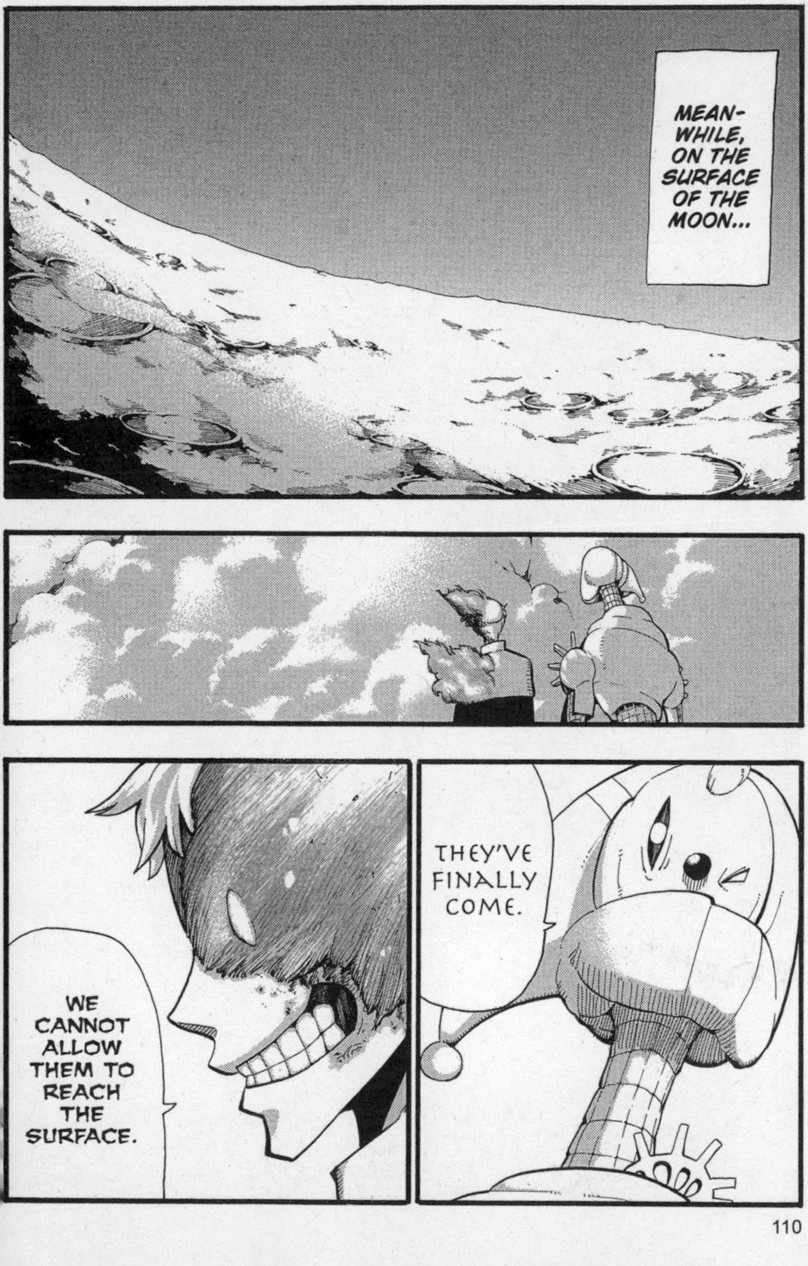
MEAN-WHILE, ON THE SURFACE OF THE MOON...
THEY'VE FINALLY COME.
WE CANNOT ALLOW THEM TO REACH THE SURFACE.

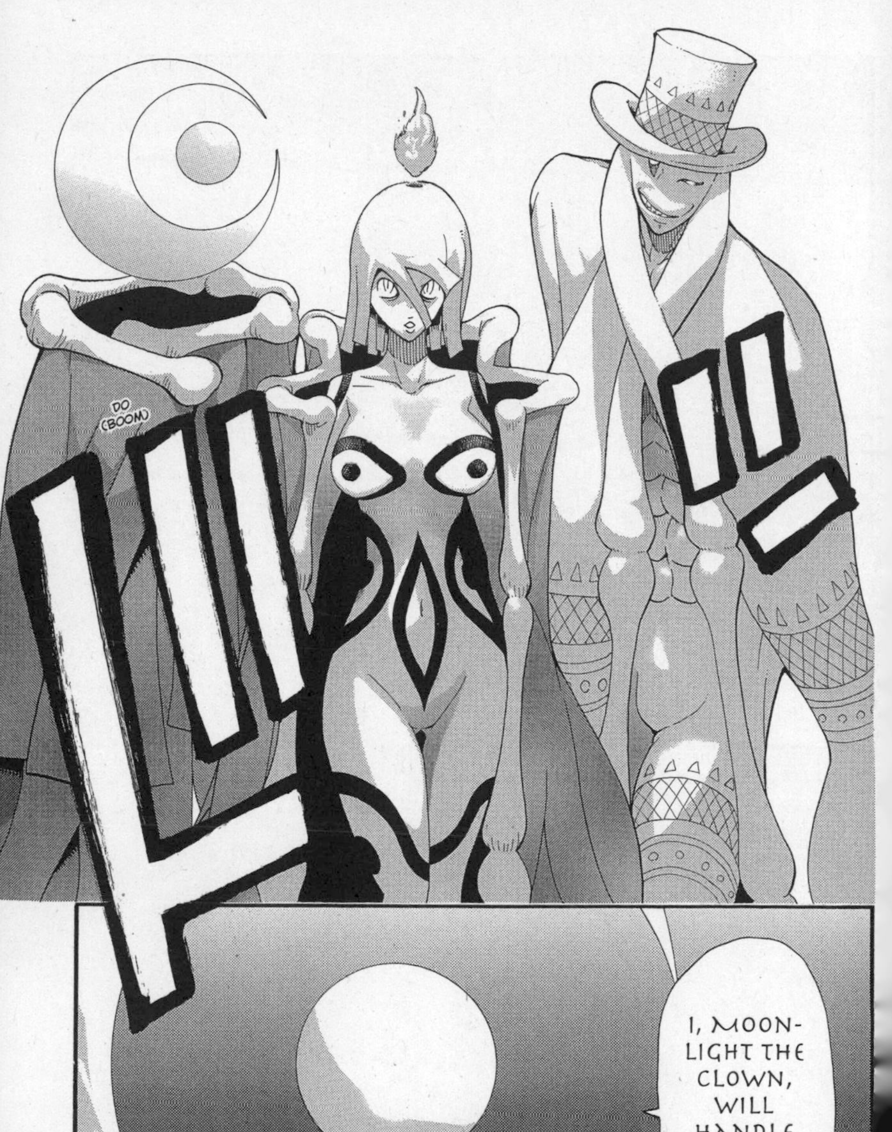
DO (BOOM)
I, MOON-LIGHT THE CLOWN, WILL HANDLE THIS.

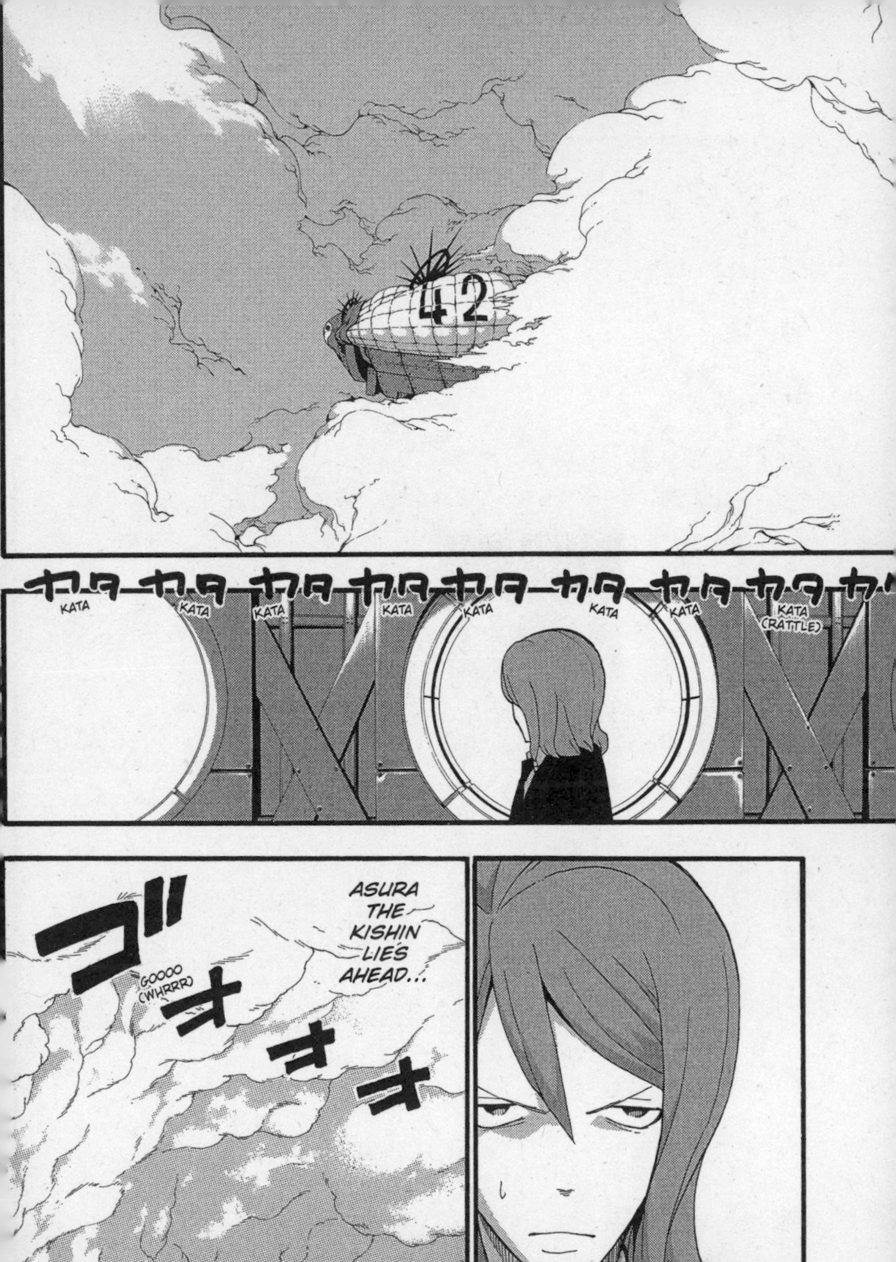
KATA
KATA
KATA
KATA
KATA
KATA
KATA
KATA (RATTLE)
ASURA THE KISHIN LIES AHEAD...
GOOOO (WHRRR)

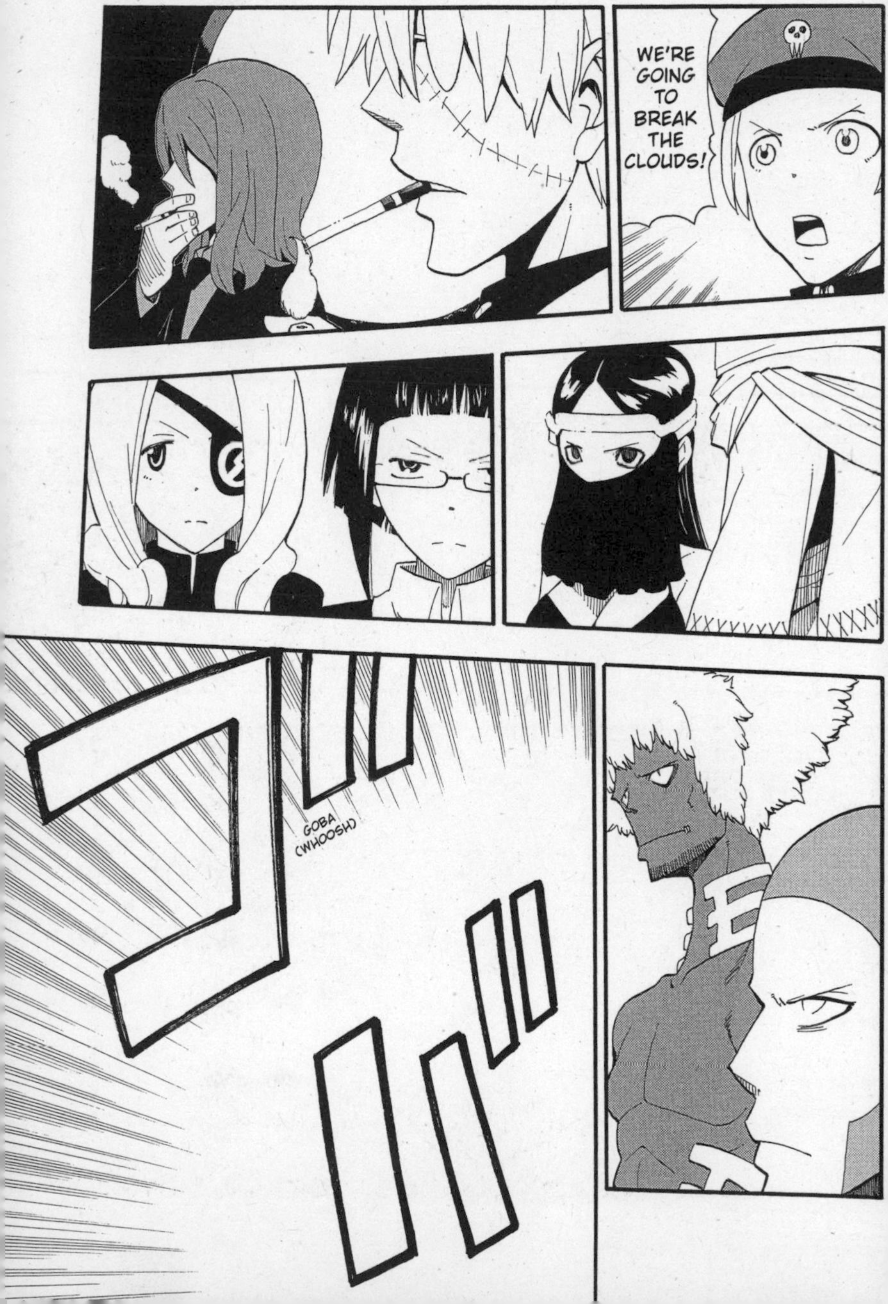
WE'RE GOING TO BREAK THE CLOUDS!
GOBA (WHOOSH)

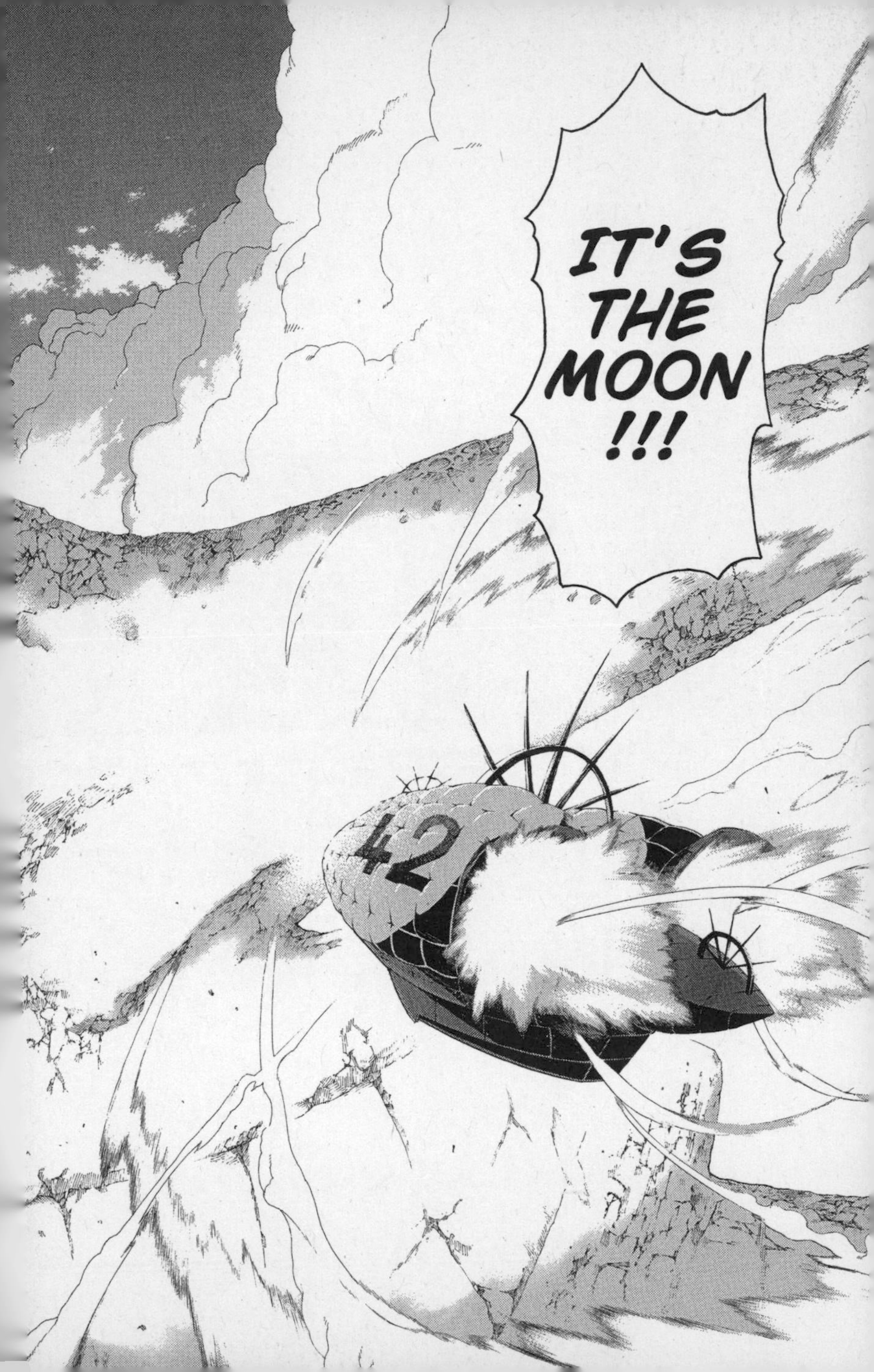
IT'S THE MOON !!!

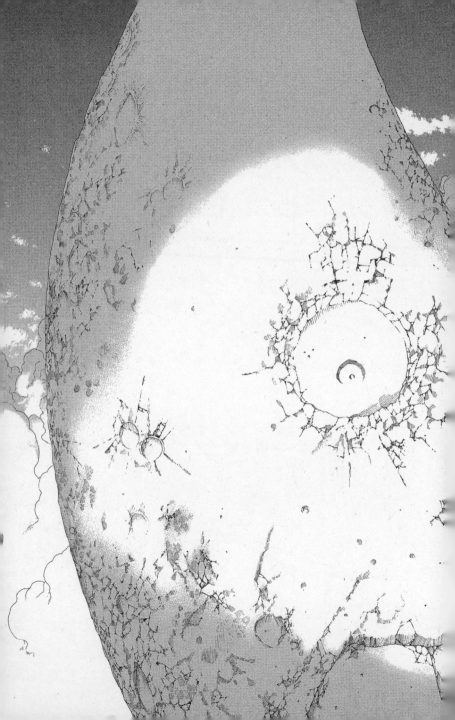

HIN
(SWSH)
HIN
HIN
HIN
ENEMY FIRE, DEAD AHEAD!!
HIN
(WHIZ)

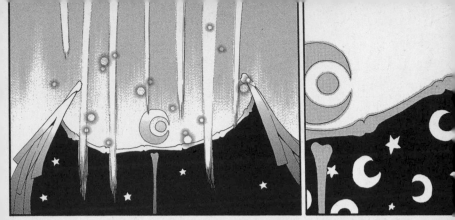

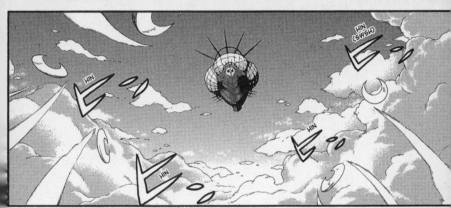

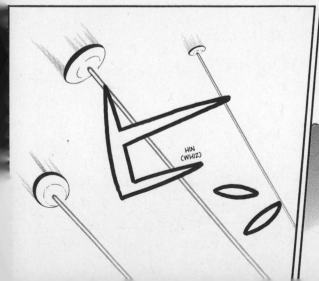

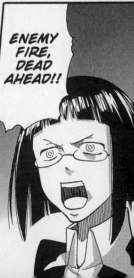

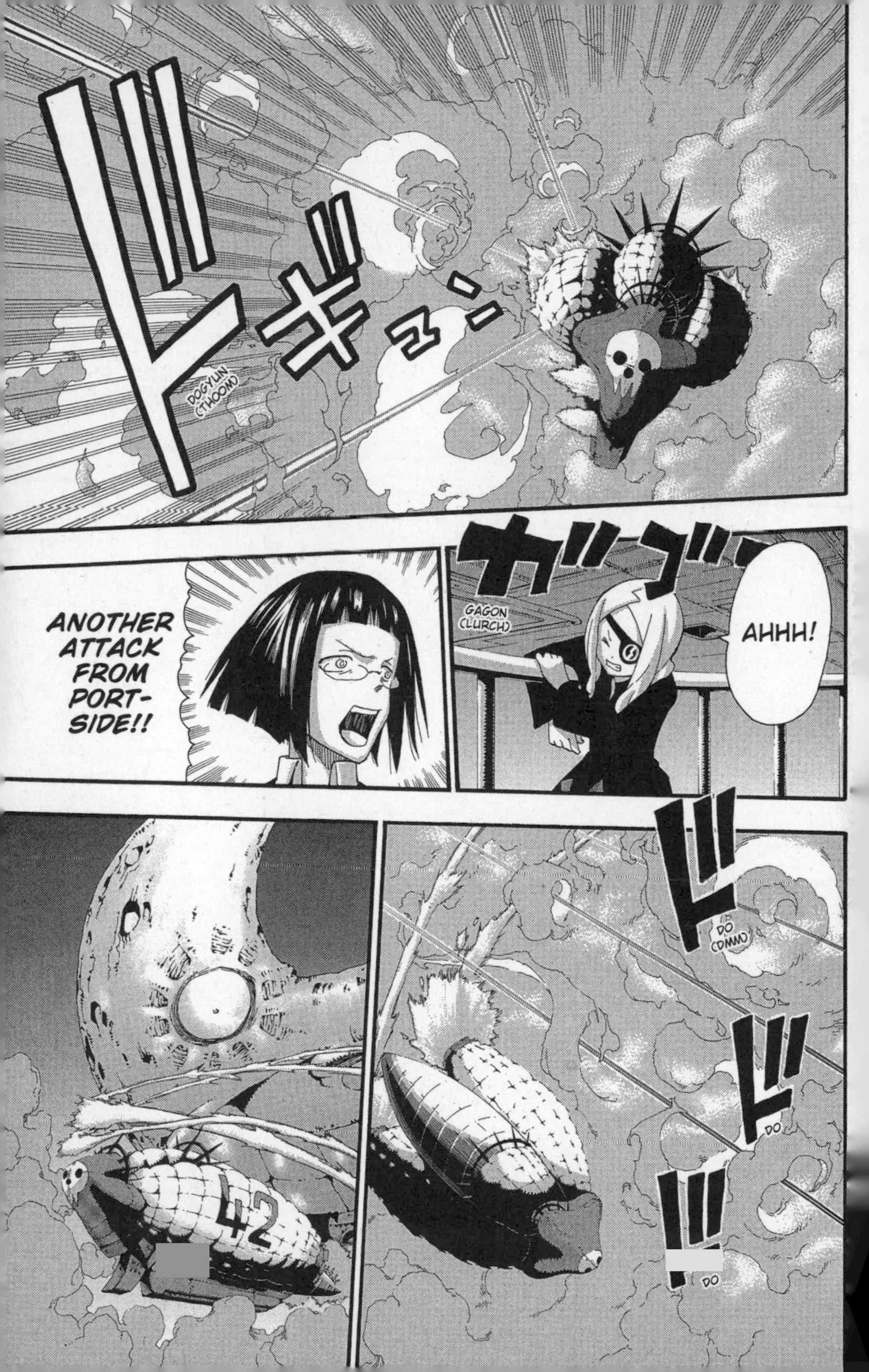
DOGYUN (THOOM)
GAGON (LURCH)
AHHH!
ANOTHER ATTACK FROM PORT-SIDE!!
DO (DMM)
DO
DO

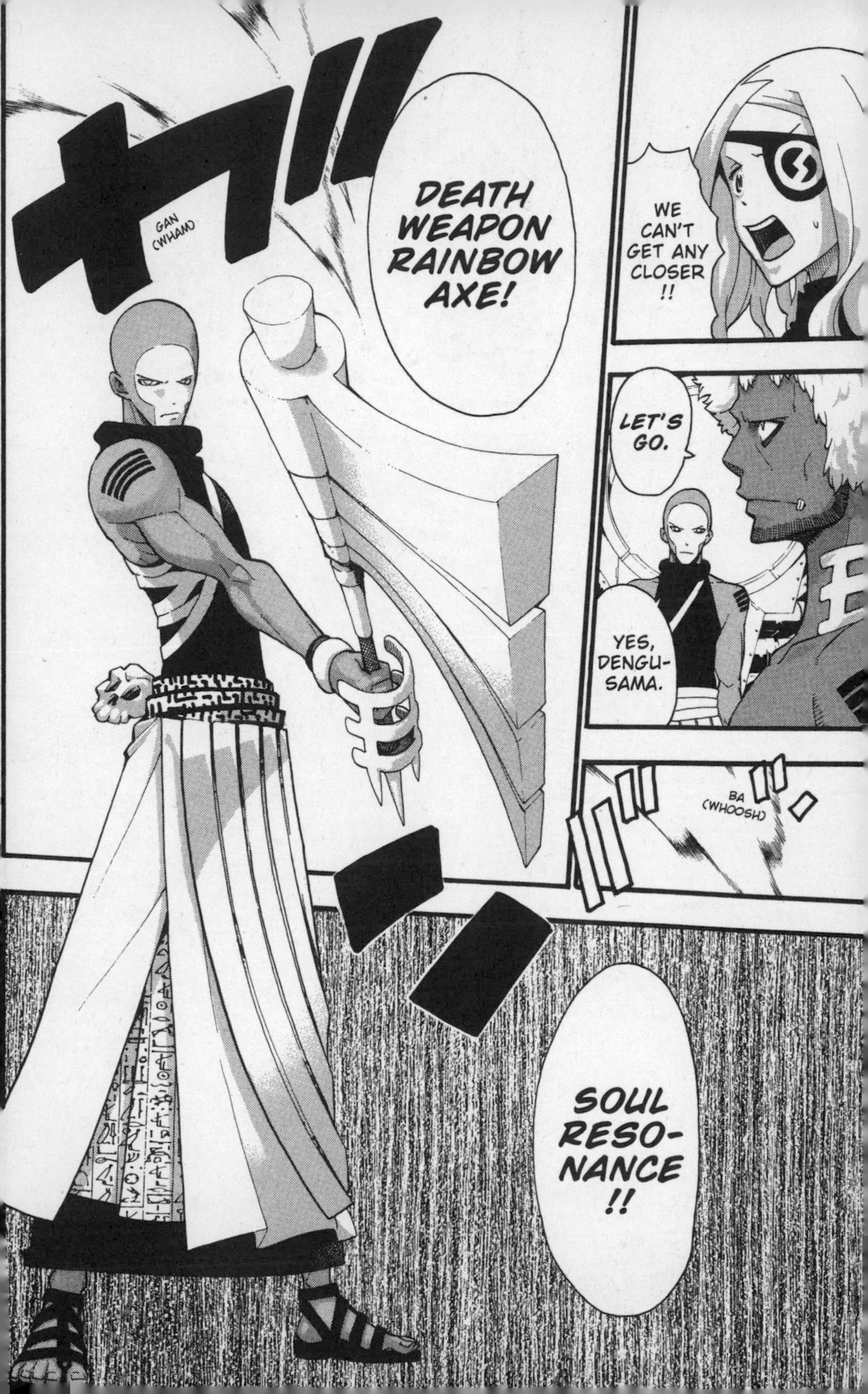
WE CAN'T GET ANY CLOSER !!
LET'S GO.
YES, DENGU-SAMA.
BA (WHOOSH)
DEATH WEAPON RAINBOW AXE!
GAN (WHAM)
SOUL RESONANCE !!

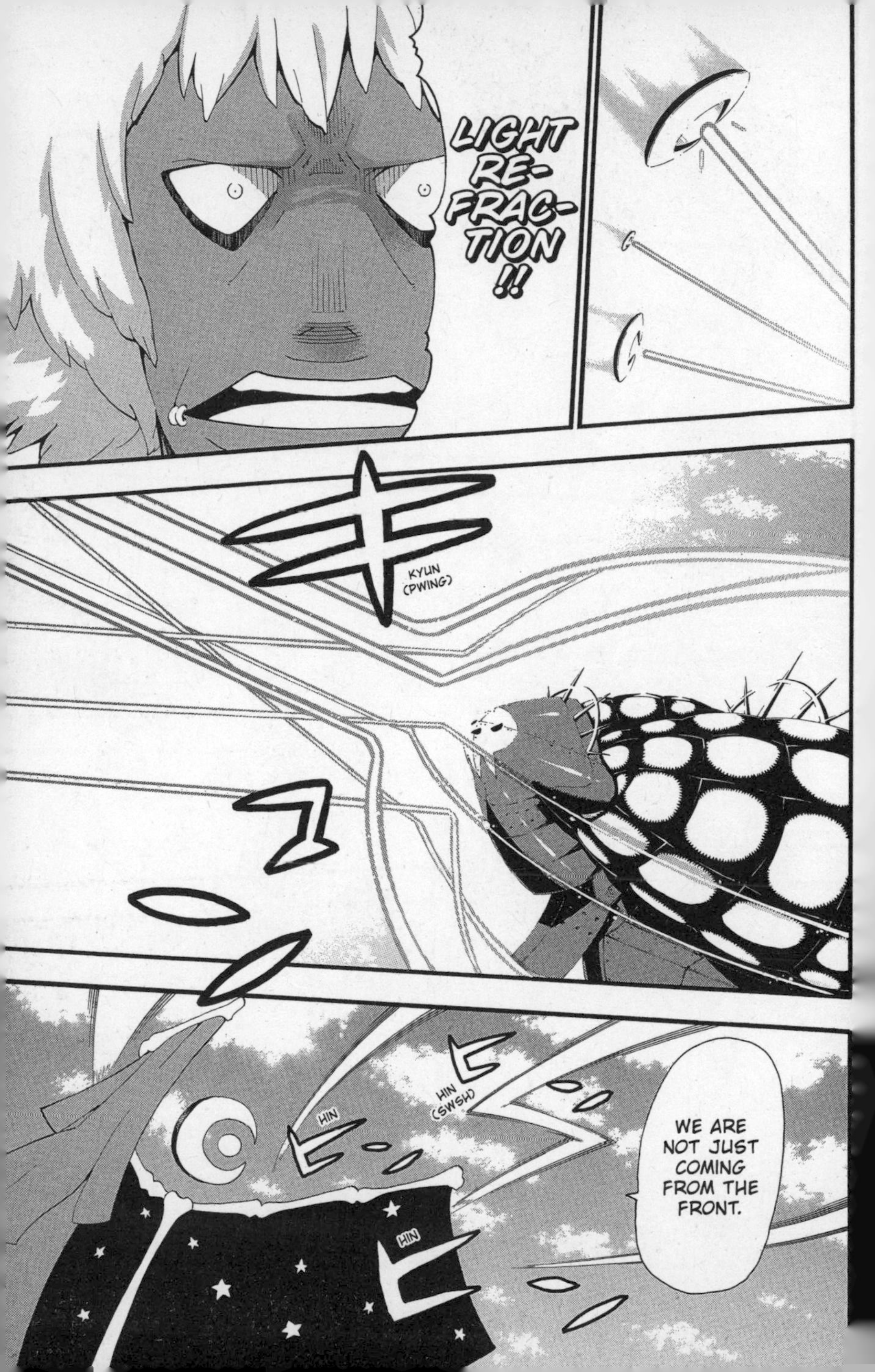
LIGHT RE-FRAC-TION!!
KYUN (PWING)
WE ARE NOT JUST COMING FROM THE FRONT.
HIN (SWSH)
HIN
HIN

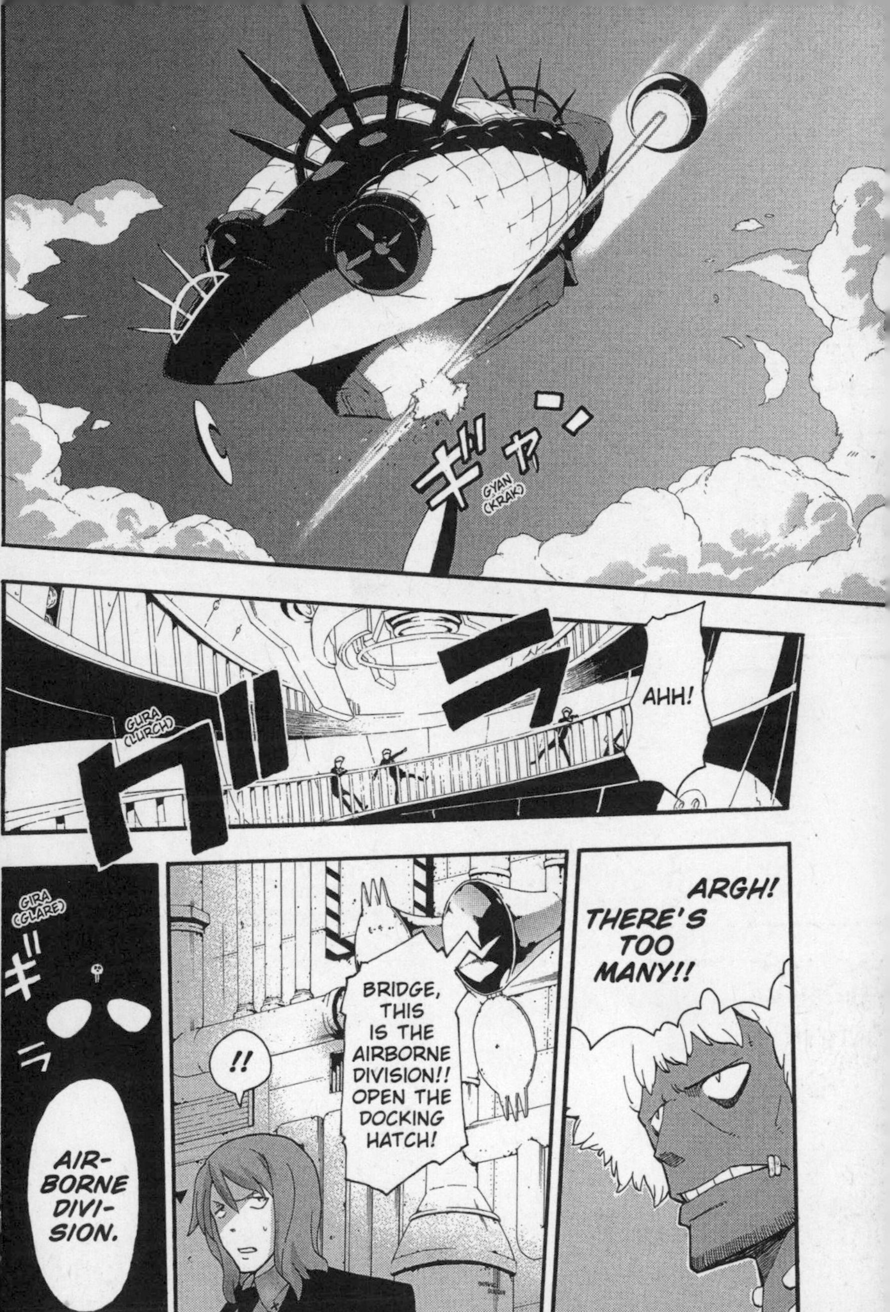
GYAN (KRAK)
GURA (LURCH)
AHH!
ARGH! THERE'S TOO MANY!!
BRIDGE, THIS IS THE AIRBORNE DIVISION!! OPEN THE DOCKING HATCH!
!!
GIRA (GLARE)
AIR-BORNE DIVI-SION.

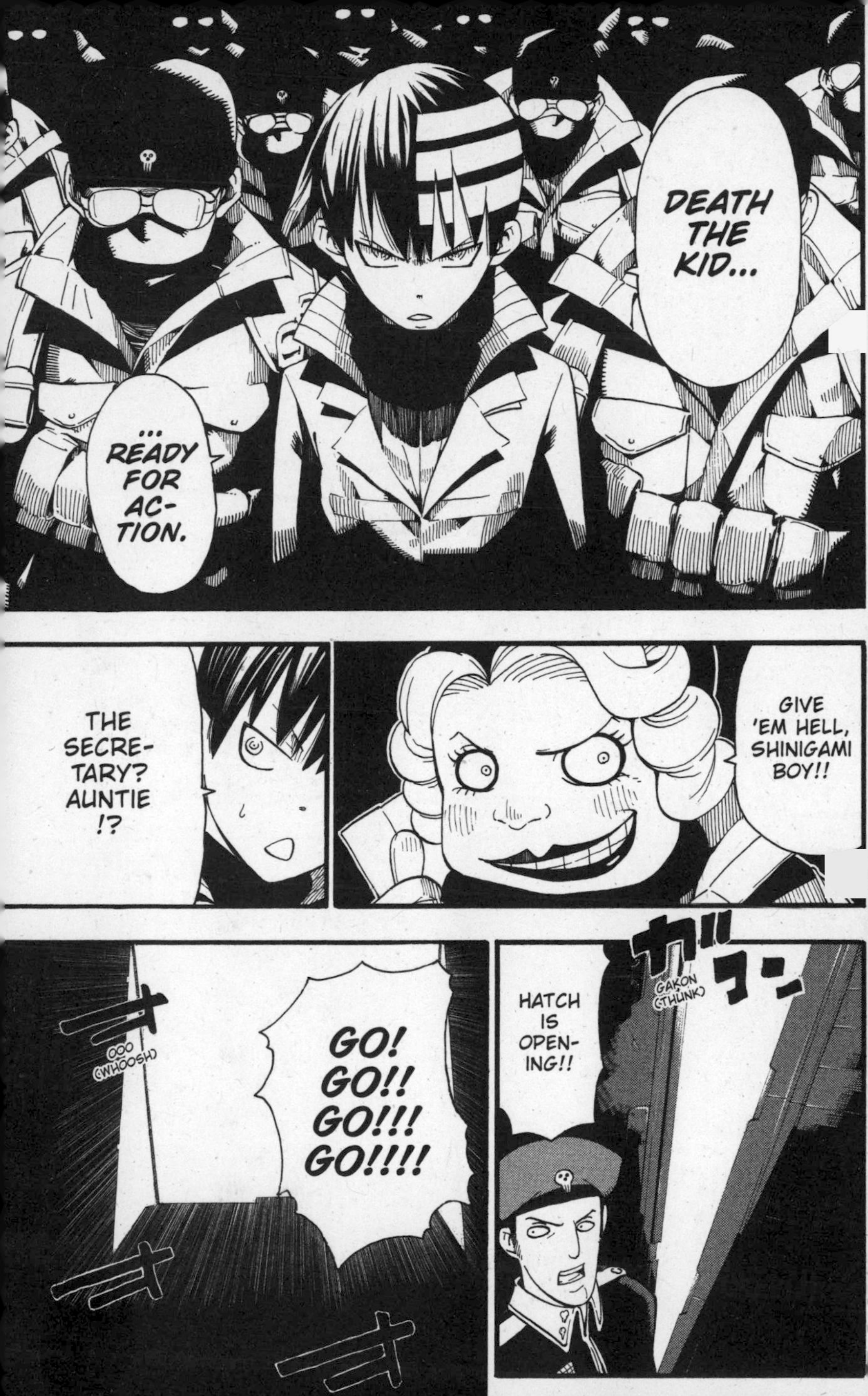
DEATH THE KID...
...READY FOR ACTION.
GIVE 'EM HELL, SHINIGAMI BOY!!
THE SECRETARY? AUNTIE!?
GAKON (THUNK)
HATCH IS OPENING!!
GO! GO!! GO!!! GO!!!!
OOO (WHOOSH)

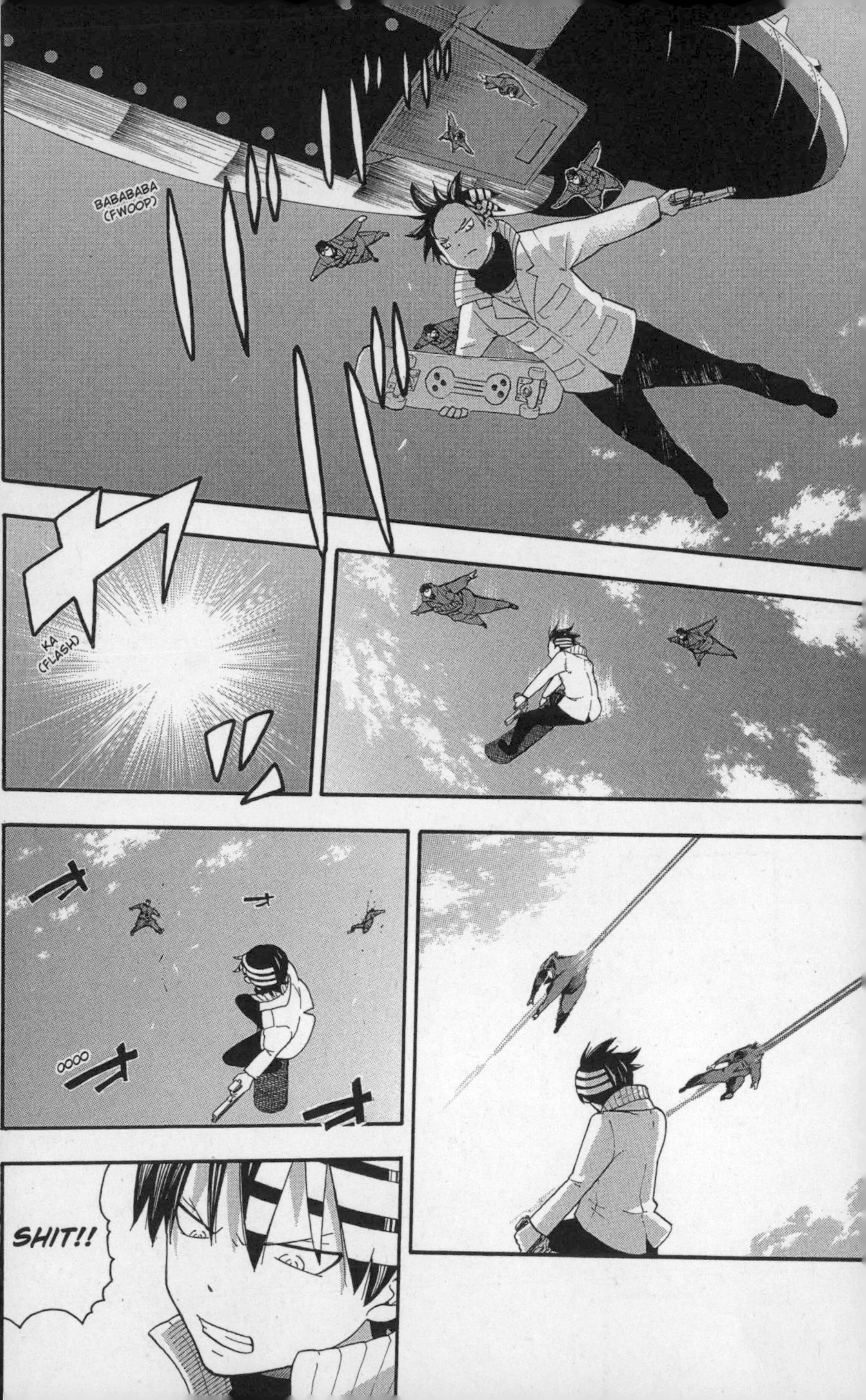
BABABABA
(FWOOP)
KA
(FLASH)
OOOO
SHIT!!

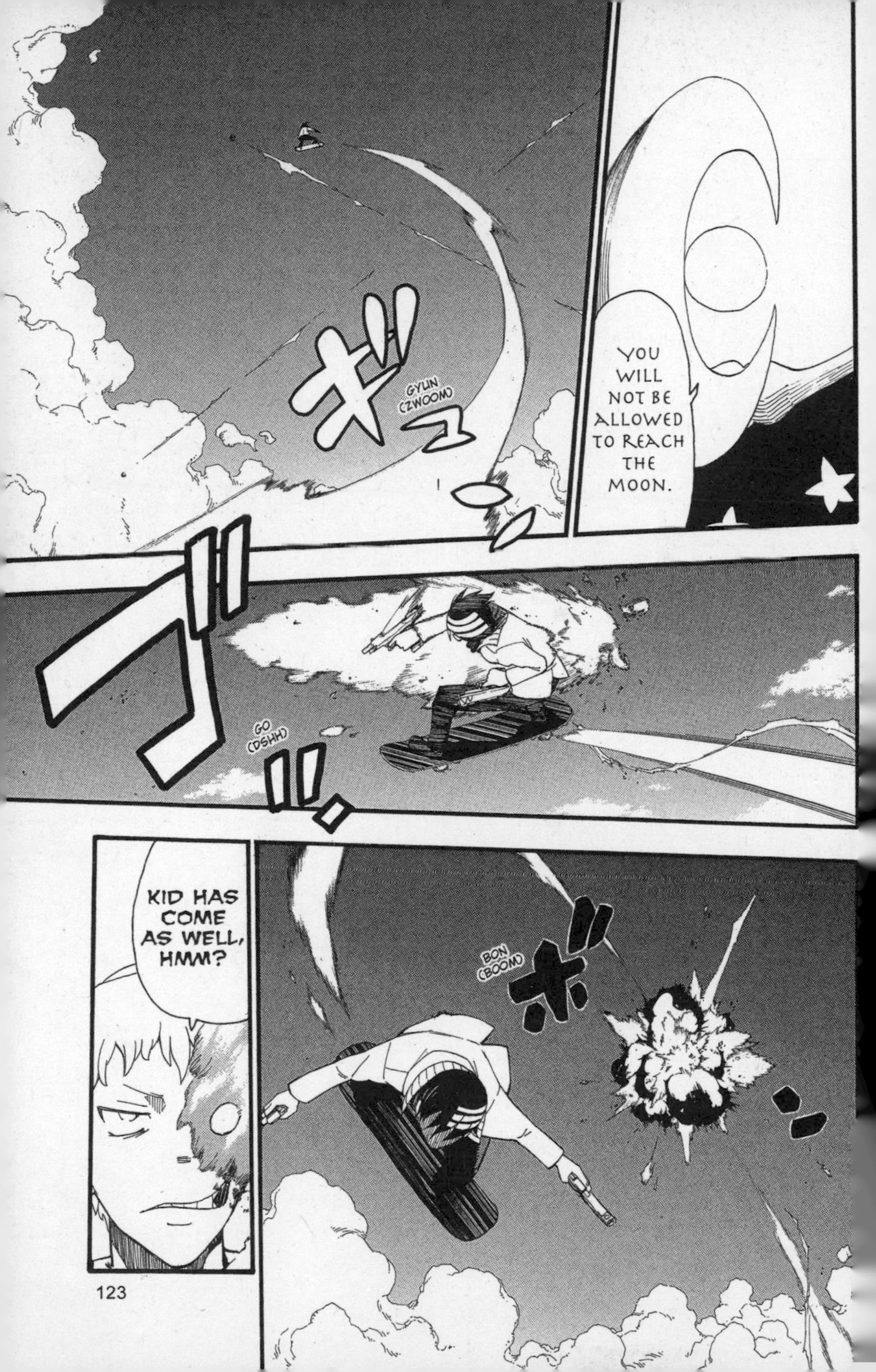
YOU WILL NOT BE ALLOWED TO REACH THE MOON.
GYUN (ZWOOM)
GO (DSHH)
BON (BOOM)
KID HAS COME AS WELL, HMM?

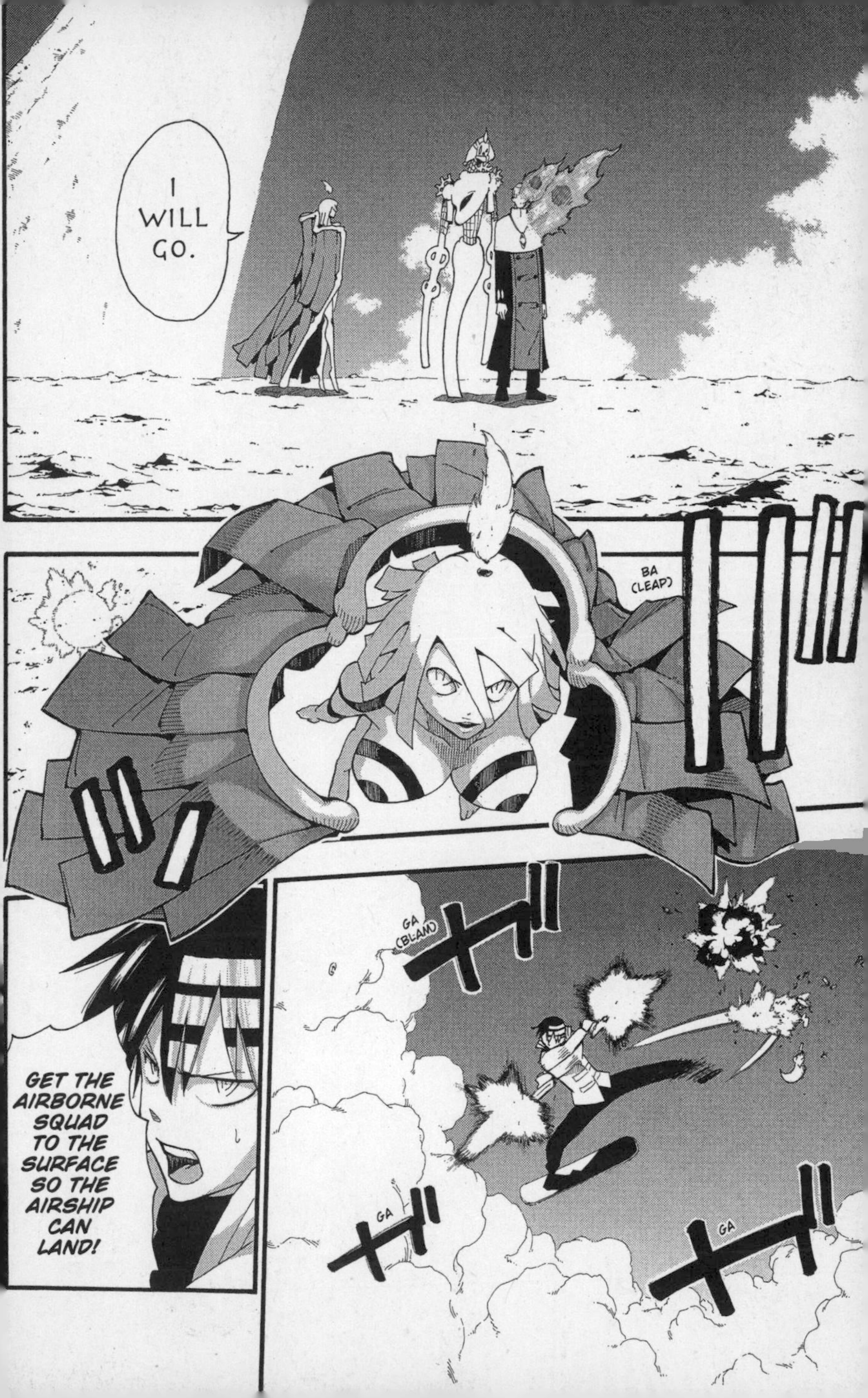
I WILL GO.
BA (LEAP)
GA (BLAM)
GA
GA
GET THE AIRBORNE SQUAD TO THE SURFACE SO THE AIRSHIP CAN LAND!

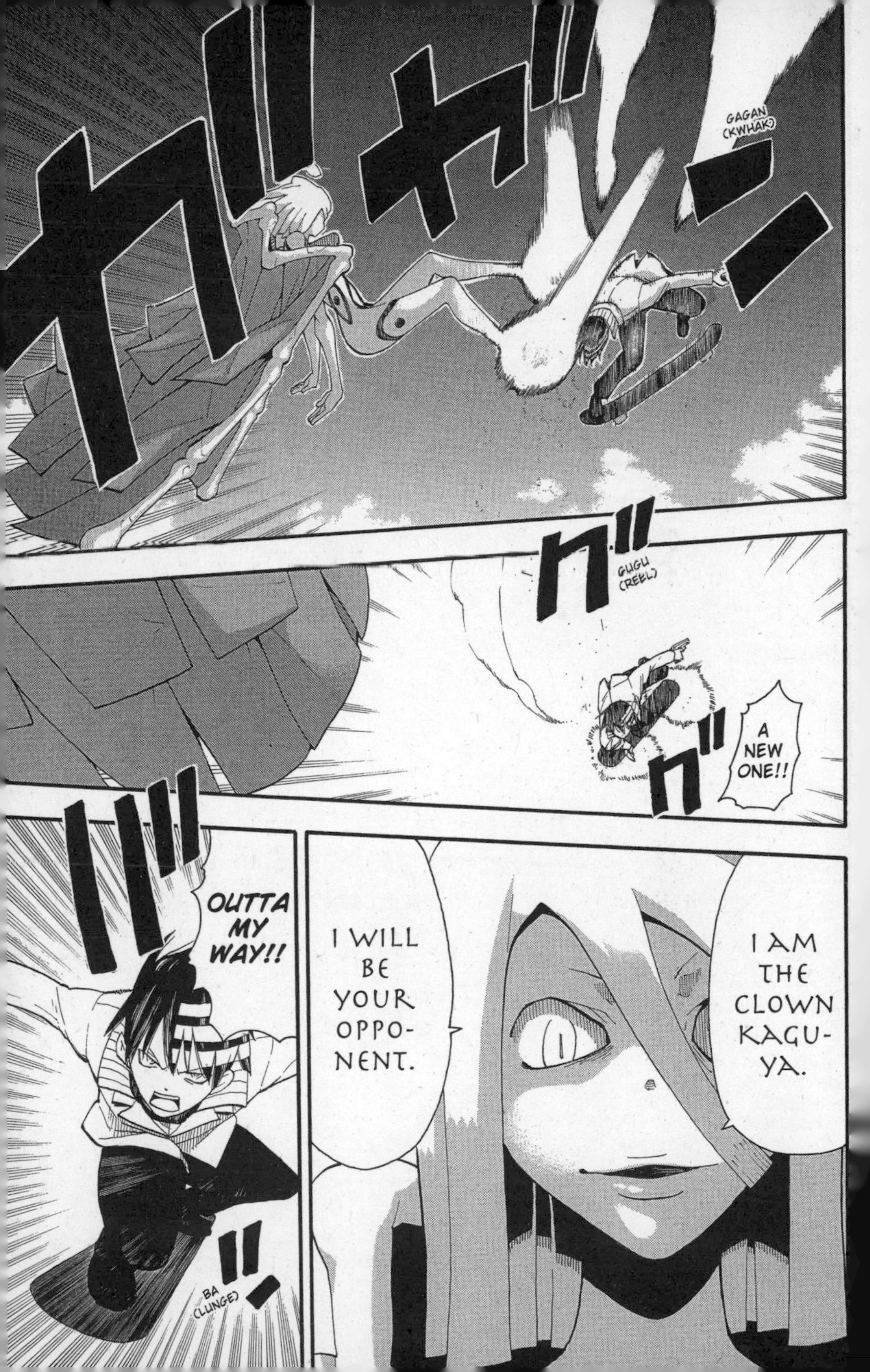
GAGAN (KWHAK)
GUGU (REEL)
A NEW ONE!!
I AM THE CLOWN KAGU-YA.
I WILL BE YOUR OPPO-NENT.
OUTTA MY WAY!!
BA (LUNGE)

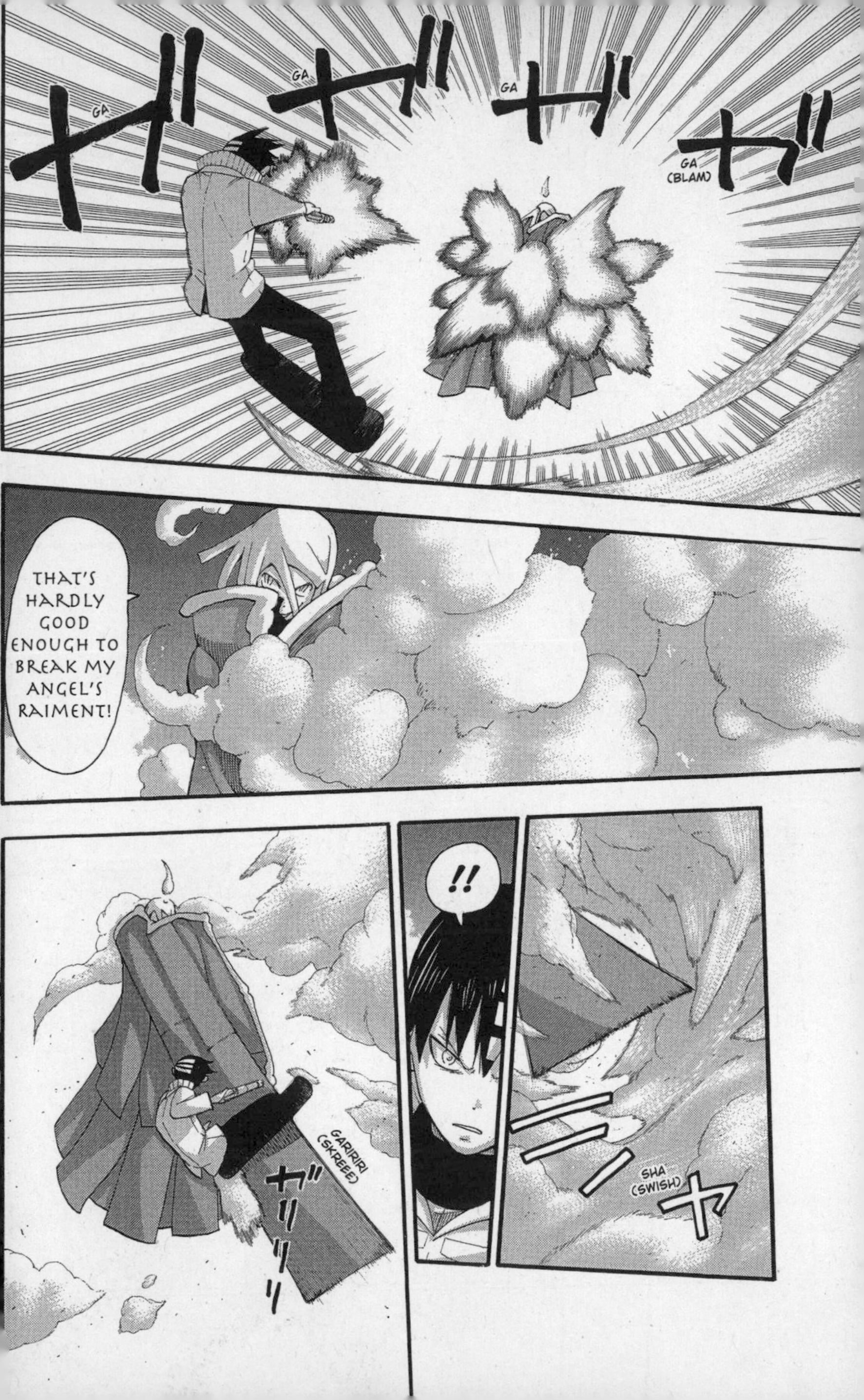
GA (BLAM)
GA
GA
GA
THAT'S HARDLY GOOD ENOUGH TO BREAK MY ANGEL'S RAIMENT!
SHA (SWISH)
!!
GARIRIRI (SKREEE)

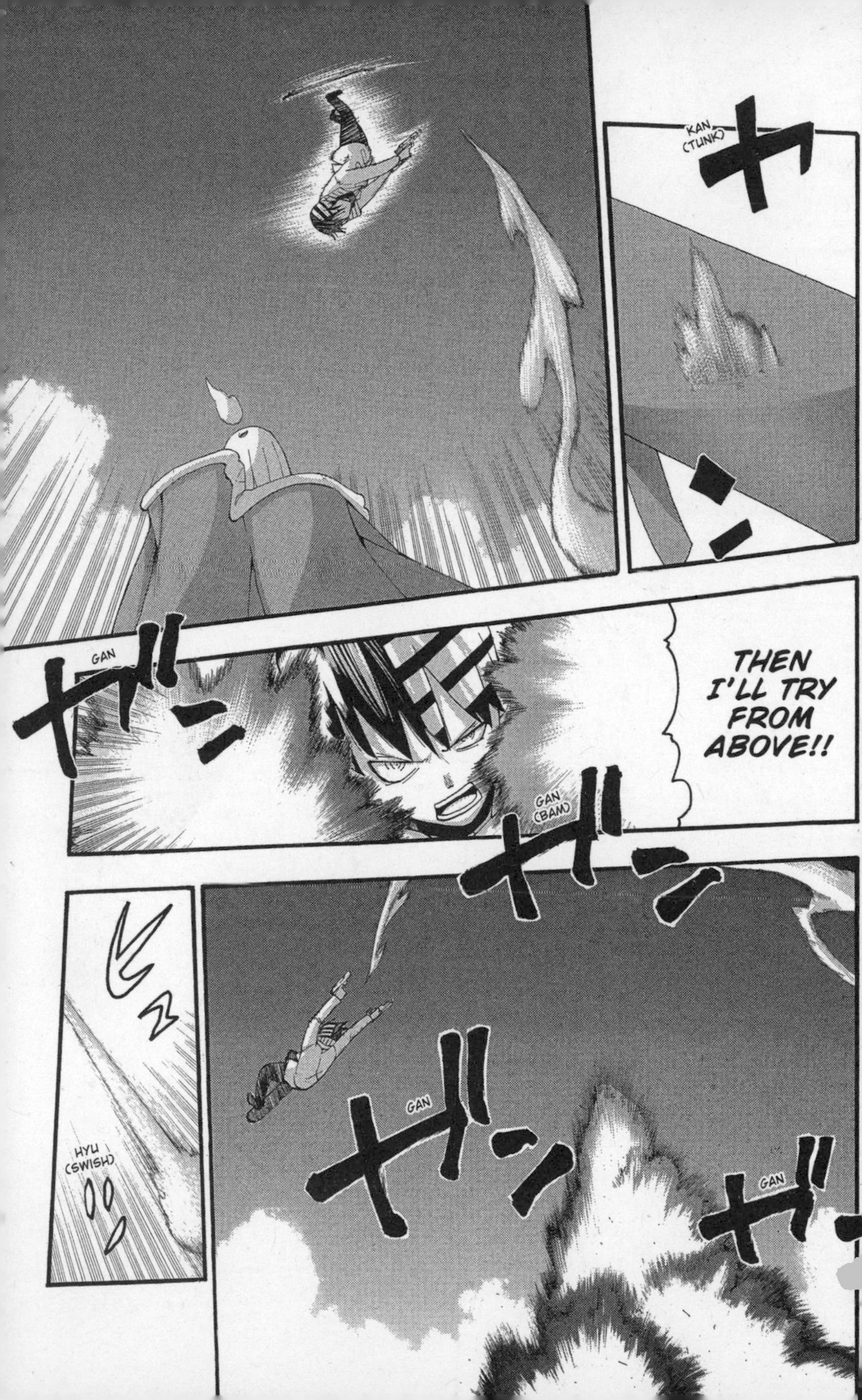
KAN (TUNK)
THEN I'LL TRY FROM ABOVE!!
GAN (BAM)
GAN
GAN
GAN
HYU (SWISH)

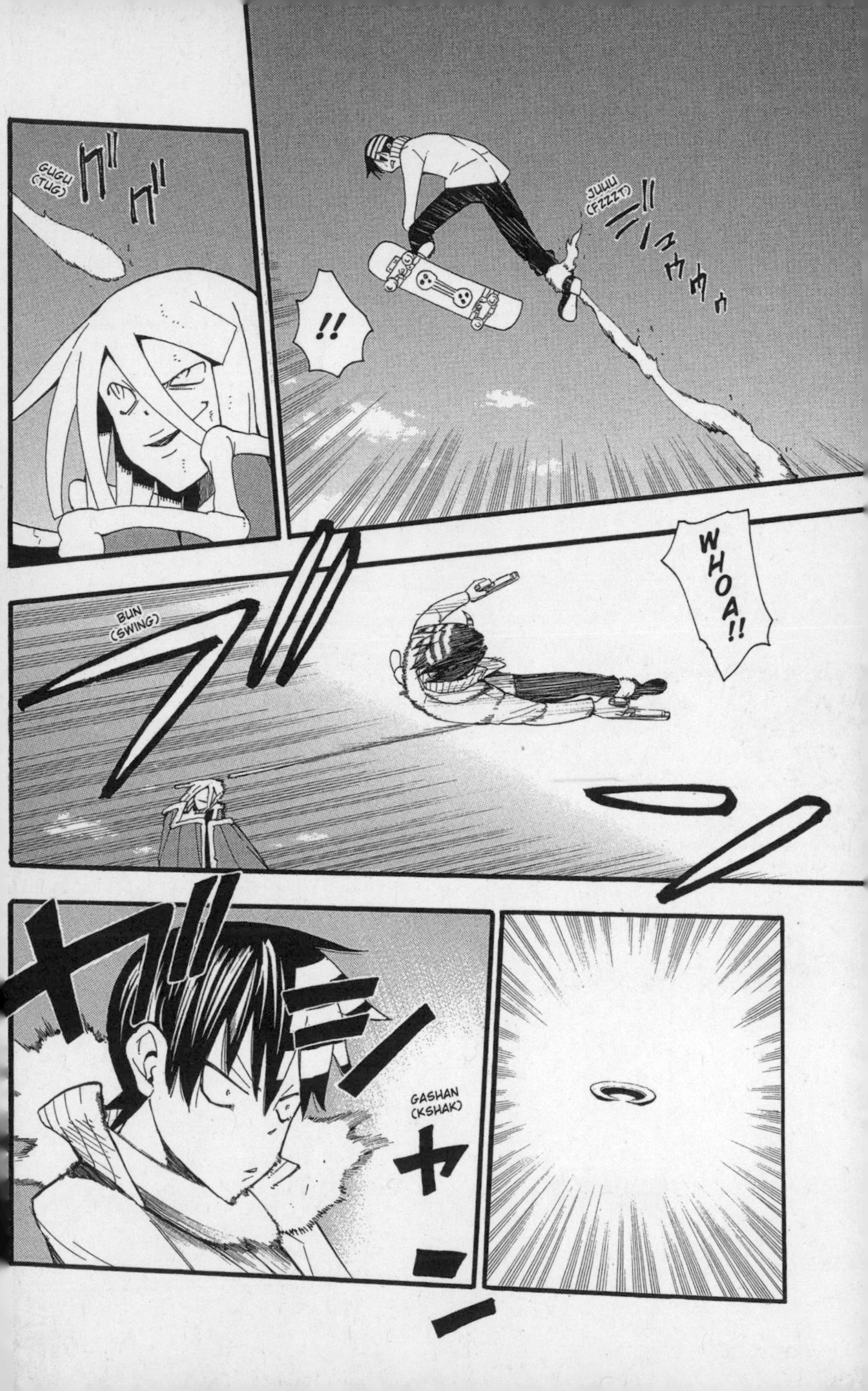
JUUU (FZZZT)
!!
GUGU (TUG)
WHOA!!
BUN (SWING)
GASHAN (KSHAK)

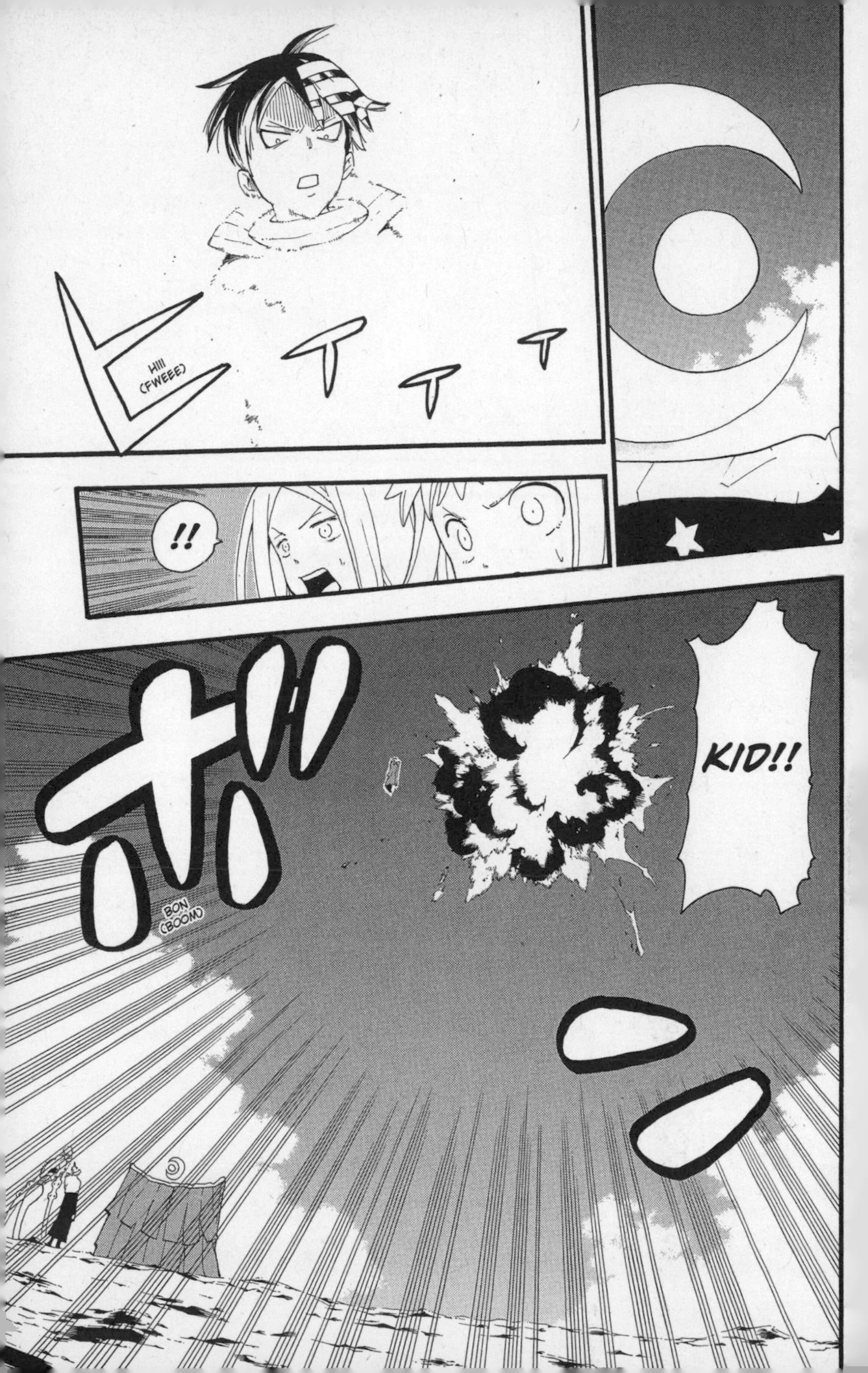
HIII (FWEEE)
!!
KID!!
BON (BOOM)

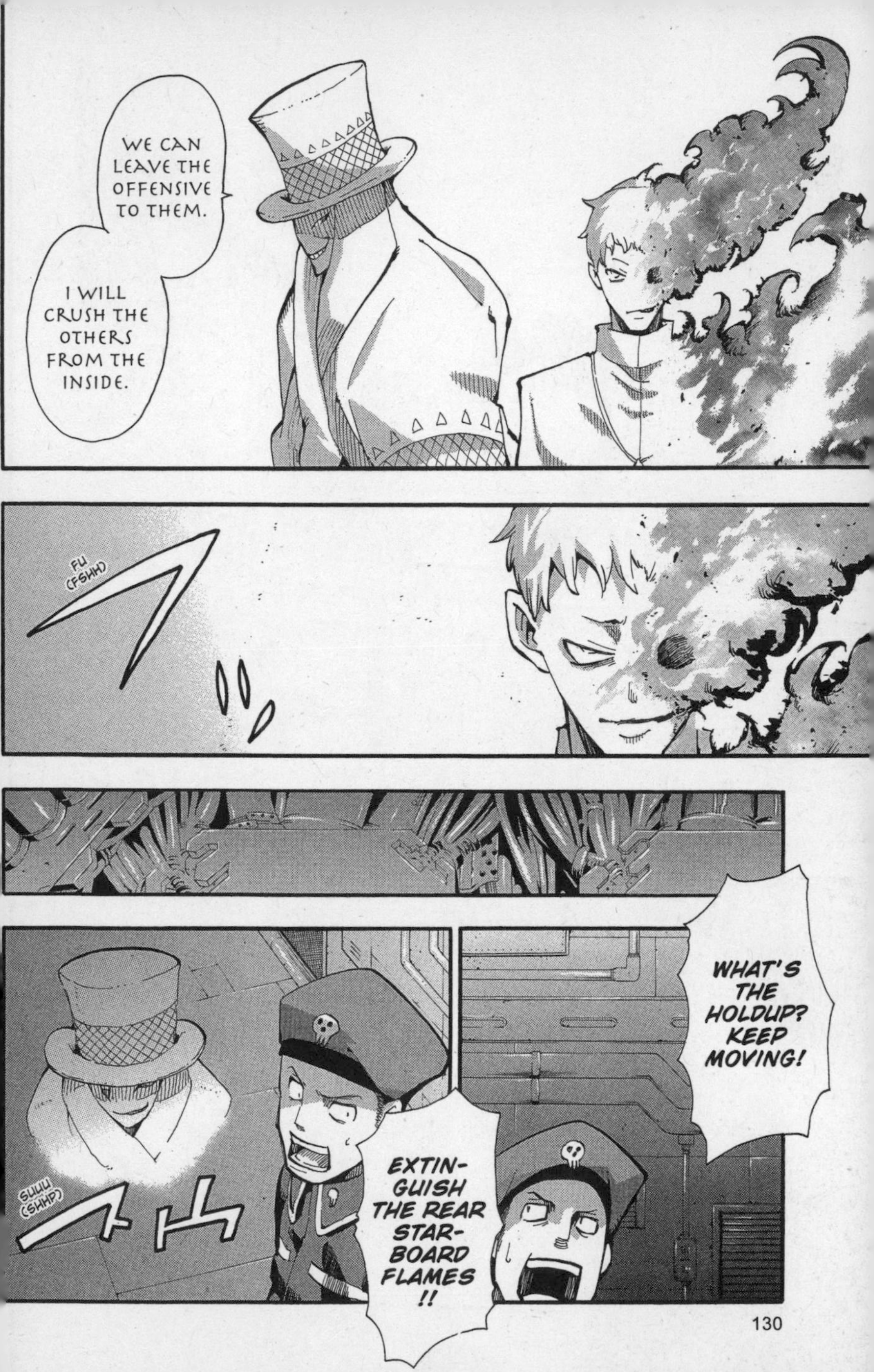
WE CAN LEAVE THE OFFENSIVE TO THEM.
I WILL CRUSH THE OTHERS FROM THE INSIDE.
FU (FSHH)
WHAT'S THE HOLDUP? KEEP MOVING!
EXTIN-GUISH THE REAR STAR-BOARD FLAMES!!
SUUU (SHHP)

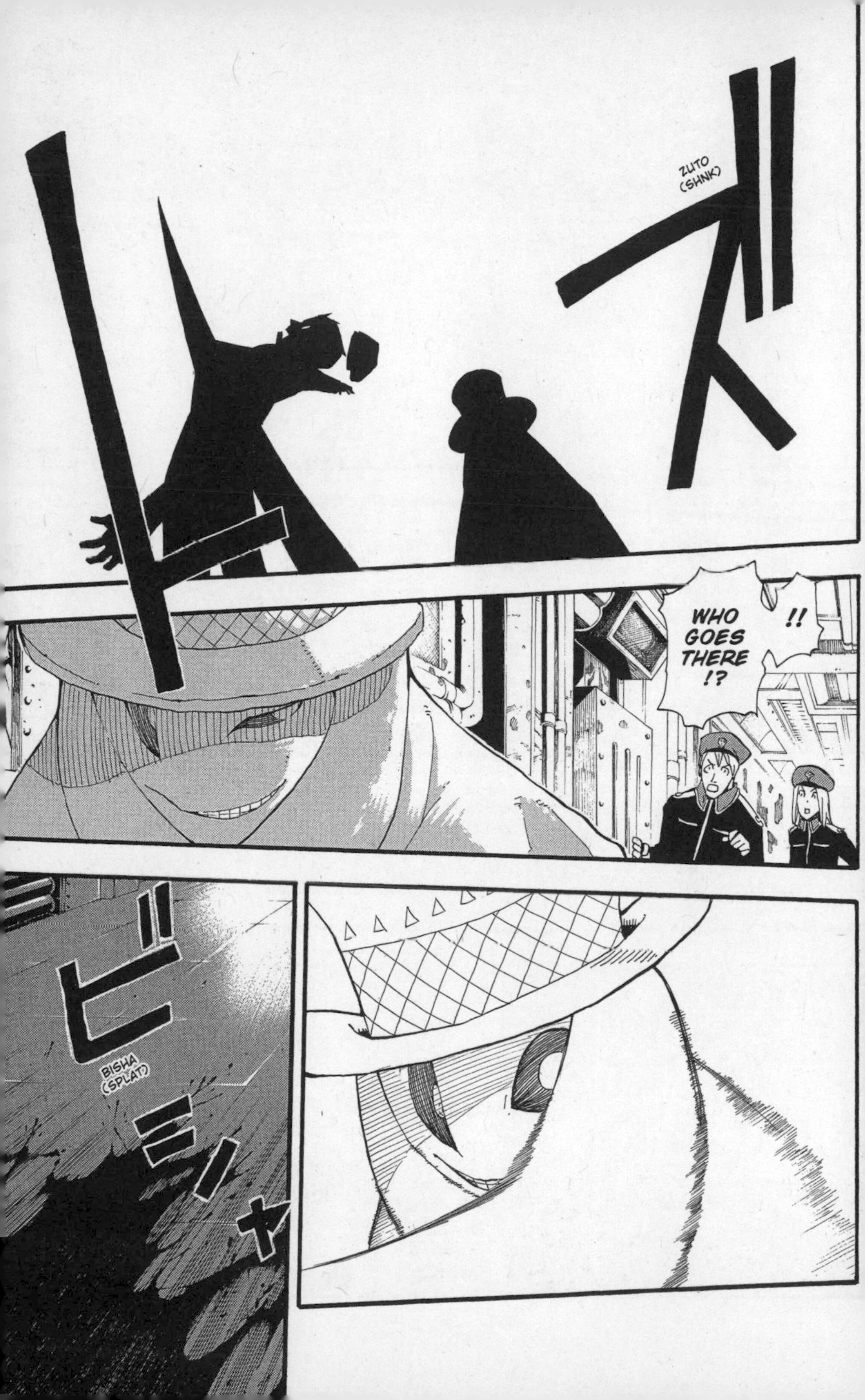
ZUTO (SHNK)
!!
WHO GOES THERE !?
BISHA (SPLAT)

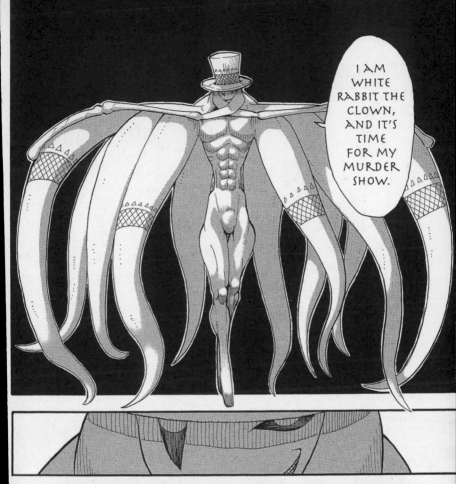

I AM WHITE RABBIT THE CLOWN, AND IT'S TIME FOR MY MURDER SHOW.

WHAT IS THIS ...?

......

WHILE WE'VE BEEN ADDRESSING THE CHAOS OUTSIDE, THE SOUL SIGNALS WITHIN THE AIRSHIP HAVE BEEN DISAPPEARING ONE BY ONE.

WHAT!?

THIS WAY!!

TA (TEK)

TA

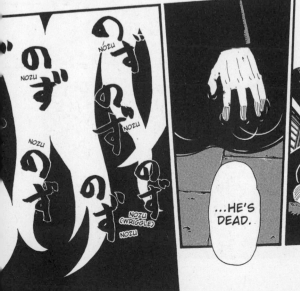

NOZU

NOZU

NOZU

NOZU

NOZU

NOZU (WRIGGLE)

NOZU

...HE'S DEAD.

ARE YOU OKAY?

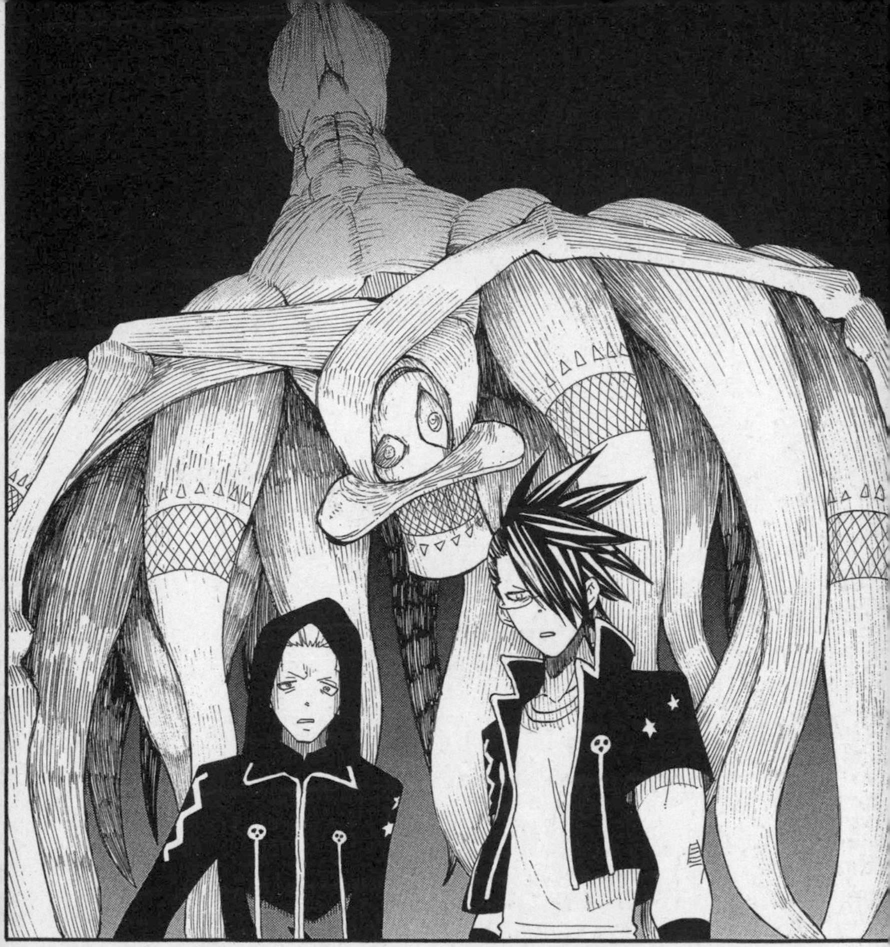
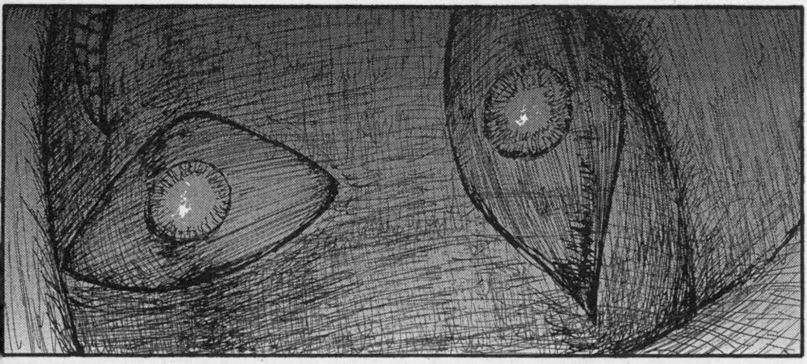

SOUL EATER

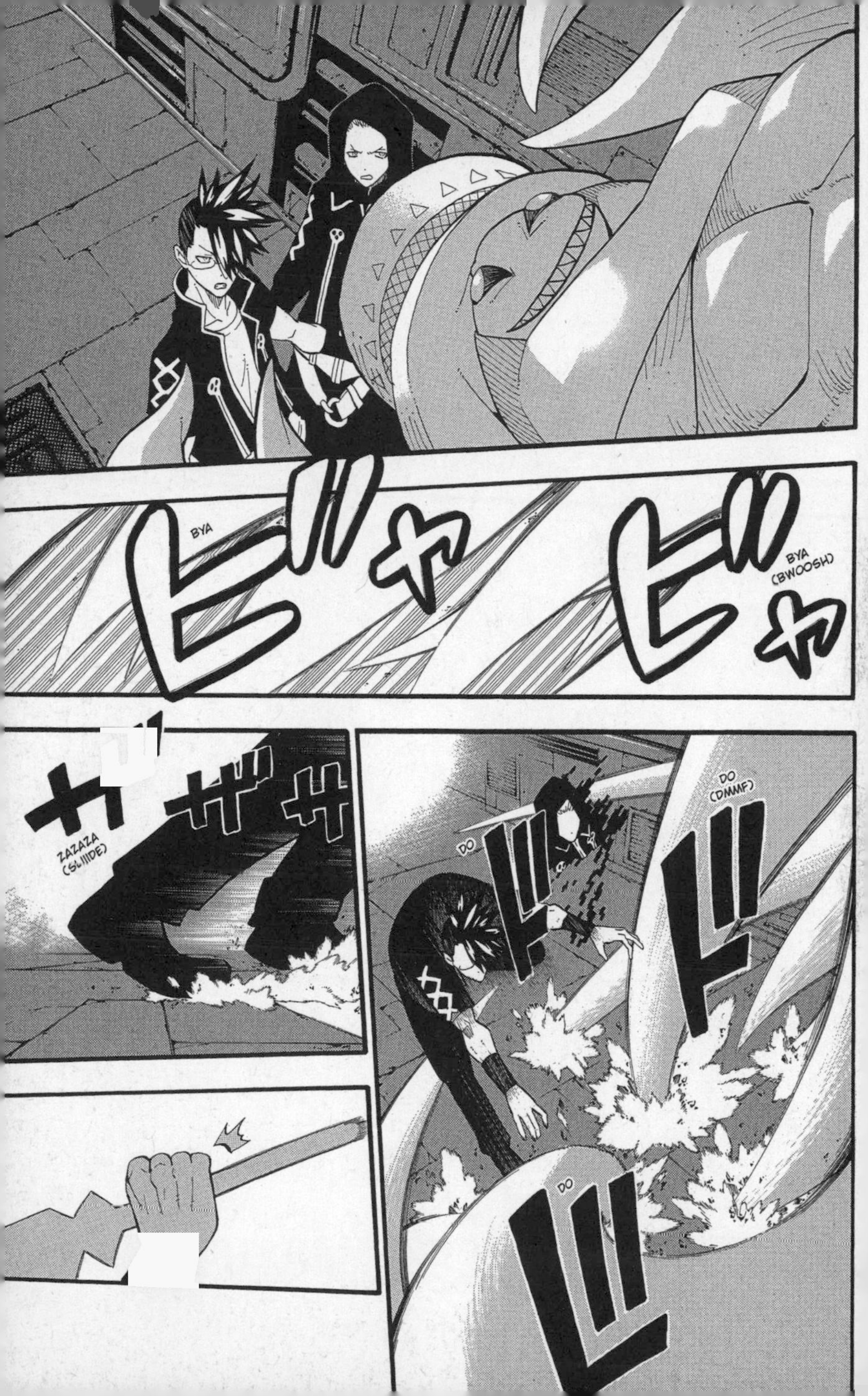
ビャ
BYA
(BWOOSH)
ビャ
BYA
ドド
DO
(DMMF)
DO
ド
DO
ザザザ
ZAZAZA
(SLIIIDE)

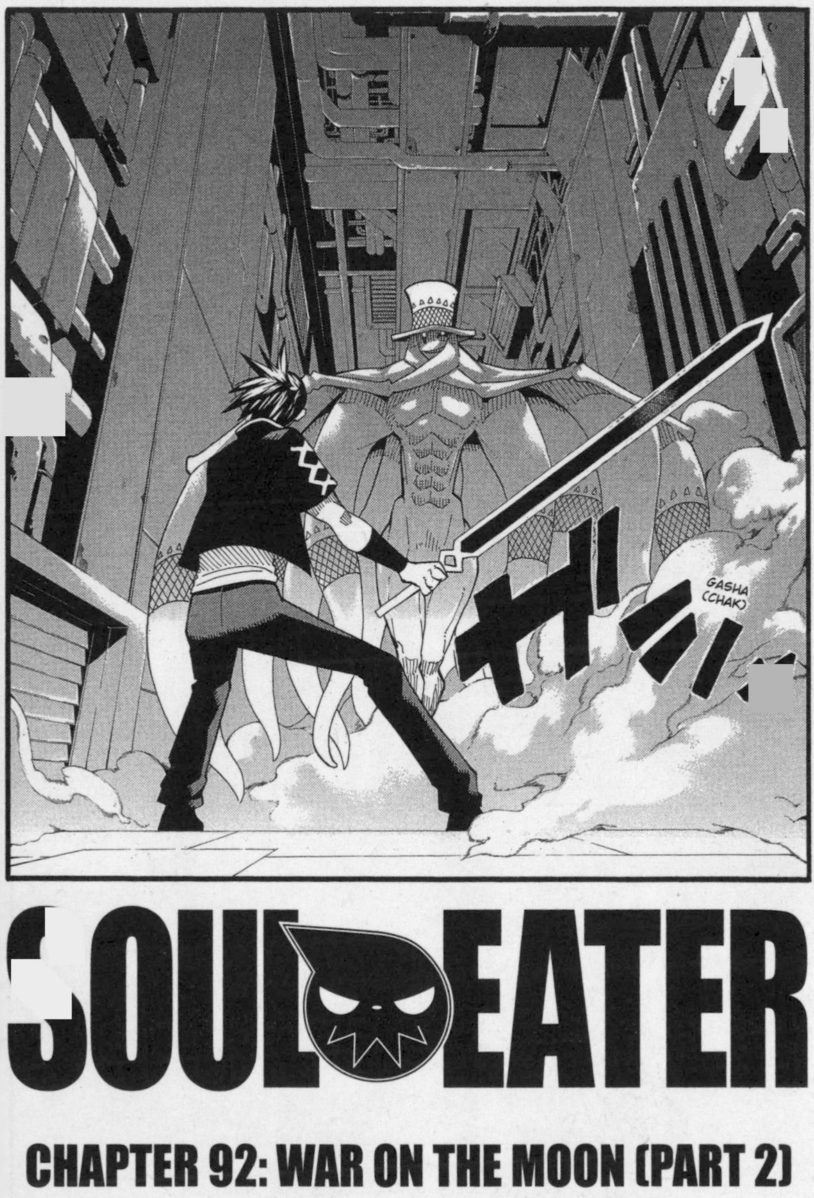
GASHA
(CHAK)

SOUL EATER

CHAPTER 92: WAR ON THE MOON (PART 2)

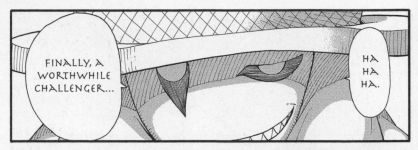

FINALLY, A WORTHWHILE CHALLENGER...

HA HA HA.

WHERE DID THIS ONE COME FROM...?

!

HURRY, HURRY! THE FIRE'S SPREADING TO THE ENGINE ROOM!!

I WISH I COULD STAY AND PLAY WITH YOU, BUT I'M IN A HURRY AS WELL.

WAIT!!

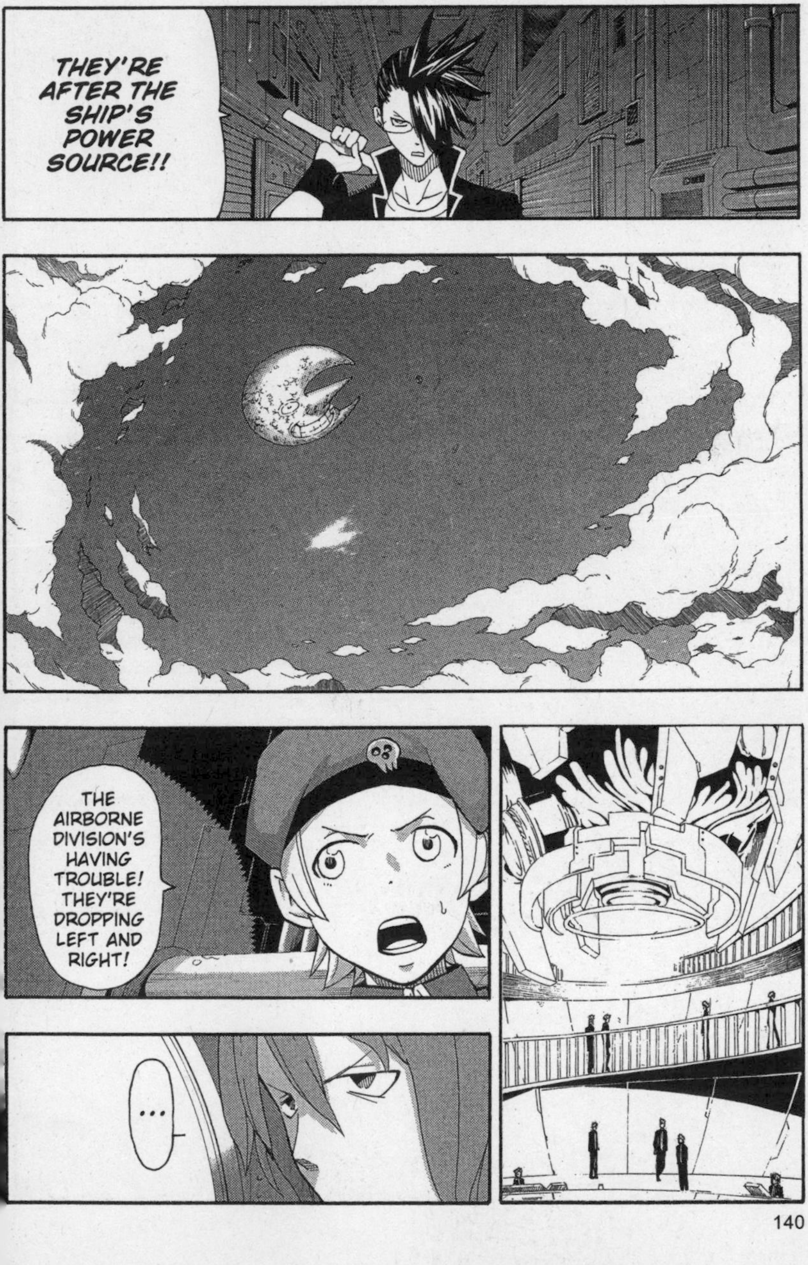
THEY'RE AFTER THE SHIP'S POWER SOURCE!!
THE AIRBORNE DIVISION'S HAVING TROUBLE! THEY'RE DROPPING LEFT AND RIGHT!
...

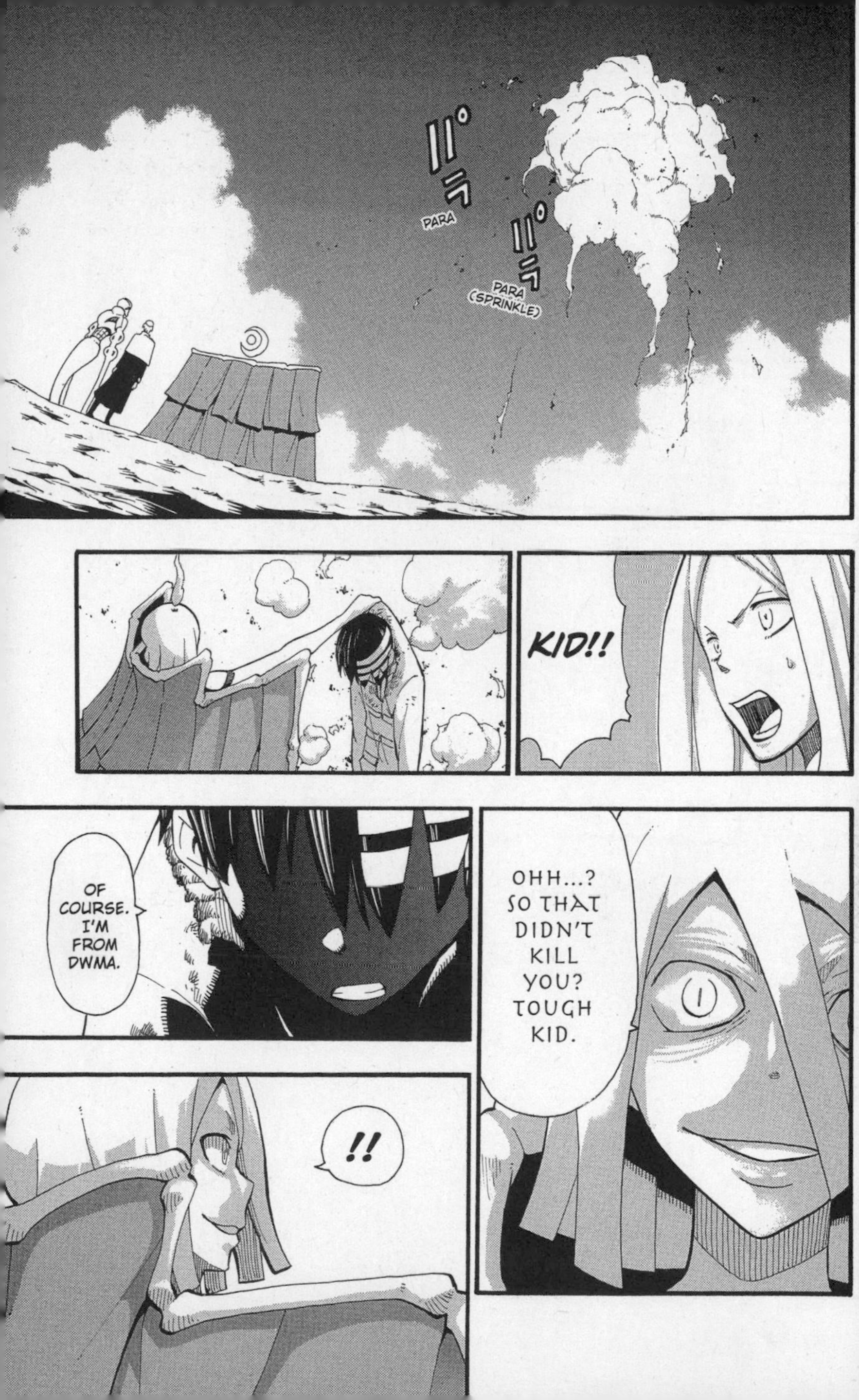
パラ
PARA
パラ
PARA (SPRINKLE)
KID!!
OHH...? SO THAT DIDN'T KILL YOU? TOUGH KID.
OF COURSE. I'M FROM DWMA.
!!

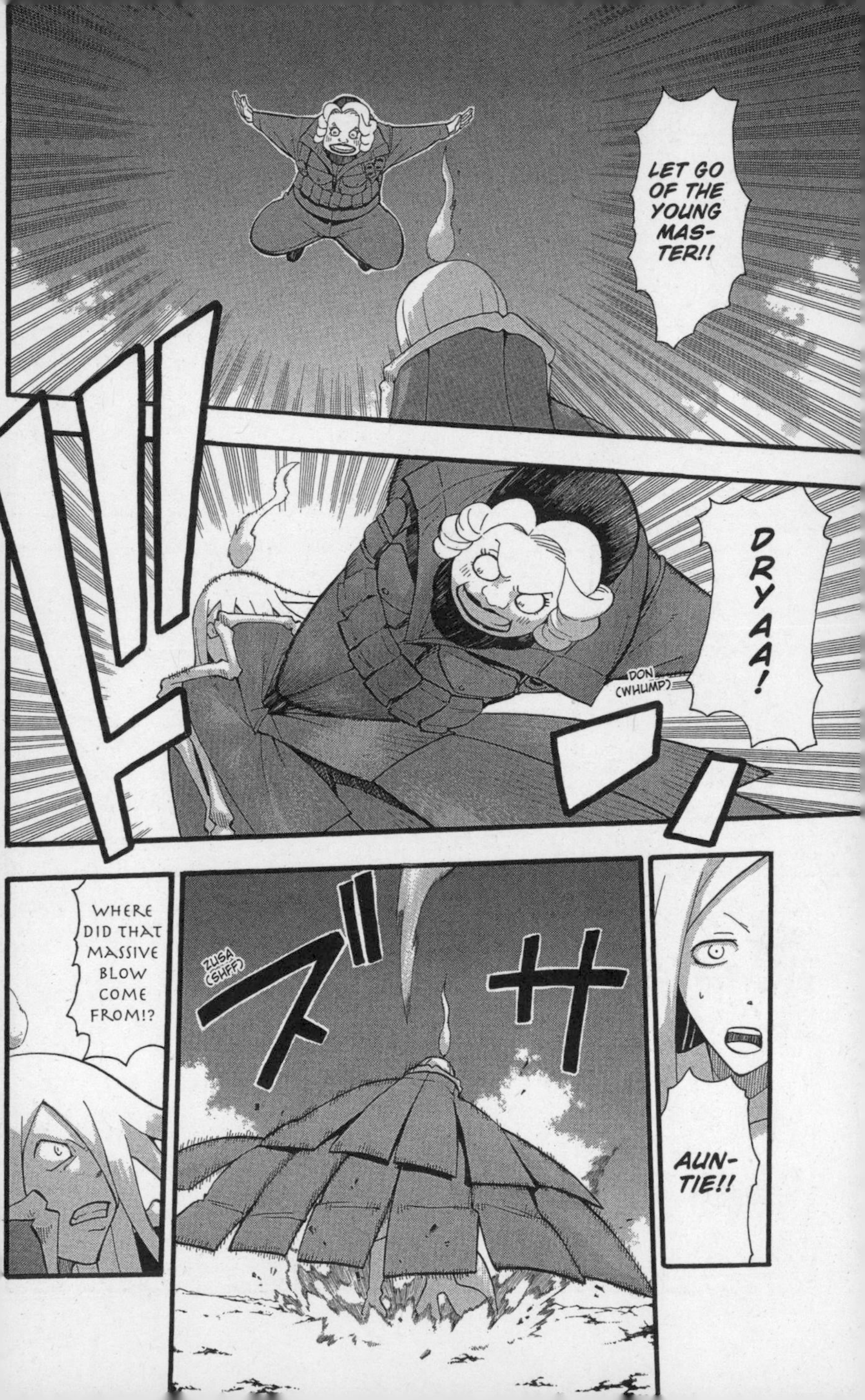
LET GO OF THE YOUNG MAS-TER!!
DRYAA!
DON (WHUMP)
AUN-TIE!!
ズサ
ZUSA (SHFF)
WHERE DID THAT MASSIVE BLOW COME FROM!?

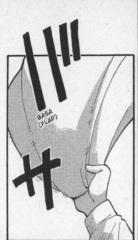

YOU ALL RIGHT?
SUTA (STEP)
THIS IS NOTHING.
DO (THUMP)
BASA (FLAP)
WE'VE GOT TO STOP THE ANTI-AIR ATTACKS...
KOOOO (WHOOOO)
...SO THE AIRBORNE TROOPS CAN LAND ON THE SURFACE.
TWO MEMBERS OF THE AIRBORNE DIVISION HAVE LANDED SAFELY.
TRANSITIONING TO OUR AIR CONTROL PLAN.

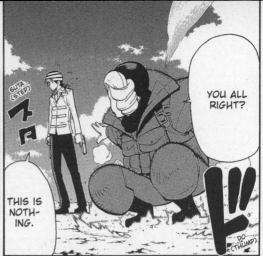

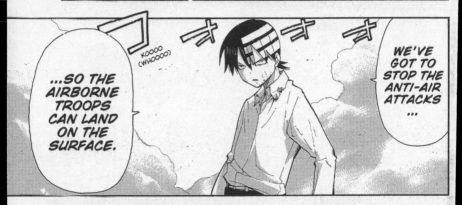

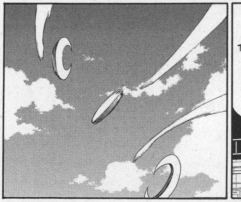

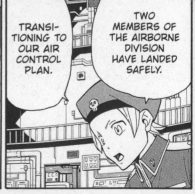

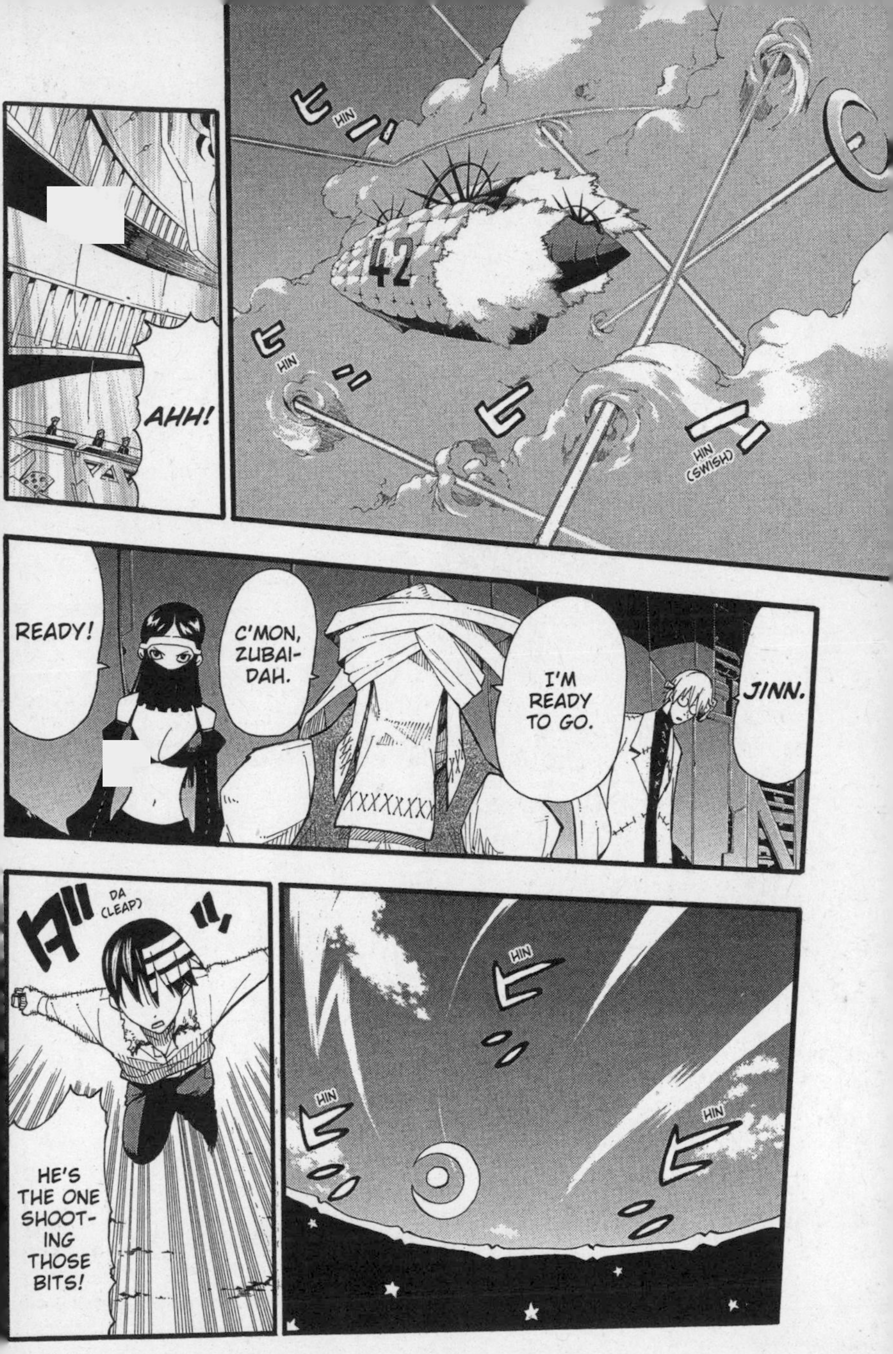
HIN
HIN
HIN (SWISH)
AHH!
JINN.
I'M READY TO GO.
C'MON, ZUBAI-DAH.
READY!
HIN
HIN
HIN
DA (LEAP)
HE'S THE ONE SHOOT-ING THOSE BITS!

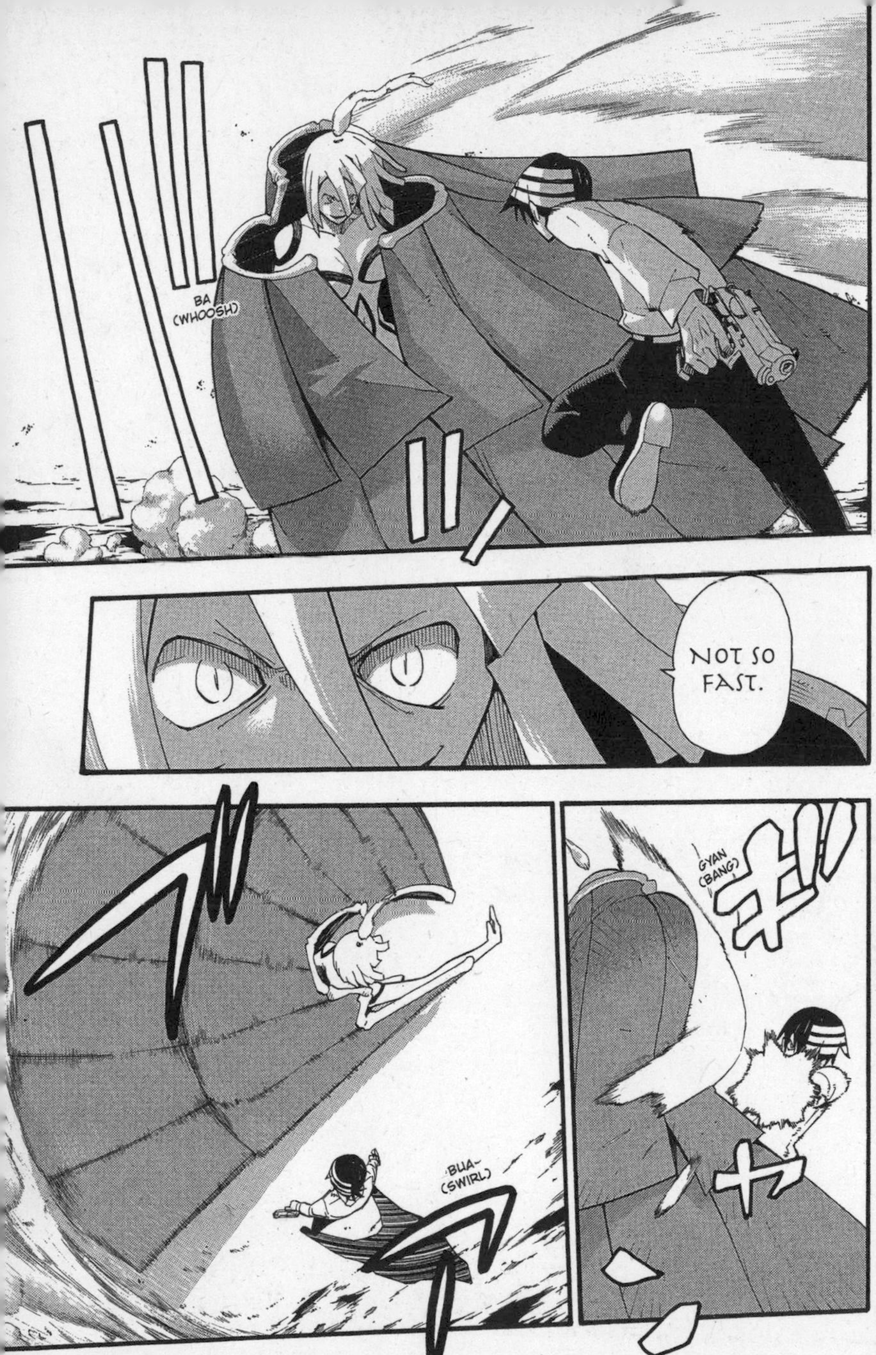
BA
(WHOOSH)
NOT SO FAST.
GYAN
(BANG)
BUA-
(SWIRL)

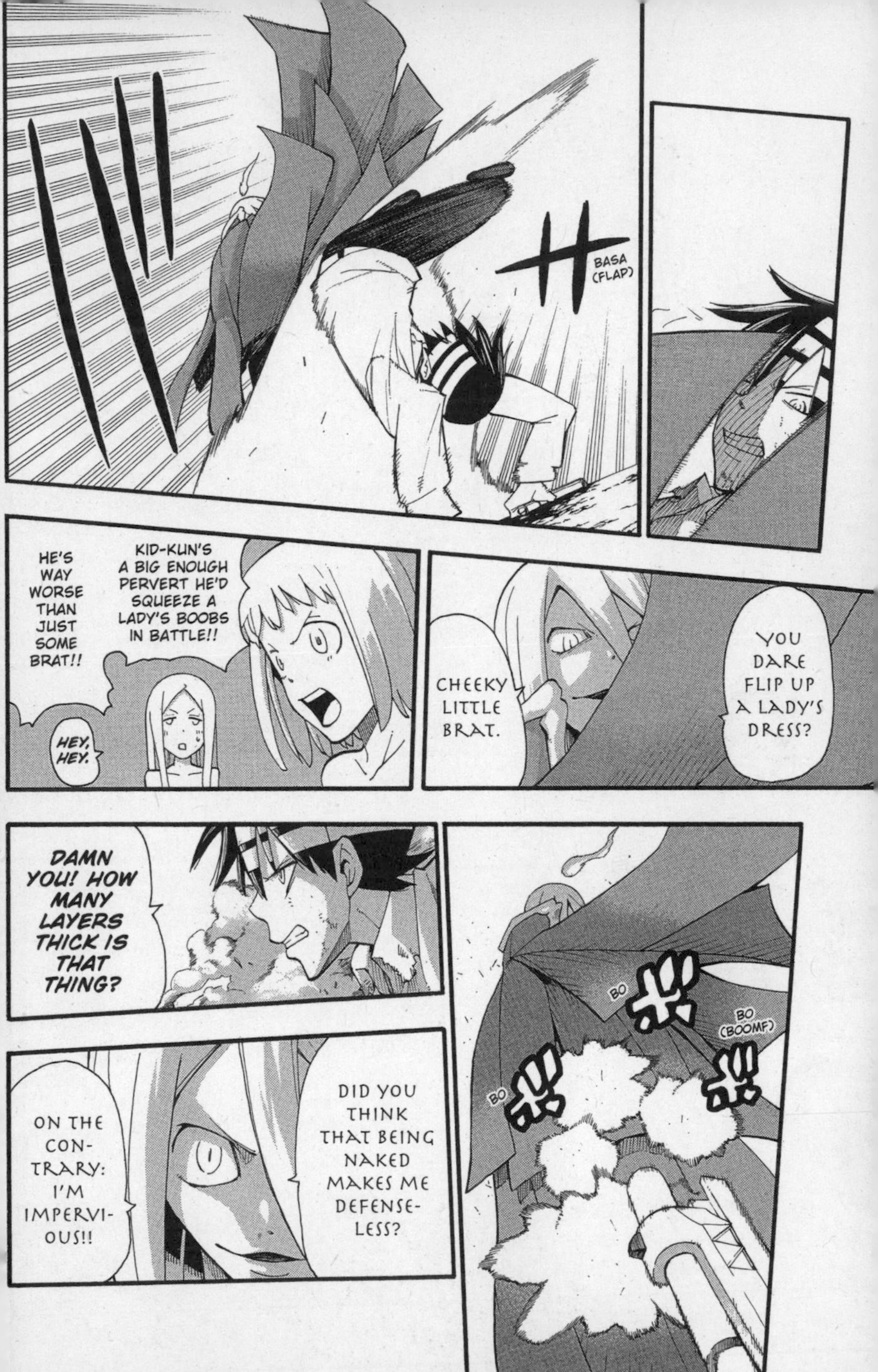
BASA (FLAP)
YOU DARE FLIP UP A LADY'S DRESS?
CHEEKY LITTLE BRAT.
KID-KUN'S A BIG ENOUGH PERVERT HE'D SQUEEZE A LADY'S BOOBS IN BATTLE!!
HE'S WAY WORSE THAN JUST SOME BRAT!!
HEY, HEY.
BO
BO (BOOMF)
BO
DAMN YOU! HOW MANY LAYERS THICK IS THAT THING?
DID YOU THINK THAT BEING NAKED MAKES ME DEFENSE-LESS?
ON THE CON-TRARY: I'M IMPERVI-OUS!!

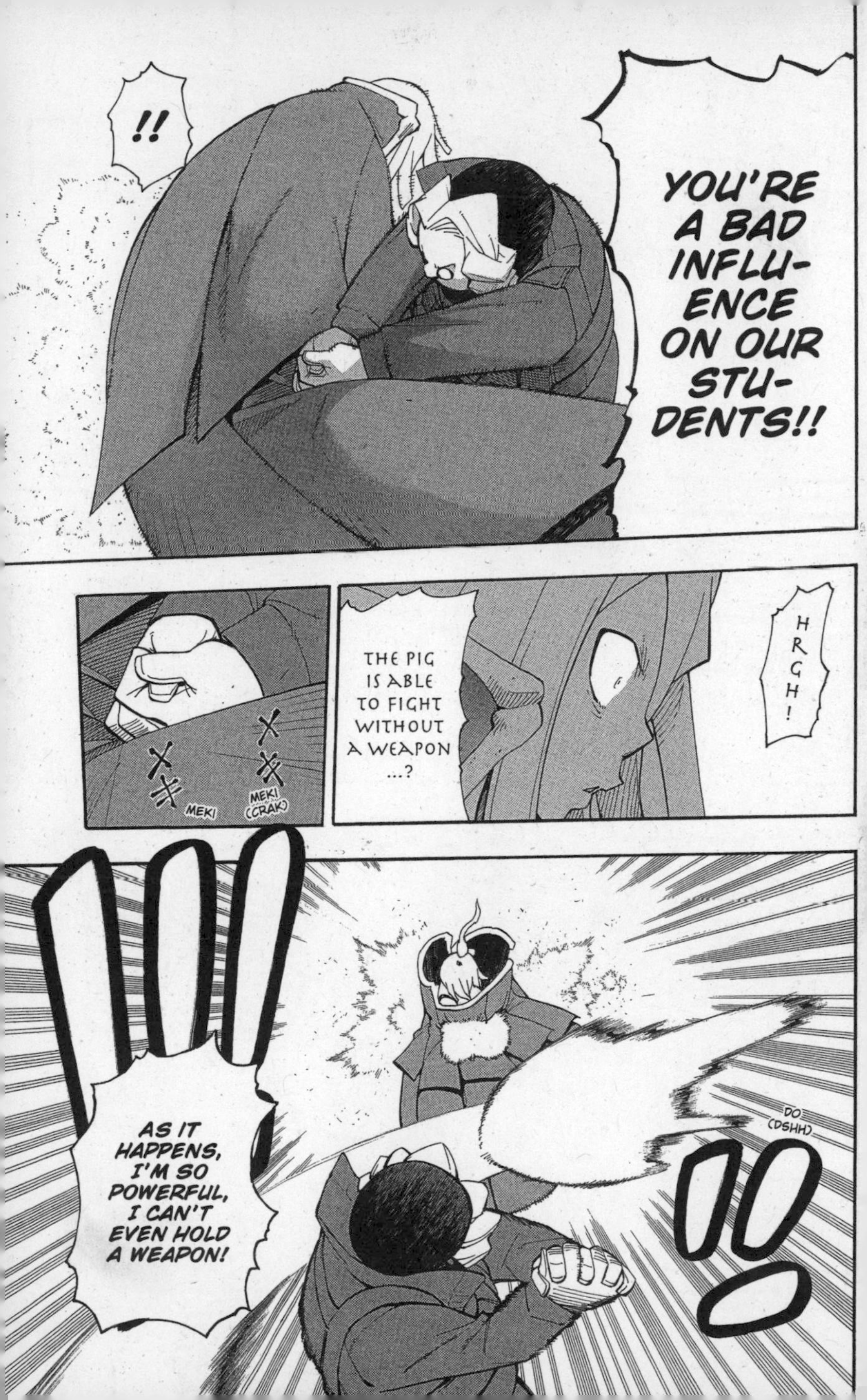
YOU'RE A BAD INFLUENCE ON OUR STUDENTS!!
!!
HRGH!
THE PIG IS ABLE TO FIGHT WITHOUT A WEAPON ...?
MEKI (CRAK)
MEKI
DO (DSHH)
AS IT HAPPENS, I'M SO POWERFUL, I CAN'T EVEN HOLD A WEAPON!

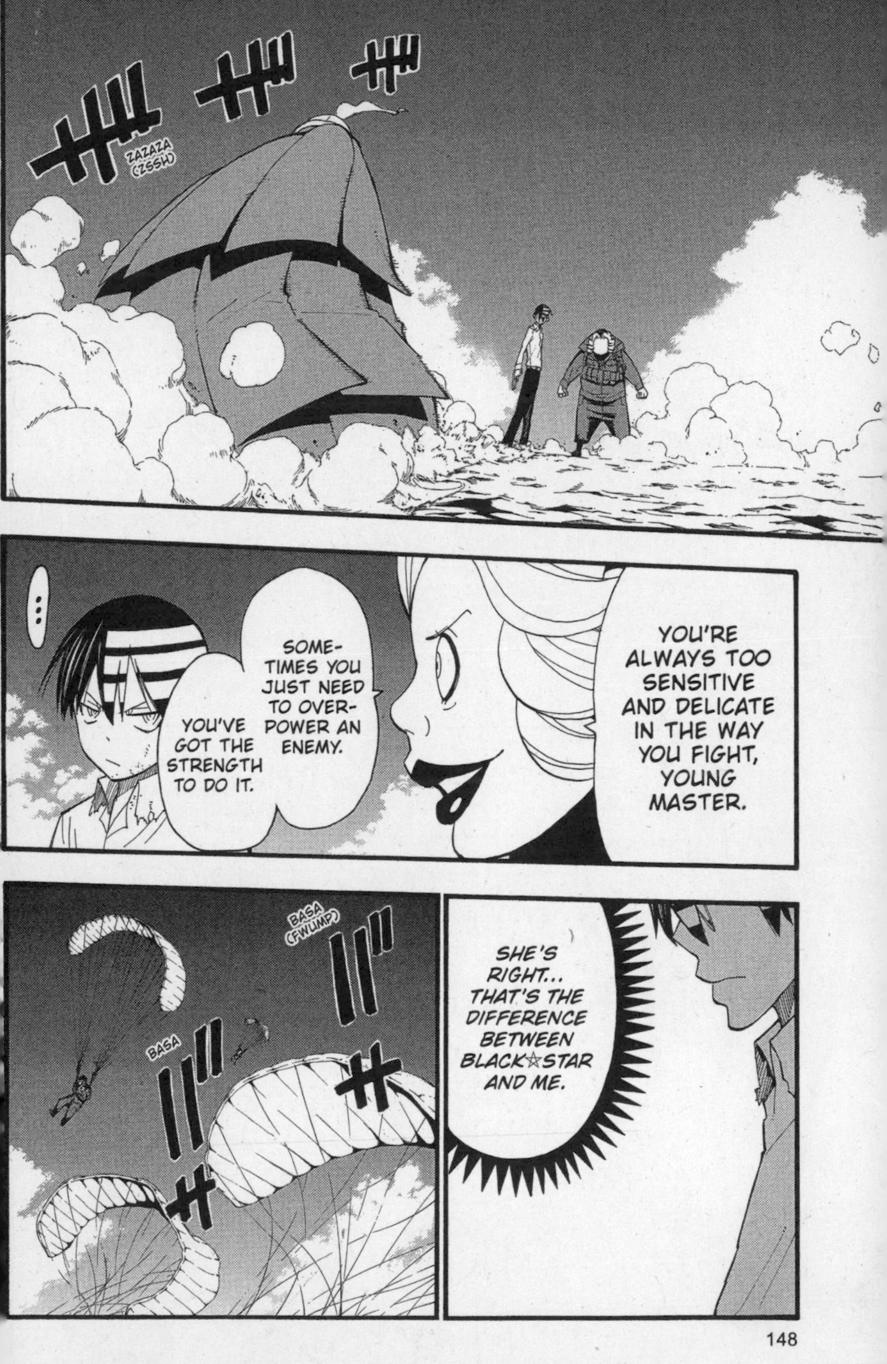
ZAZAZA (ZSSH)
YOU'RE ALWAYS TOO SENSITIVE AND DELICATE IN THE WAY YOU FIGHT, YOUNG MASTER.
SOME-TIMES YOU JUST NEED TO OVER-POWER AN ENEMY.
YOU'VE GOT THE STRENGTH TO DO IT.
...
SHE'S RIGHT... THAT'S THE DIFFERENCE BETWEEN BLACK☆STAR AND ME.
BASA (FWUMP)
BASA

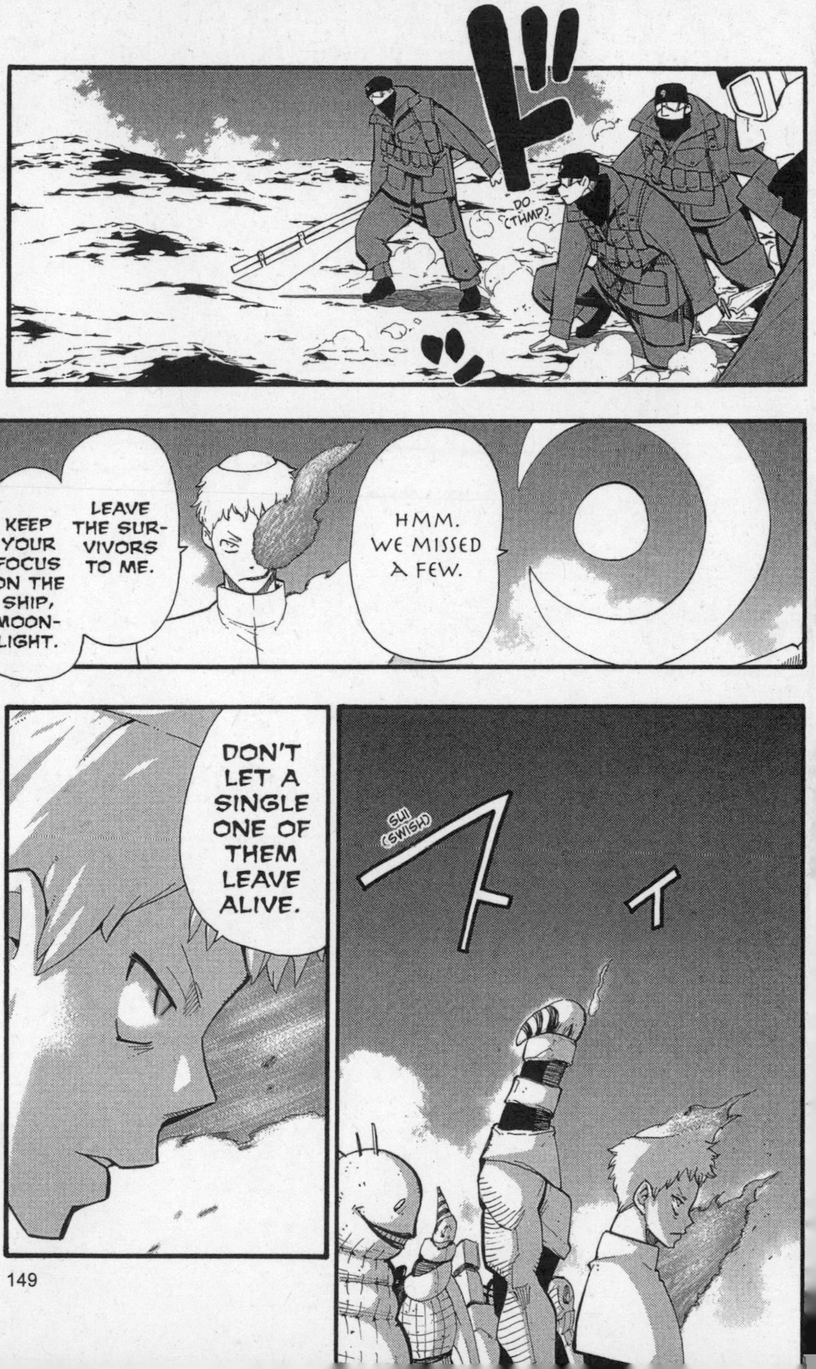
DO (THMP)
HMM. WE MISSED A FEW.
LEAVE THE SURVIVORS TO ME.
KEEP YOUR FOCUS ON THE SHIP, MOONLIGHT.
SUI (SWISH)
DON'T LET A SINGLE ONE OF THEM LEAVE ALIVE.

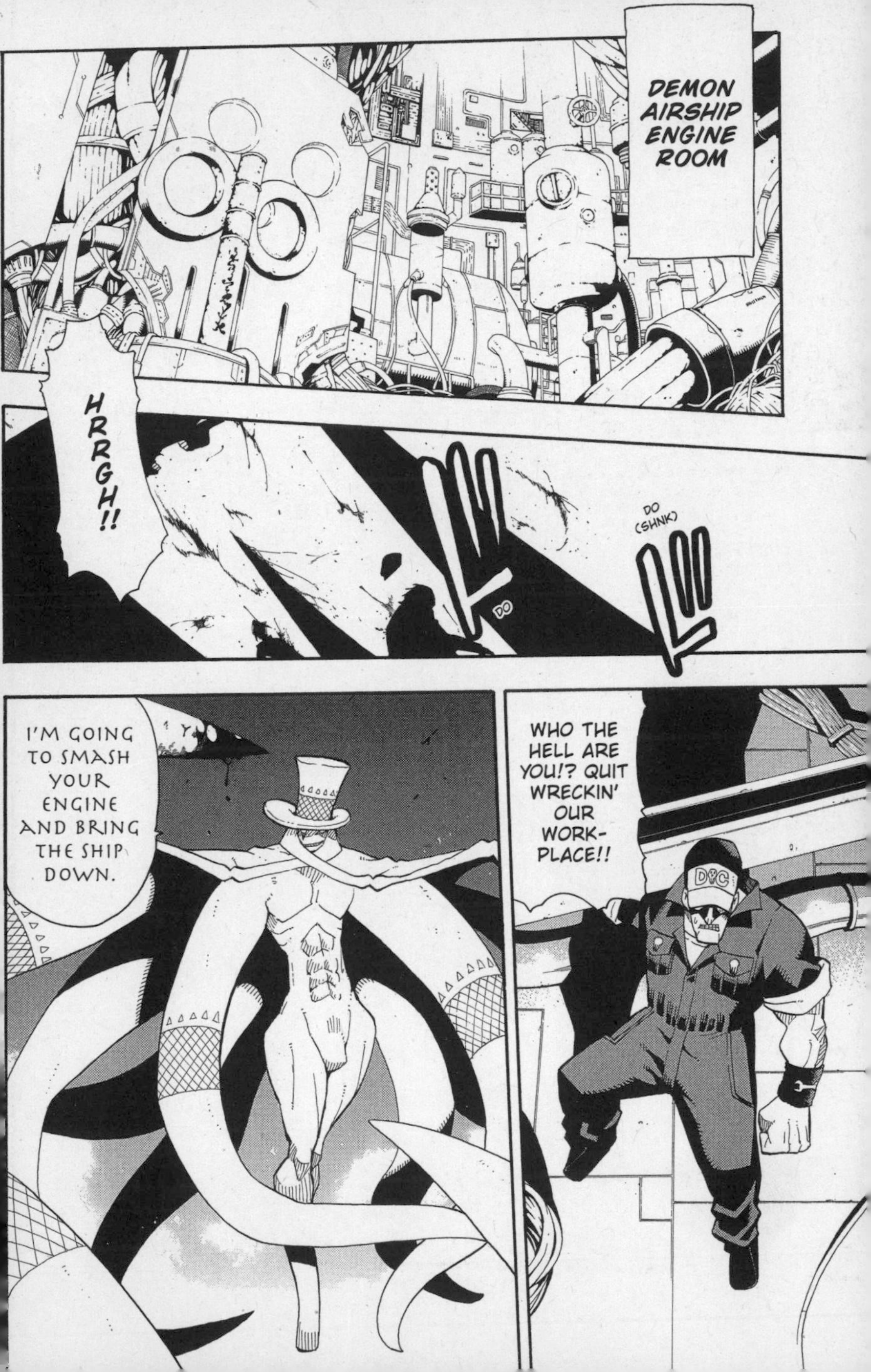
DEMON AIRSHIP ENGINE ROOM
DO (SHNK)
DO
HRRGH!!
WHO THE HELL ARE YOU!? QUIT WRECKIN' OUR WORK-PLACE!!
I'M GOING TO SMASH YOUR ENGINE AND BRING THE SHIP DOWN.

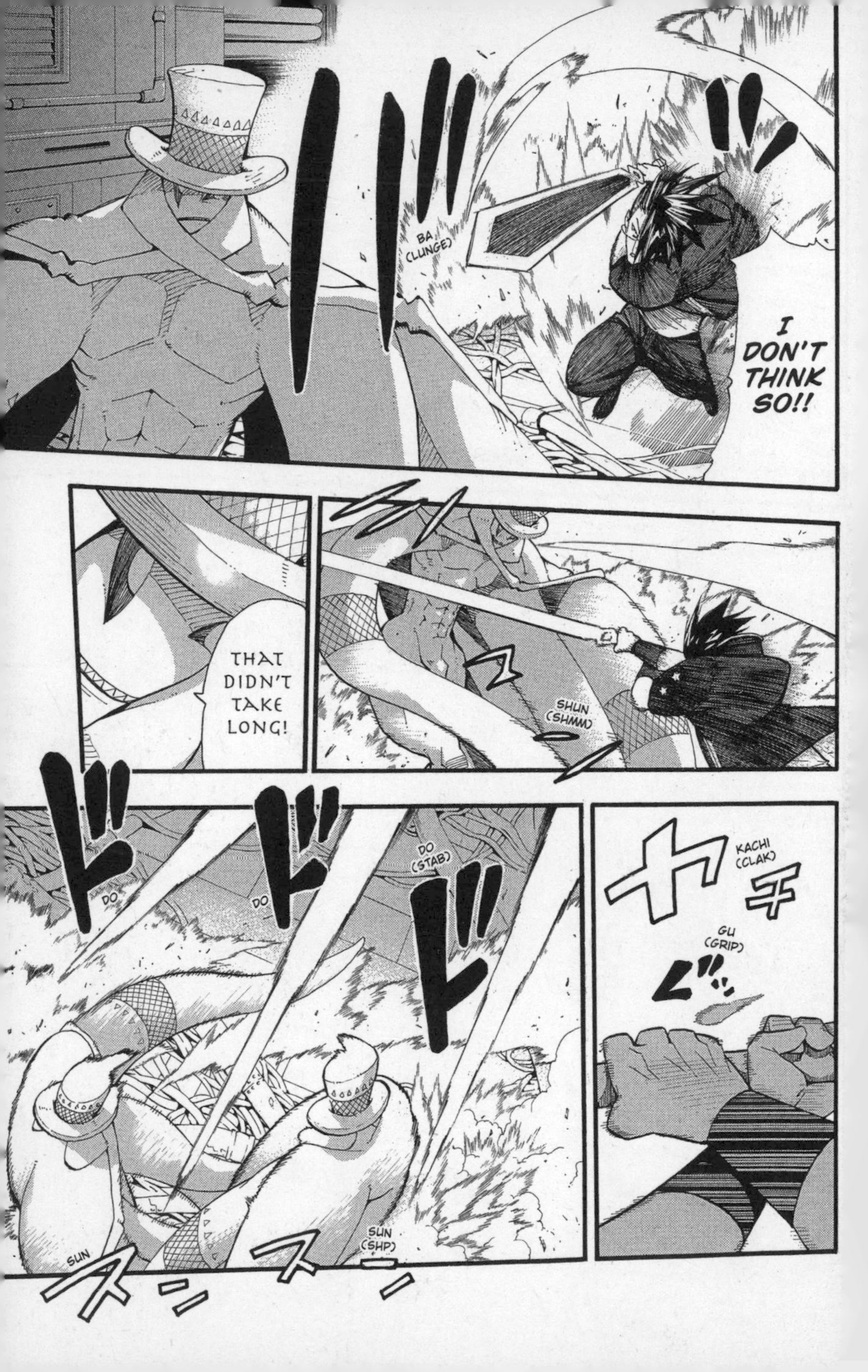
BA (LUNGE)
I DON'T THINK SO!!
SHUN (SHMM)
THAT DIDN'T TAKE LONG!
KACHI (CLAK)
GU (GRIP)
DO (STAB)
DO
DO
SUN (SHP)
SUN

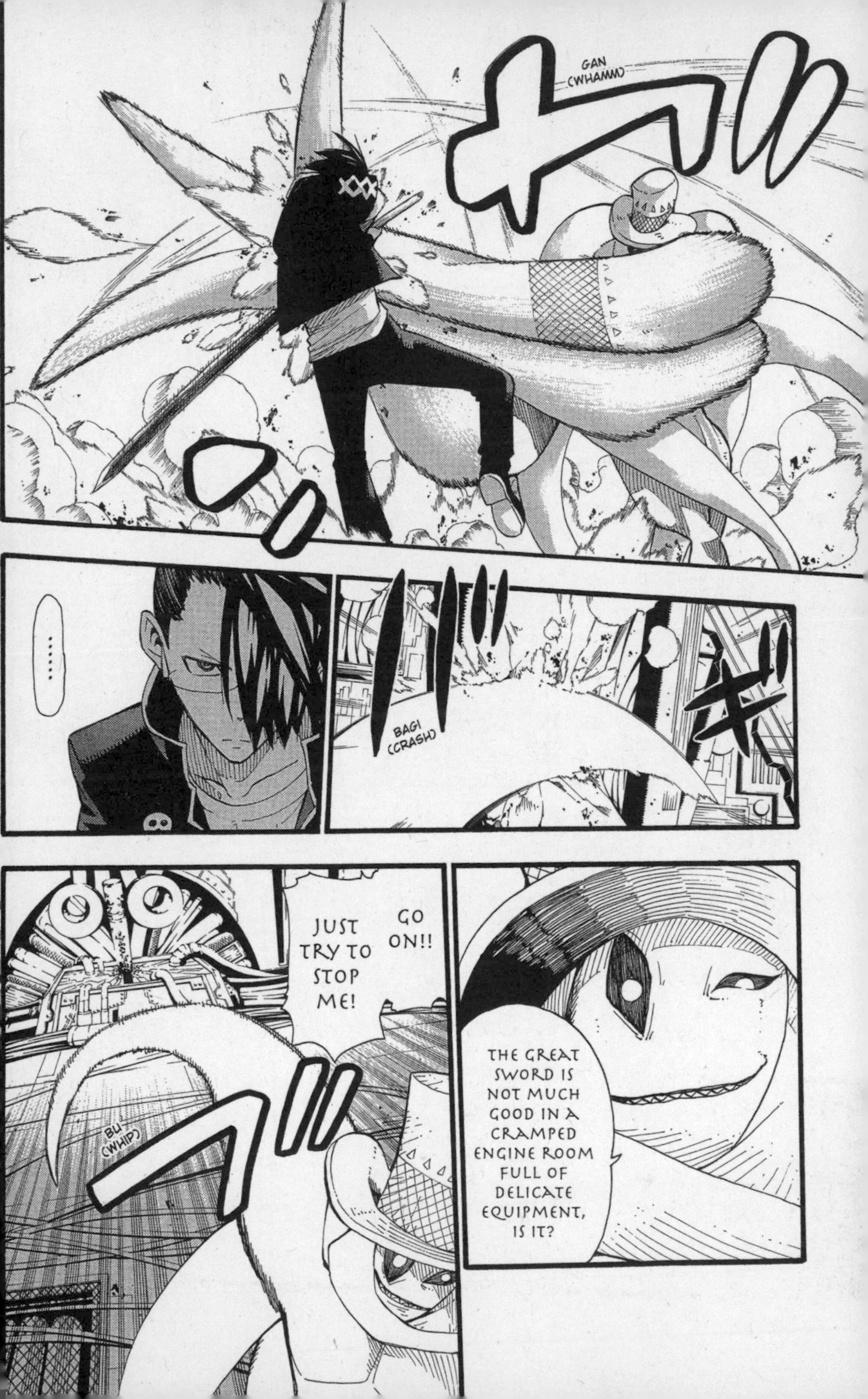
GAN (WHAMM)
BAGI (CRASH)
......
THE GREAT SWORD IS NOT MUCH GOOD IN A CRAMPED ENGINE ROOM FULL OF DELICATE EQUIPMENT, IS IT?
GO ON!!
JUST TRY TO STOP ME!
BU (WHIP)

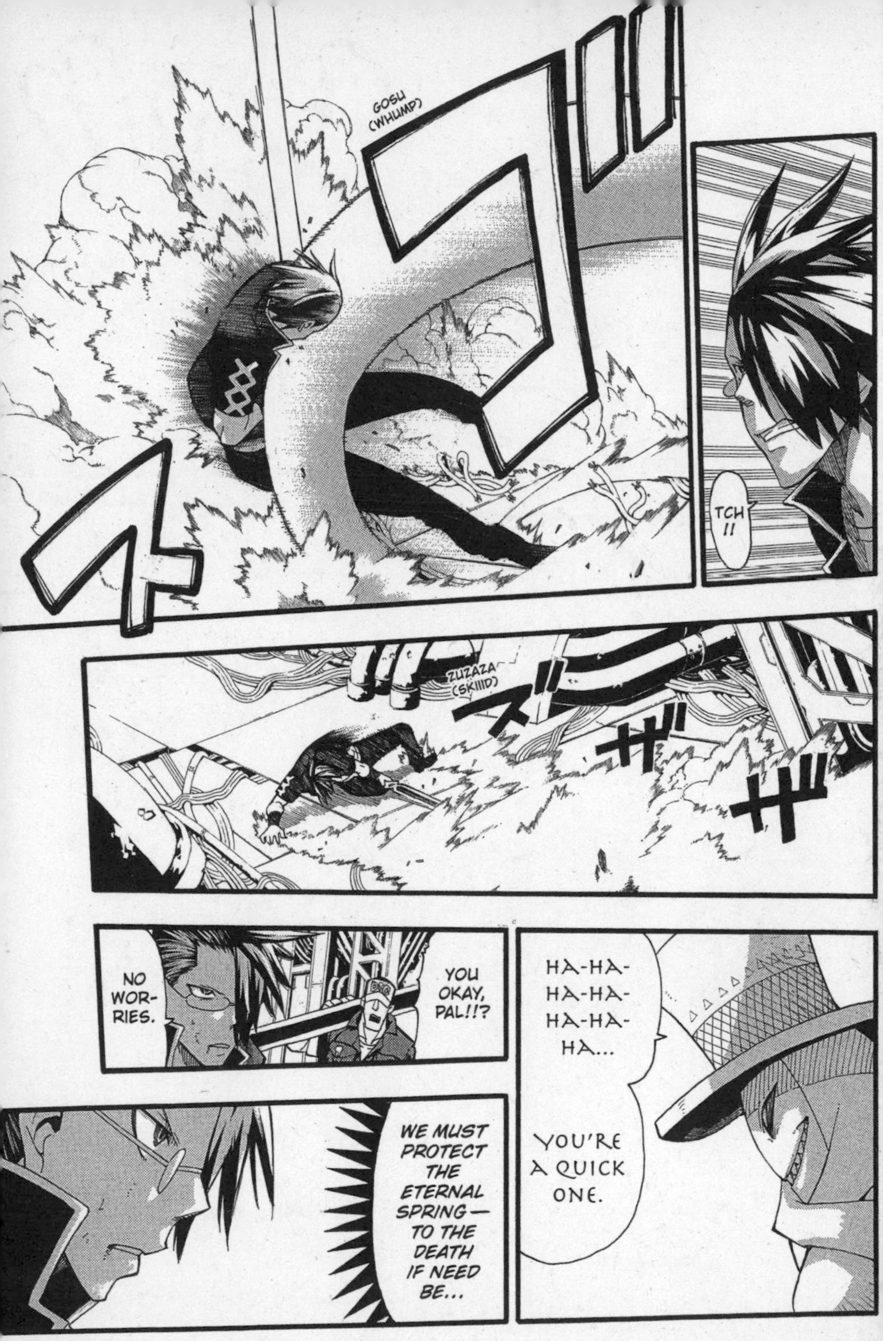
TCH!!
GOSU (WHUMP)
ZUZAZA (SKIIID)
HA-HA-HA-HA-HA-HA-HA...
YOU'RE A QUICK ONE.
YOU OKAY, PAL!!?
NO WORRIES.
WE MUST PROTECT THE ETERNAL SPRING—TO THE DEATH IF NEED BE...

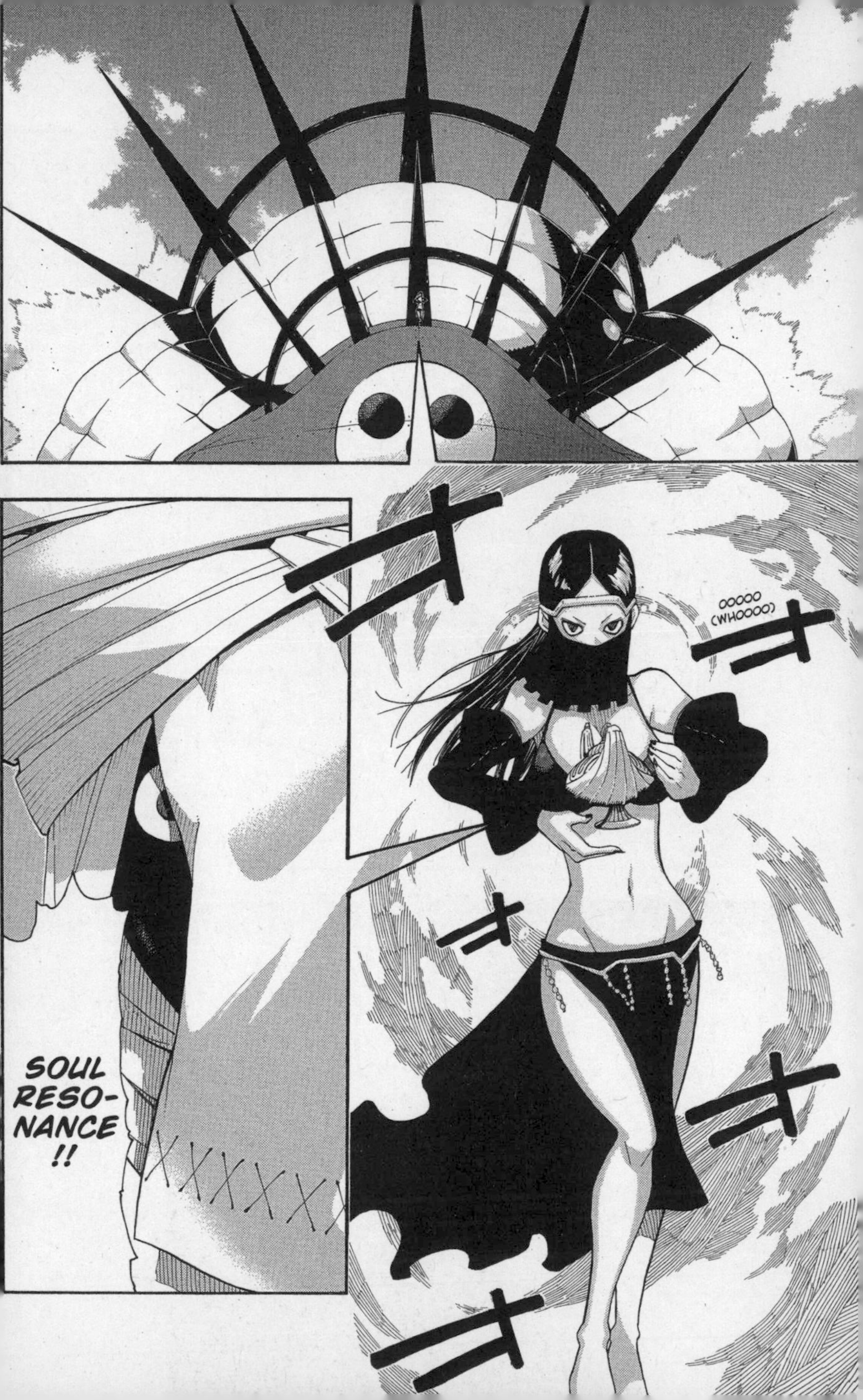
OOOOO
(WHOOOO)
SOUL
RESO-
NANCE
!!

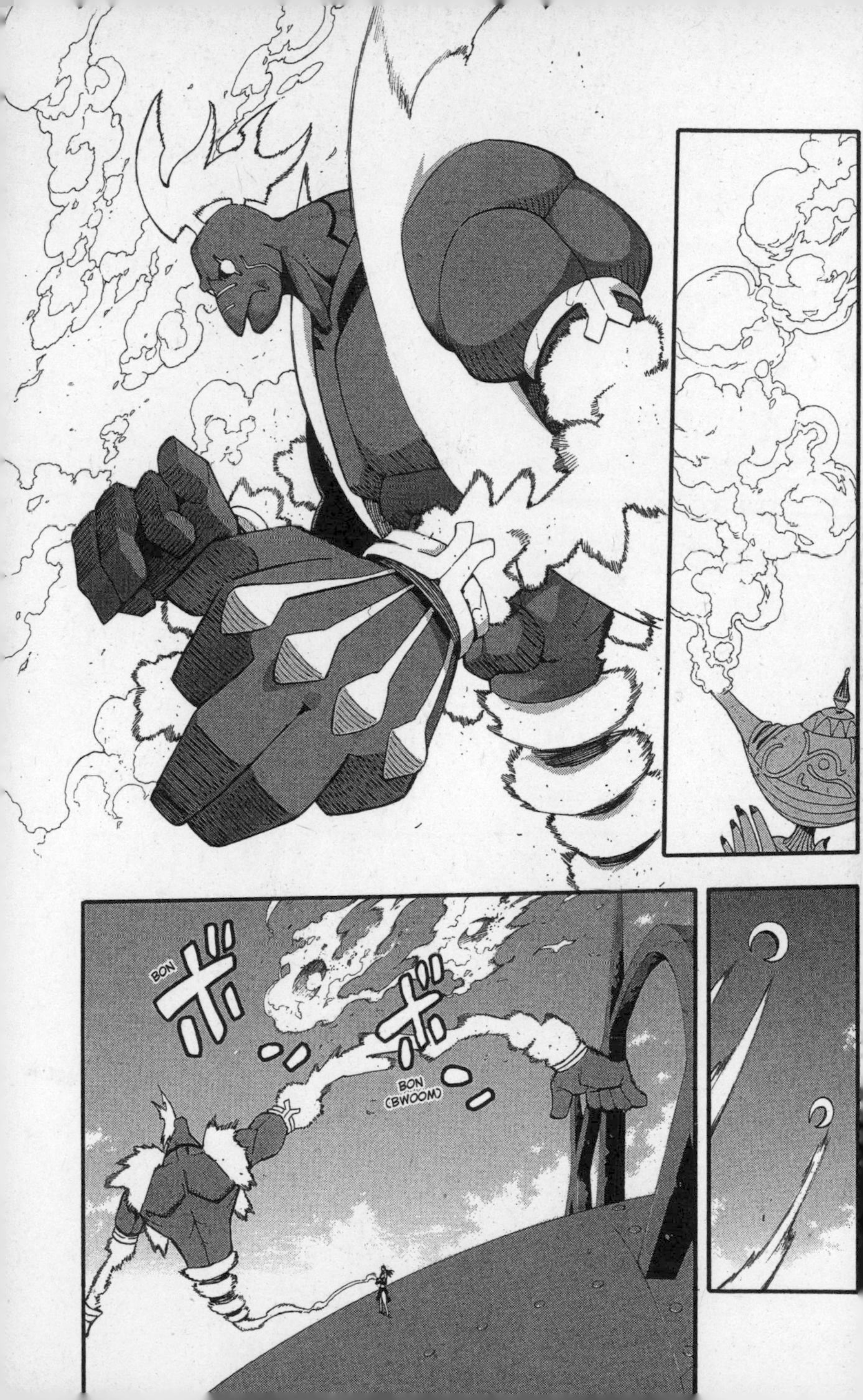
BON
BON (BWOOM)

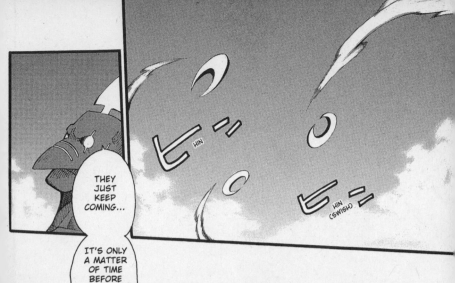

THEY JUST KEEP COMING...

IT'S ONLY A MATTER OF TIME BEFORE THE SHIP GOES DOWN!!

HURRY UP, AIRBORNE DIVISION!!

WE HAVE TO WIPE THEM ALL OUT!!

OOOO (WHOOM)

LIZ, PATTY!

DOSA (THUMP)

!

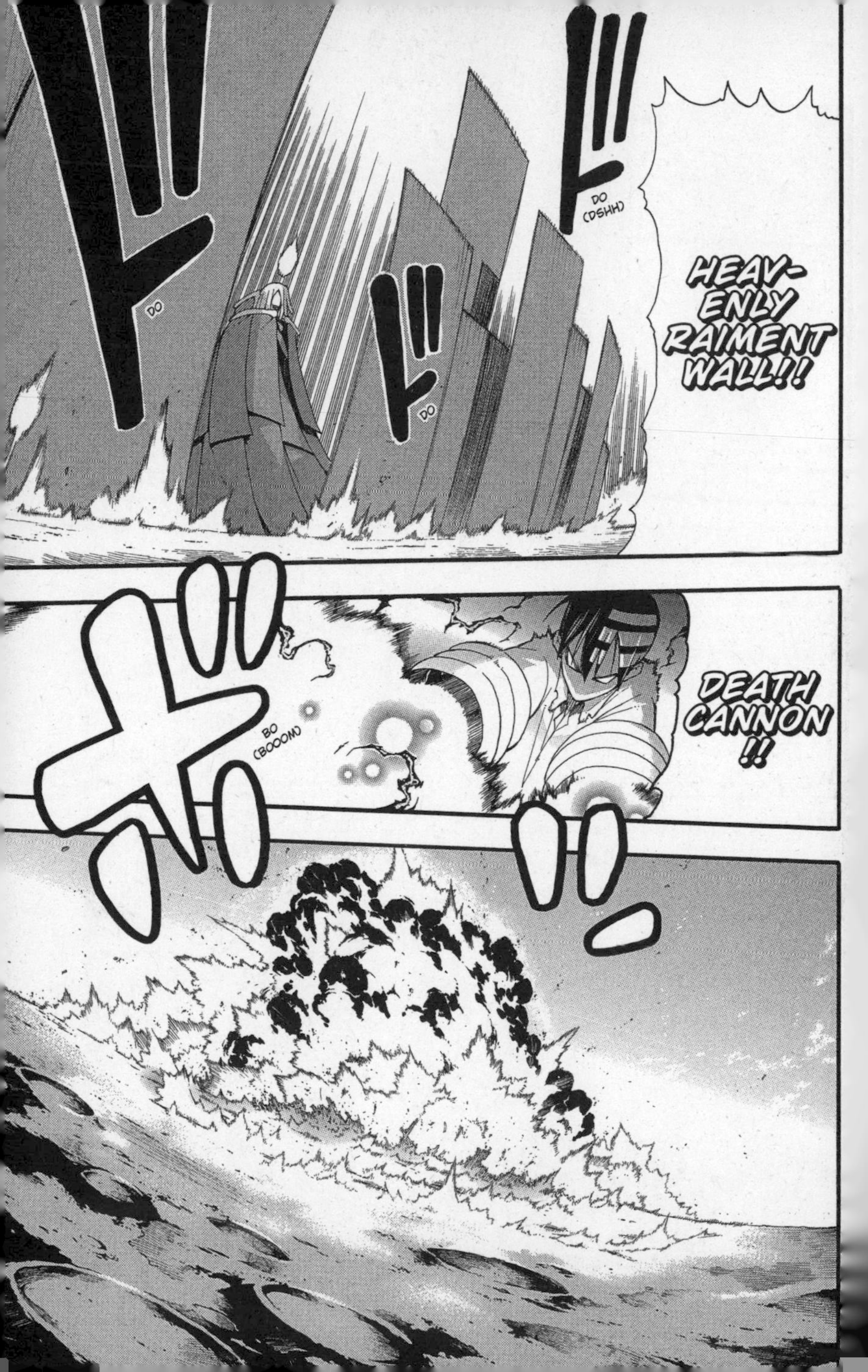
HEAV-ENLY RAIMENT WALL!!
DO (DSHH)
DO
DO
DEATH CANNON!!
BO (BOOOM)

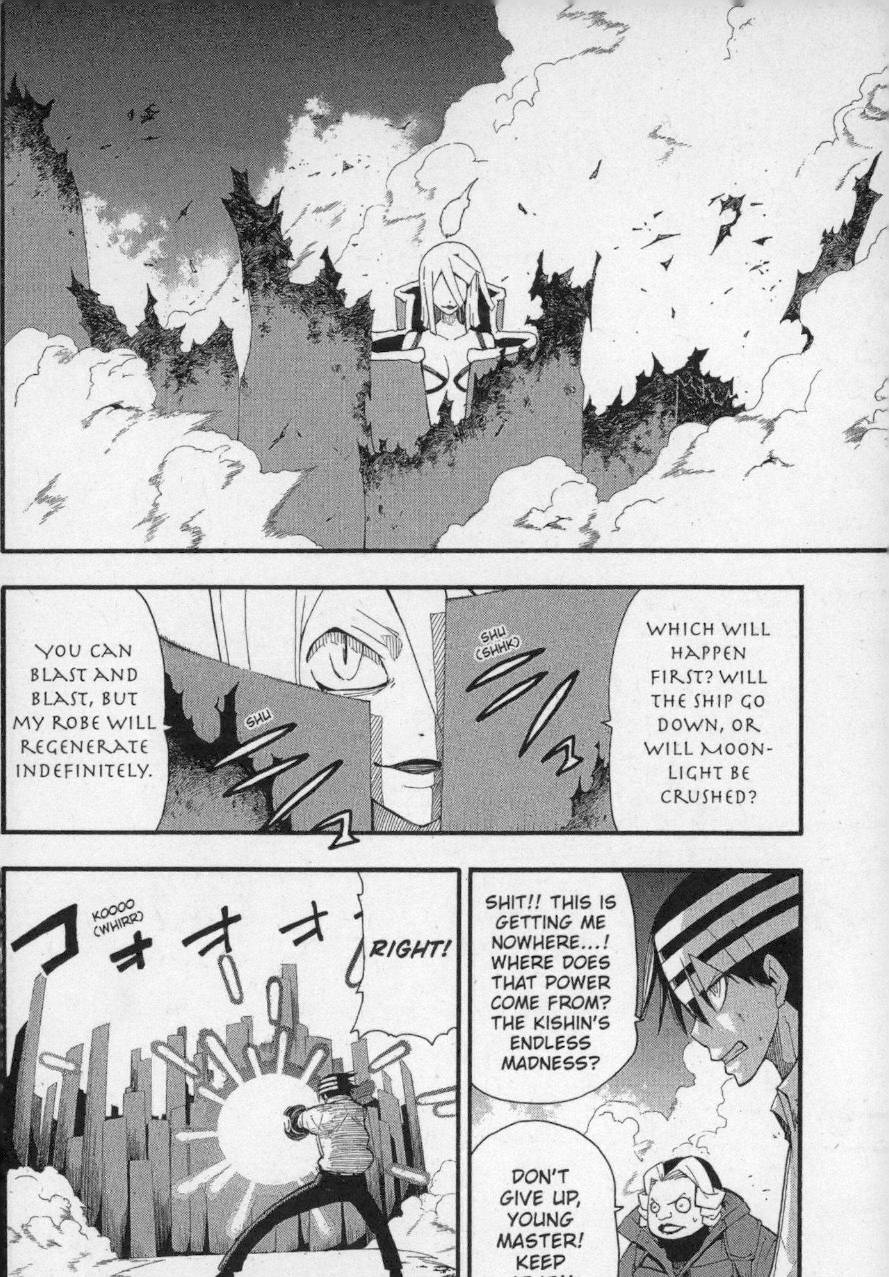
WHICH WILL HAPPEN FIRST? WILL THE SHIP GO DOWN, OR WILL MOON-LIGHT BE CRUSHED?
SHU (SHHK)
YOU CAN BLAST AND BLAST, BUT MY ROBE WILL REGENERATE INDEFINITELY.
SHU
SHIT!! THIS IS GETTING ME NOWHERE...! WHERE DOES THAT POWER COME FROM? THE KISHIN'S ENDLESS MADNESS?
DON'T GIVE UP, YOUNG MASTER! KEEP AT IT!!
RIGHT!
KOOOO (WHIRR)

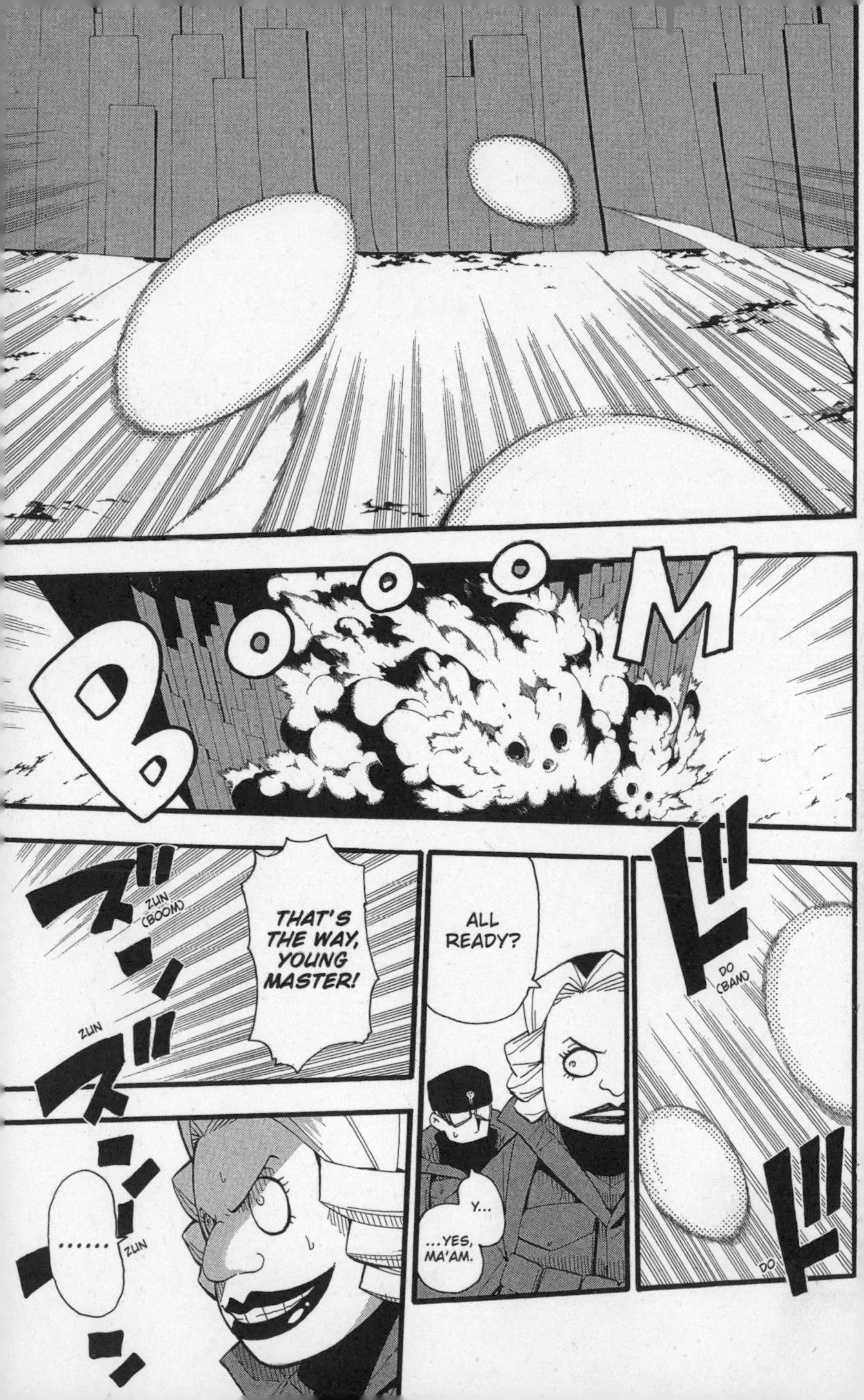
BOOOOM
DO (BAM)
DO
ALL READY?
Y...
...YES, MA'AM.
ZUN (BOOM)
THAT'S THE WAY, YOUNG MASTER!
ZUN
......
ZUN

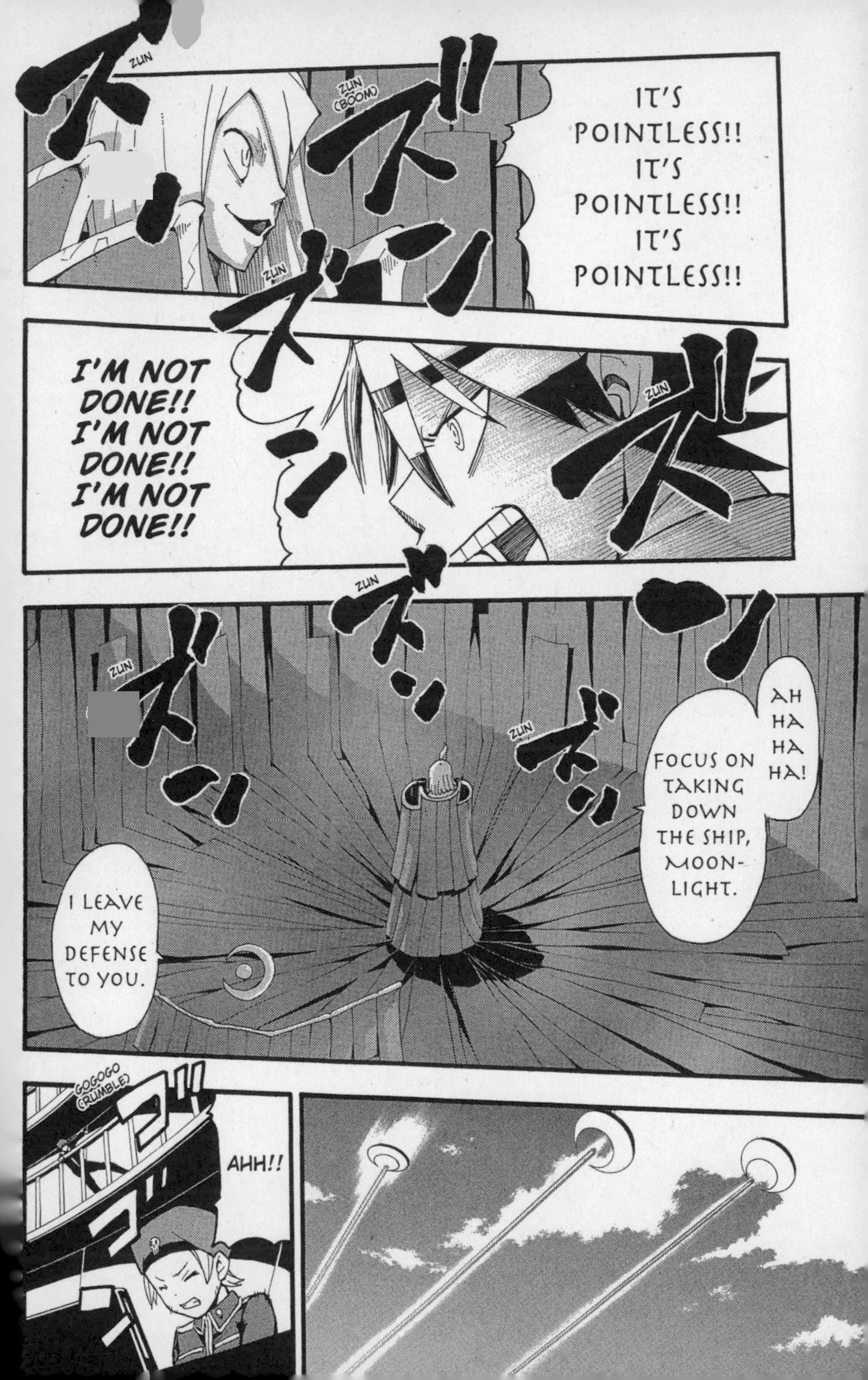
IT'S POINTLESS!! IT'S POINTLESS!! IT'S POINTLESS!!
ZUN (BOOM)
ZUN
ZUN
ZUN
I'M NOT DONE!! I'M NOT DONE!! I'M NOT DONE!!
ZUN
AH HA HA HA!
FOCUS ON TAKING DOWN THE SHIP, MOON-LIGHT.
ZUN
ZUN
I LEAVE MY DEFENSE TO YOU.
AHH!!
GOGOGO (RUMBLE)

SHU
(SWISH)

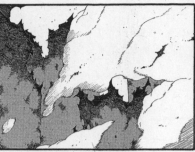

I ONLY
HAVE ONE
SHOT AT
THIS...!!

......

I'VE GOT
TO MOVE
SIMULTA-
NEOUSLY
WITH HIS
NEXT
BLAST!!

GU
(SQUEEZE)

BLAM

CHIRA
(PEEK)

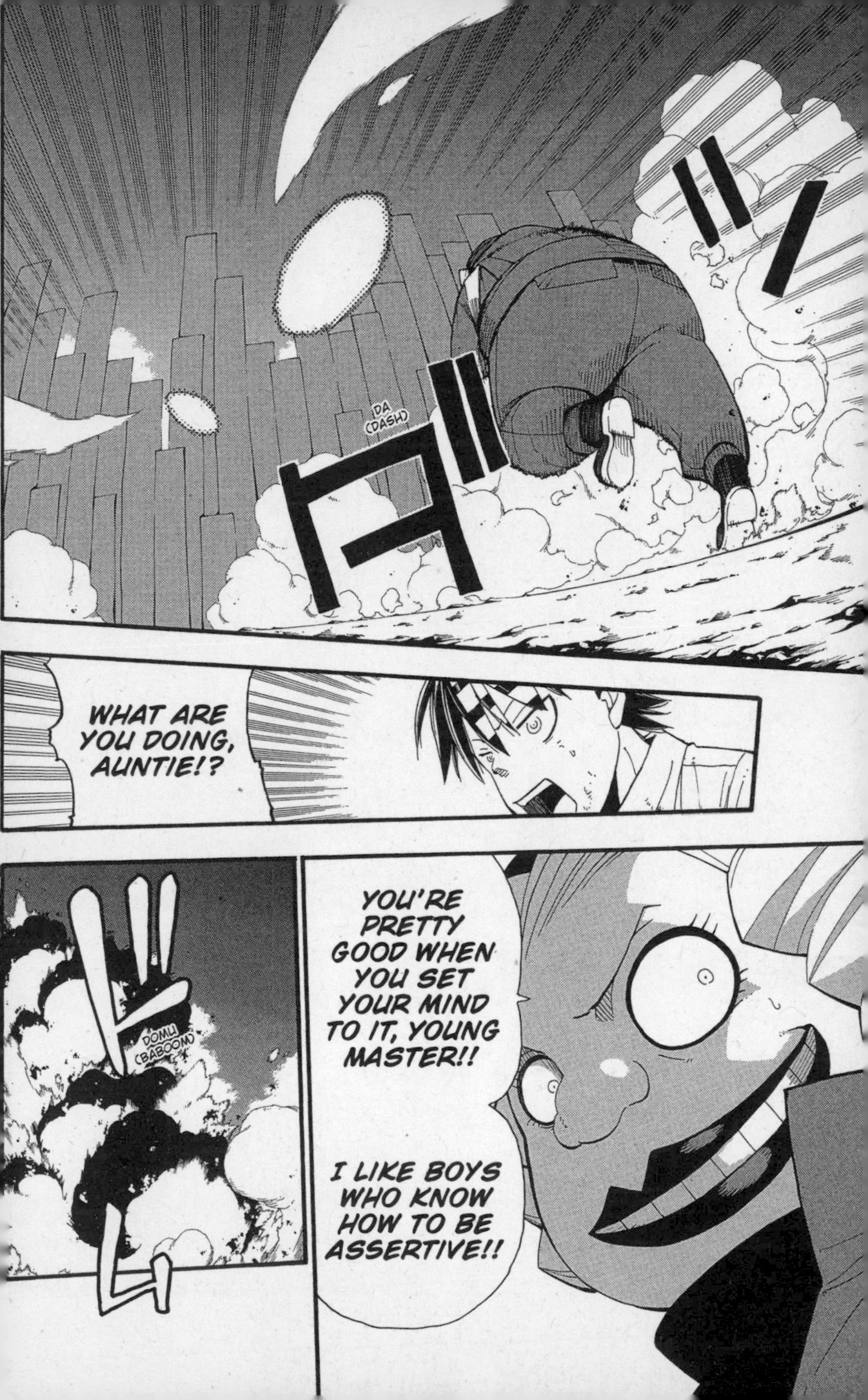
DA (DASH)
WHAT ARE YOU DOING, AUNTIE!?
YOU'RE PRETTY GOOD WHEN YOU SET YOUR MIND TO IT, YOUNG MASTER!!
I LIKE BOYS WHO KNOW HOW TO BE ASSERTIVE!!
DOMU (BABOOM)

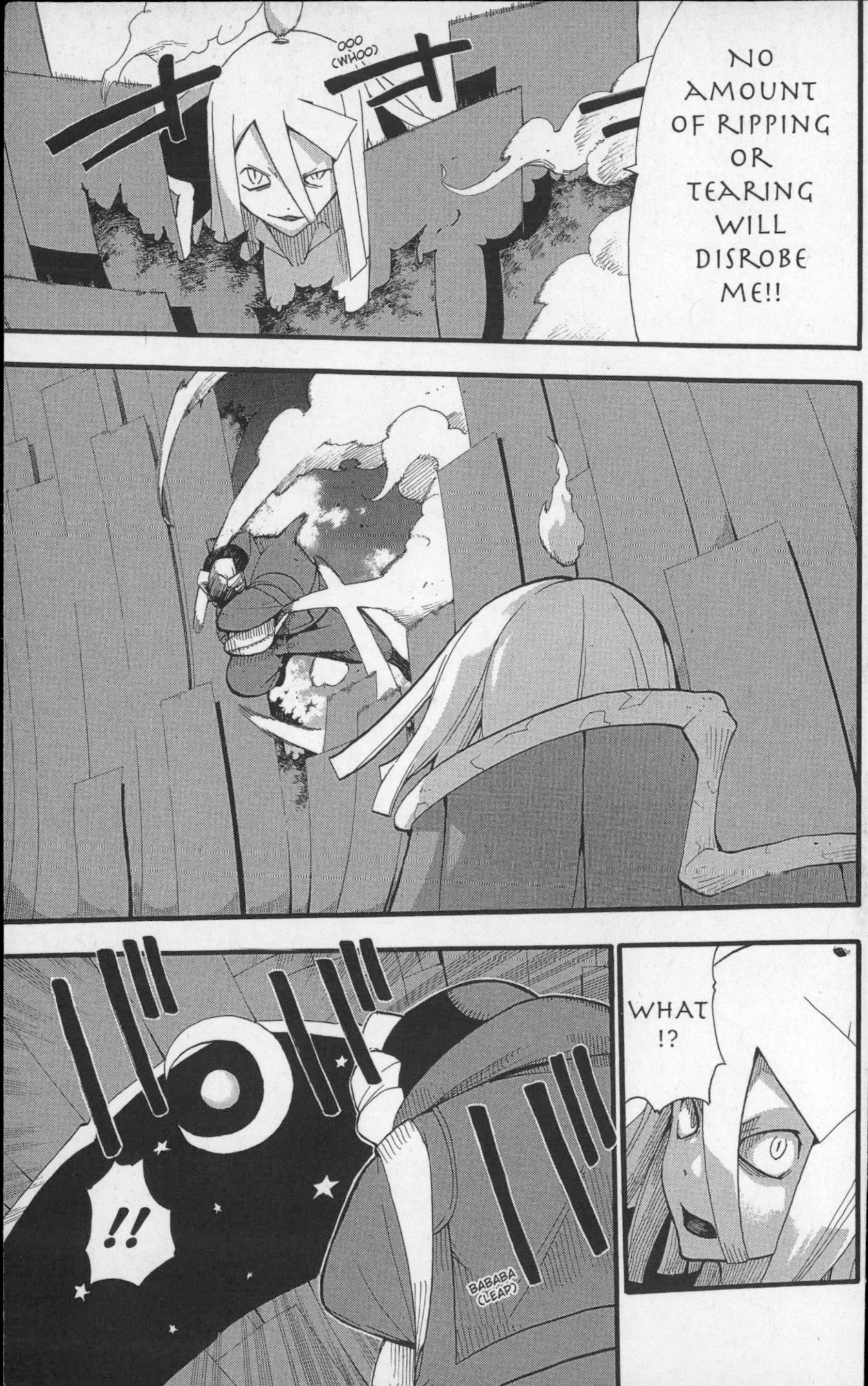
NO AMOUNT OF RIPPING OR TEARING WILL DISROBE ME!!
OOO (WHOO)
WHAT !?
!!
BABABA (LEAP)

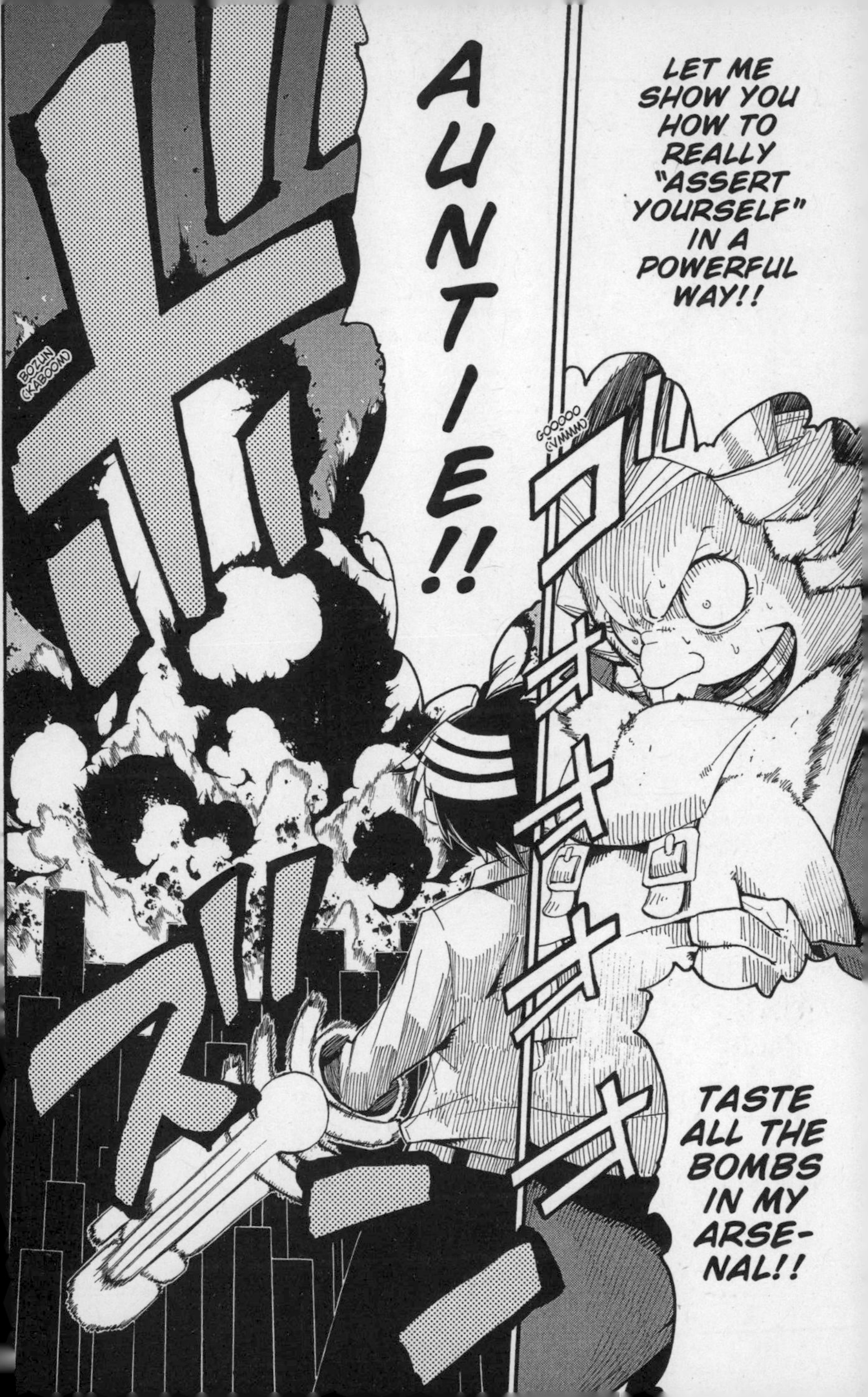
LET ME SHOW YOU HOW TO REALLY "ASSERT YOURSELF" IN A POWERFUL WAY!!
AUNTIE!!
GOOOOO (VMMMM)
TASTE ALL THE BOMBS IN MY ARSE-NAL!!
BOZUN (KABOOM)

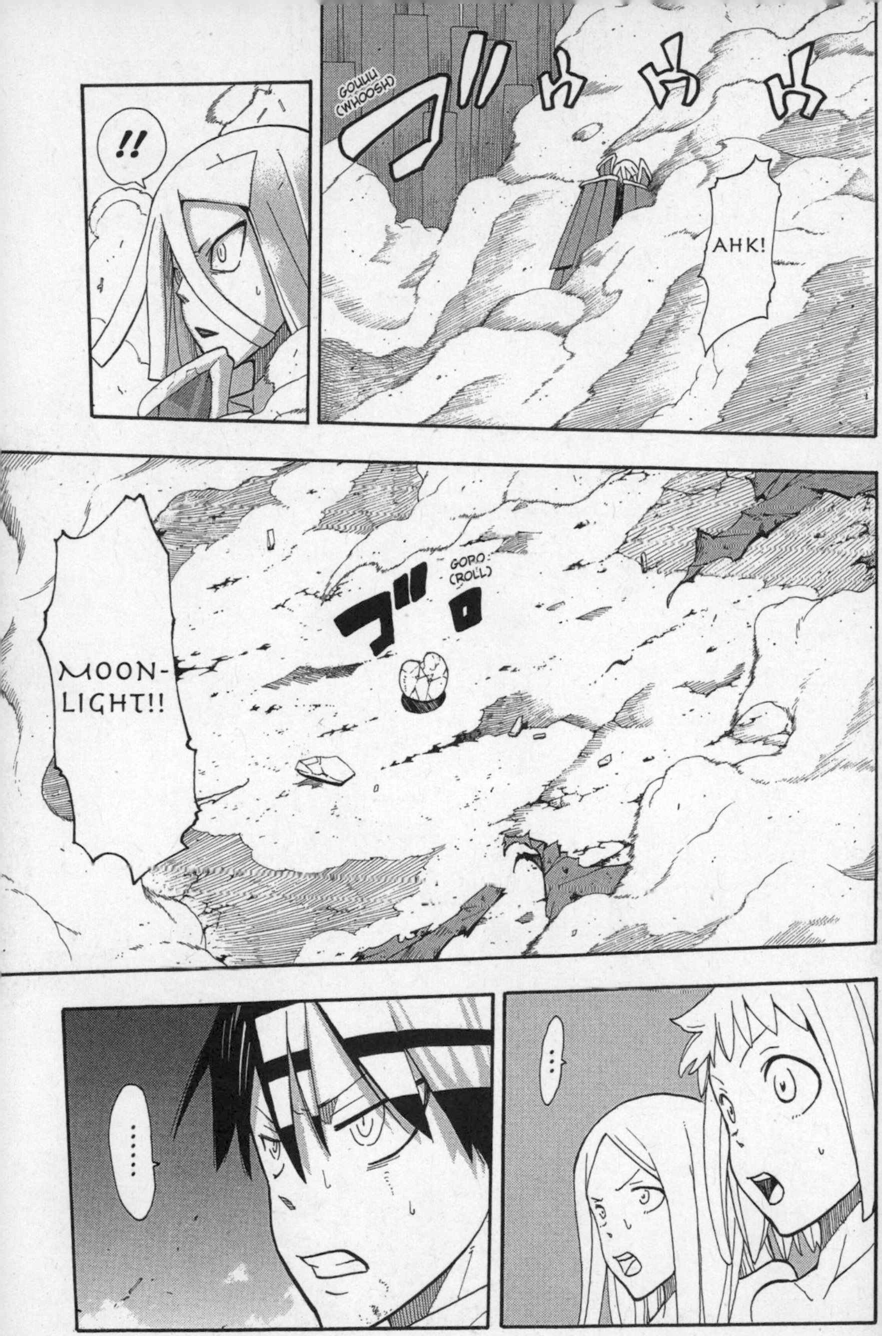
GOUUU (WHOOSH)
AHK!
!!
GORO (ROLL)
MOON-LIGHT!!
...
......

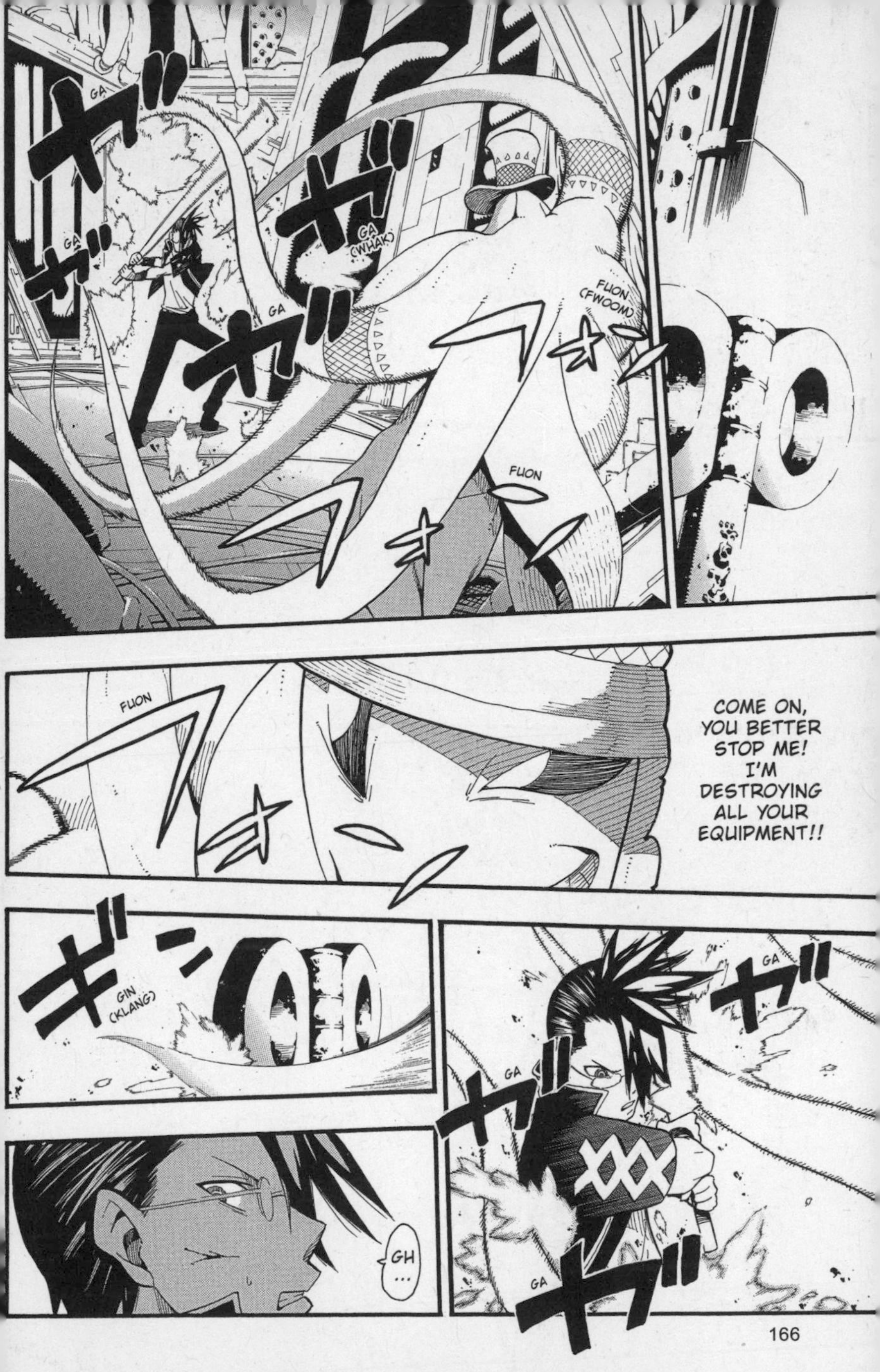
GA
GA (WHAK)
GA
GA
FUON (FWOOM)
FUON
COME ON, YOU BETTER STOP ME! I'M DESTROYING ALL YOUR EQUIPMENT!!
FUON
GA
GA
GA
GIN (KLANG)
GH ...

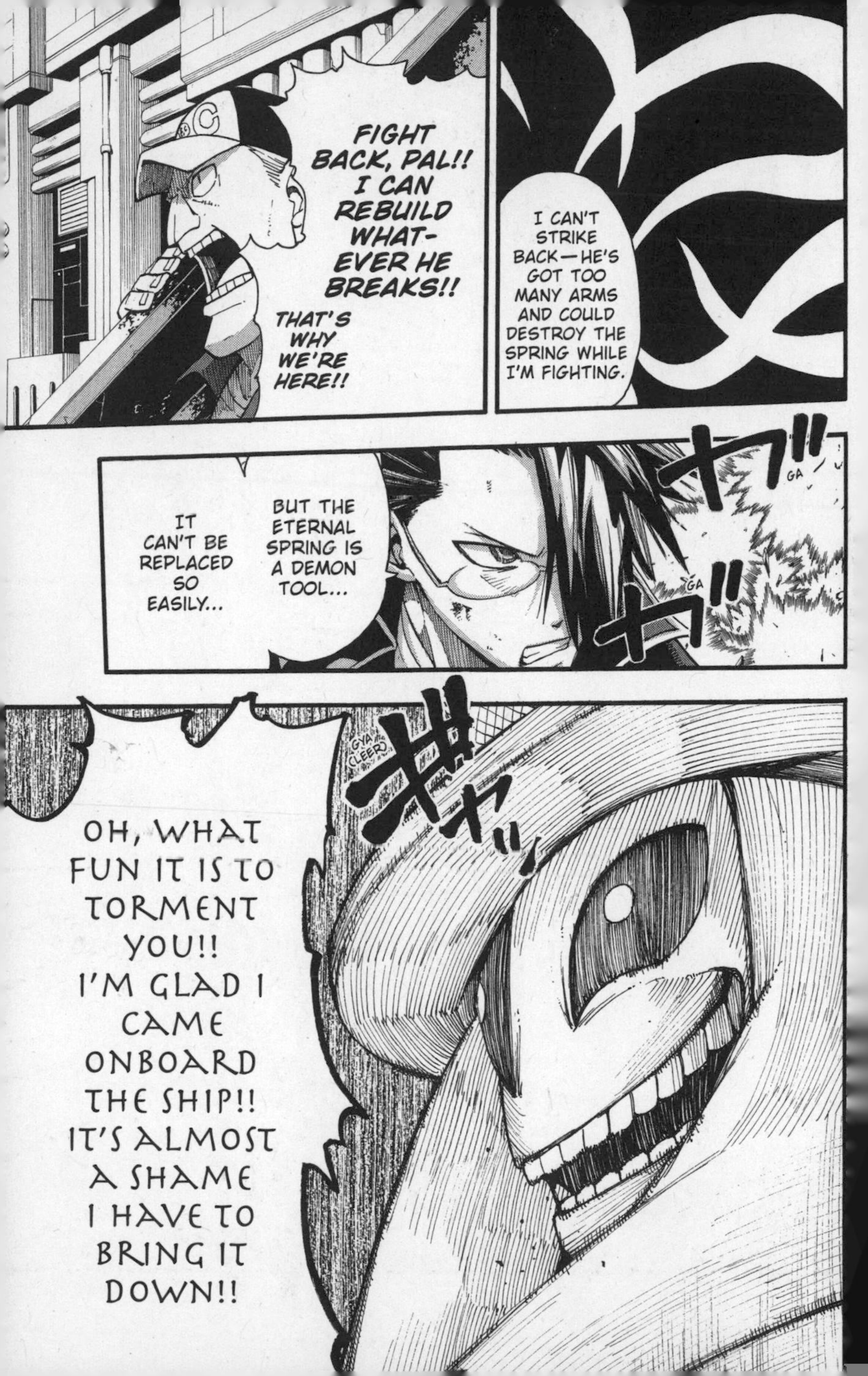
I CAN'T STRIKE BACK—HE'S GOT TOO MANY ARMS AND COULD DESTROY THE SPRING WHILE I'M FIGHTING.
FIGHT BACK, PAL!! I CAN REBUILD WHATEVER HE BREAKS!!
THAT'S WHY WE'RE HERE!!
GA
GA
BUT THE ETERNAL SPRING IS A DEMON TOOL...
IT CAN'T BE REPLACED SO EASILY...
GYA (CLEER)
OH, WHAT FUN IT IS TO TORMENT YOU!! I'M GLAD I CAME ONBOARD THE SHIP!! IT'S ALMOST A SHAME I HAVE TO BRING IT DOWN!!

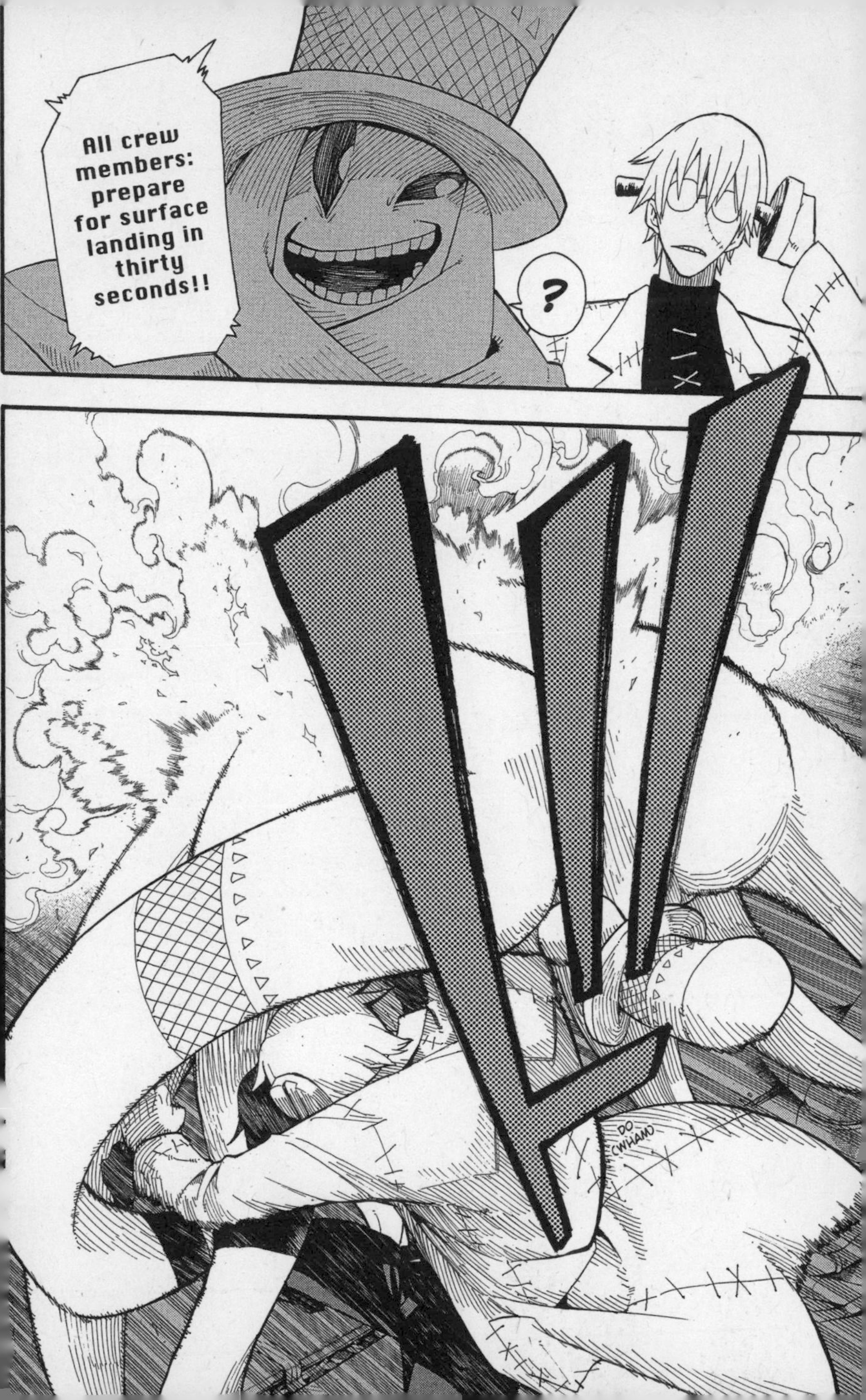
All crew members: prepare for surface landing in thirty seconds!!
?
DO CWHAM

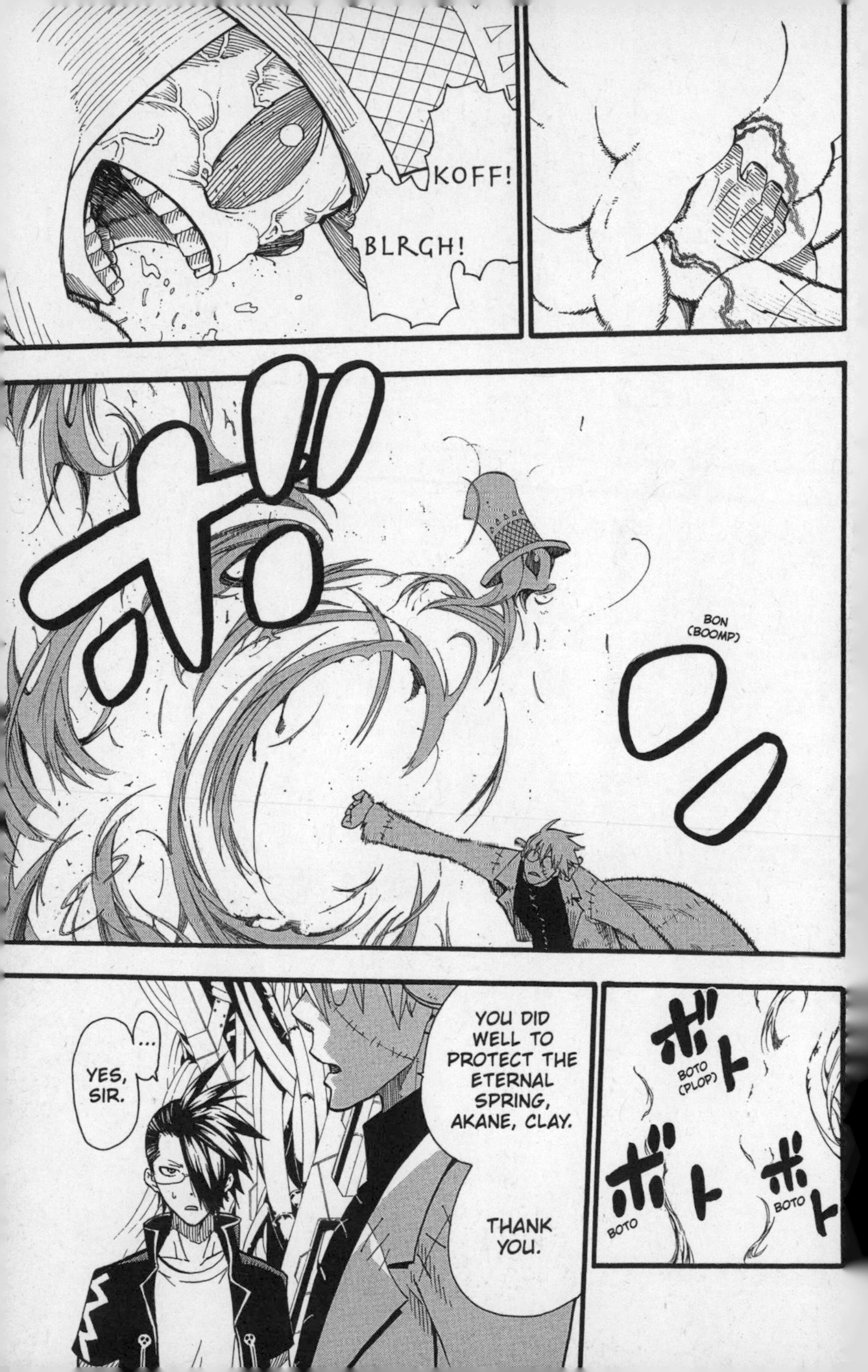
KOFF!
BLRGH!
ボン
BON (BOOMP)
ボト
BOTO (PLOP)
ボト
BOTO
ボト
BOTO
YOU DID WELL TO PROTECT THE ETERNAL SPRING, AKANE, CLAY.
THANK YOU.
...
YES, SIR.

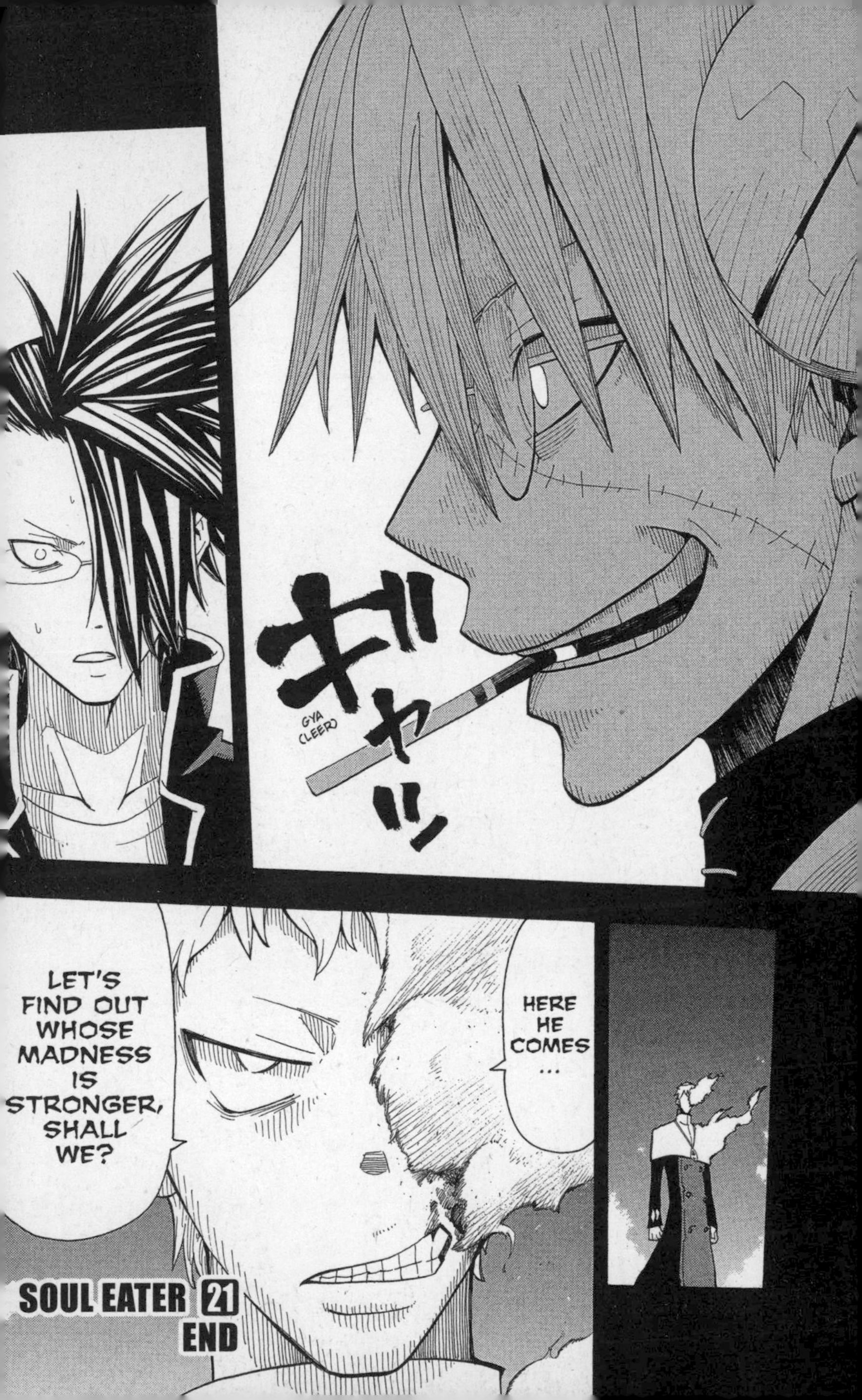
ギャッ
GYA (LEER)
HERE HE COMES...
LET'S FIND OUT WHOSE MADNESS IS STRONGER, SHALL WE?
SOUL EATER 21 END

SOUL EATER

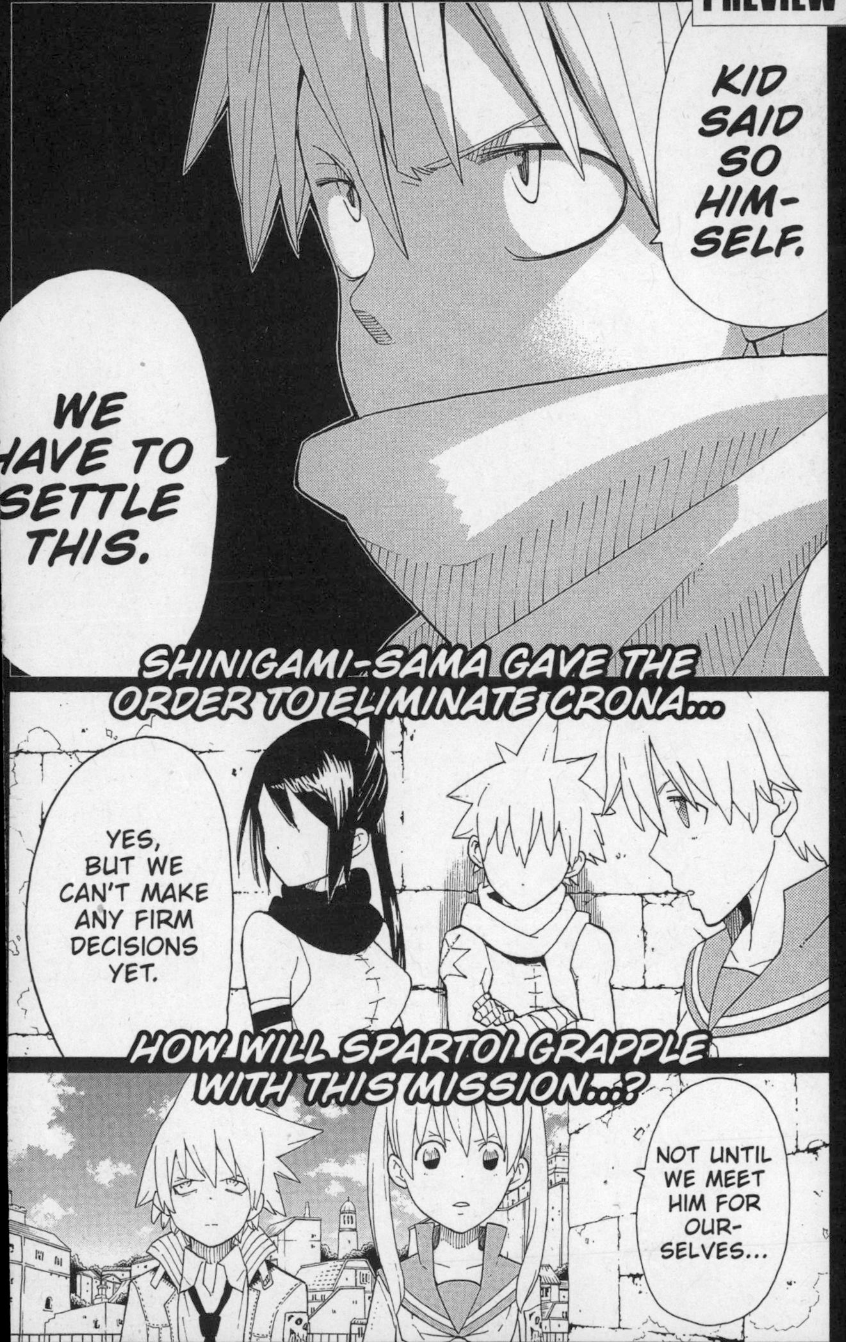
KID SAID SO HIM-SELF.
WE HAVE TO SETTLE THIS.
SHINIGAMI-SAMA GAVE THE ORDER TO ELIMINATE CRONA...
YES, BUT WE CAN'T MAKE ANY FIRM DECISIONS YET.
HOW WILL SPARTOI GRAPPLE WITH THIS MISSION...?
NOT UNTIL WE MEET HIM FOR OUR-SELVES...

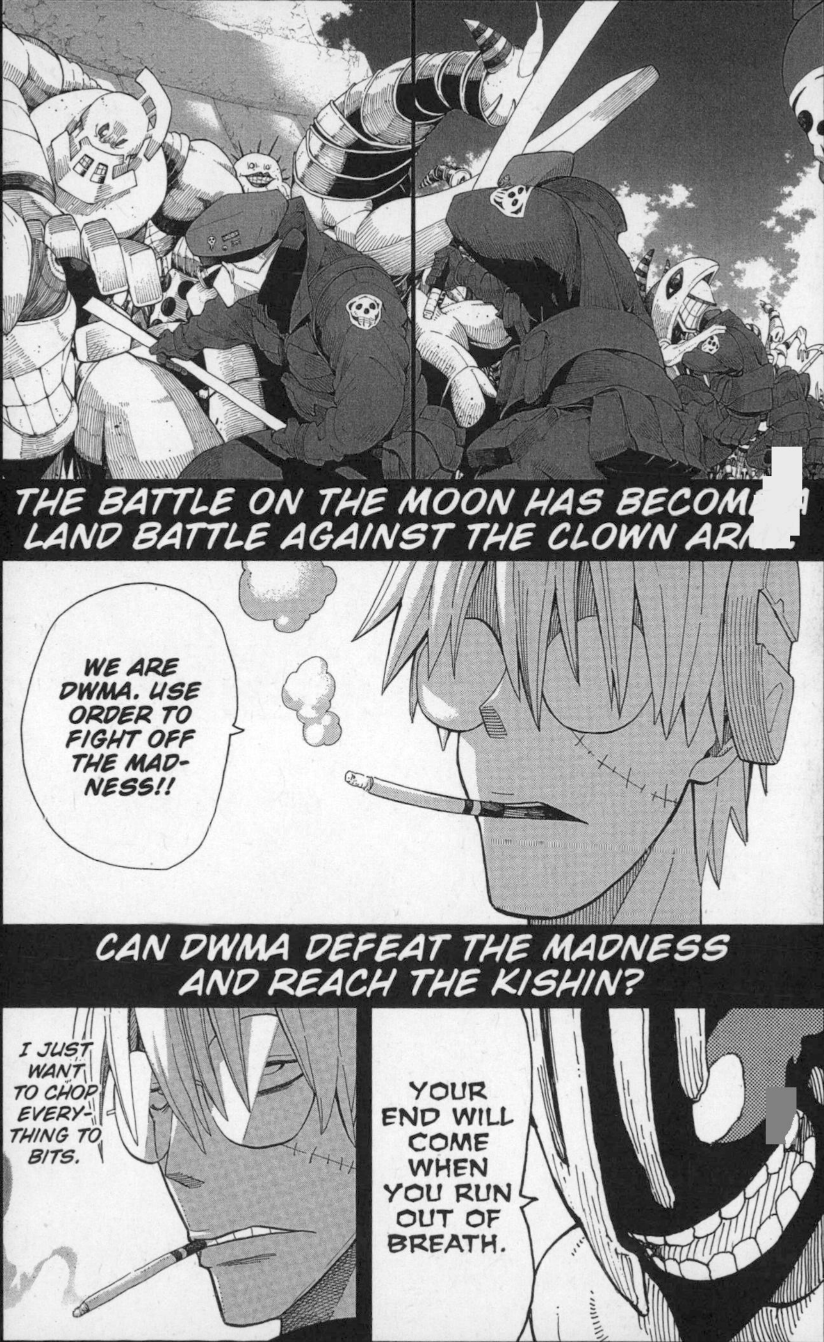
THE BATTLE ON THE MOON HAS BECOM A LAND BATTLE AGAINST THE CLOWN AR
WE ARE DWMA. USE ORDER TO FIGHT OFF THE MAD-NESS!!
CAN DWMA DEFEAT THE MADNESS AND REACH THE KISHIN?
YOUR END WILL COME WHEN YOU RUN OUT OF BREATH.
I JUST WANT TO CHOP EVERY-THING TO BITS.

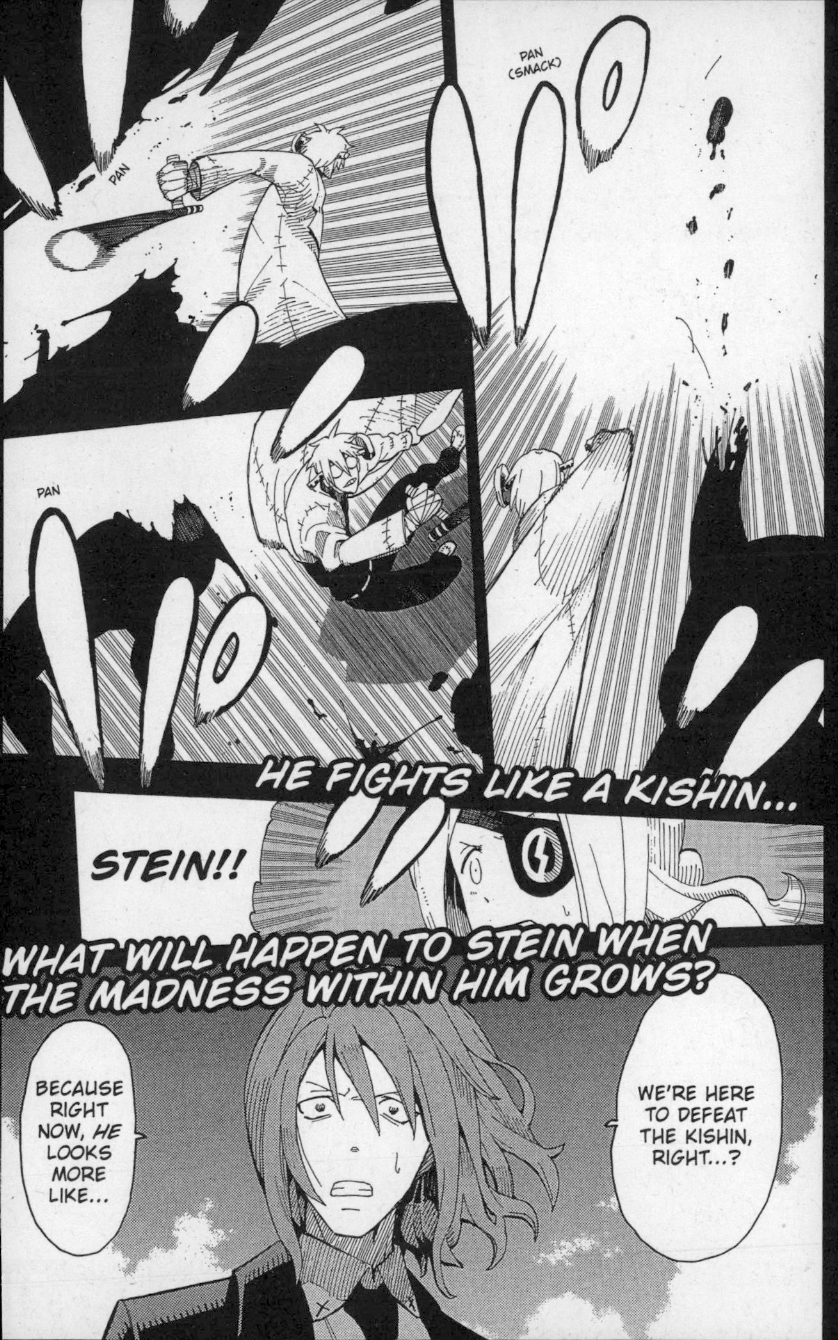
PAN (SMACK)
PAN
PAN
HE FIGHTS LIKE A KISHIN...
STEIN!!
WHAT WILL HAPPEN TO STEIN WHEN THE MADNESS WITHIN HIM GROWS?
WE'RE HERE TO DEFEAT THE KISHIN, RIGHT...?
BECAUSE RIGHT NOW, *HE* LOOKS MORE LIKE...

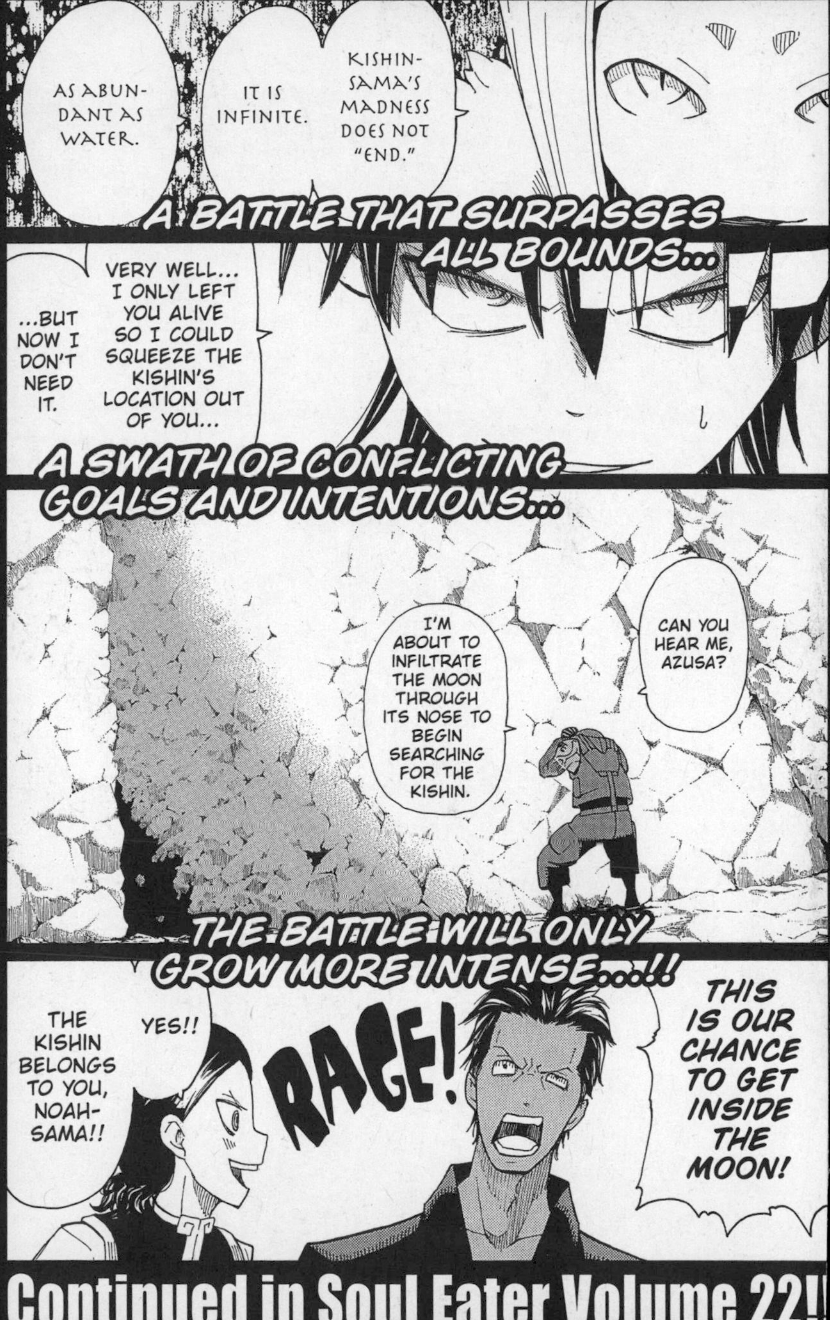
KISHIN-SAMA'S MADNESS DOES NOT "END."
IT IS INFINITE.
AS ABUNDANT AS WATER.
A BATTLE THAT SURPASSES ALL BOUNDS...
VERY WELL... I ONLY LEFT YOU ALIVE SO I COULD SQUEEZE THE KISHIN'S LOCATION OUT OF YOU...
...BUT NOW I DON'T NEED IT.
A SWATH OF CONFLICTING GOALS AND INTENTIONS...
CAN YOU HEAR ME, AZUSA?
I'M ABOUT TO INFILTRATE THE MOON THROUGH ITS NOSE TO BEGIN SEARCHING FOR THE KISHIN.
THE BATTLE WILL ONLY GROW MORE INTENSE...!!
THIS IS OUR CHANCE TO GET INSIDE THE MOON!
RAGE!
YES!!
THE KISHIN BELONGS TO YOU, NOAH-SAMA!!

Continued in Soul Eater Volume 22!!

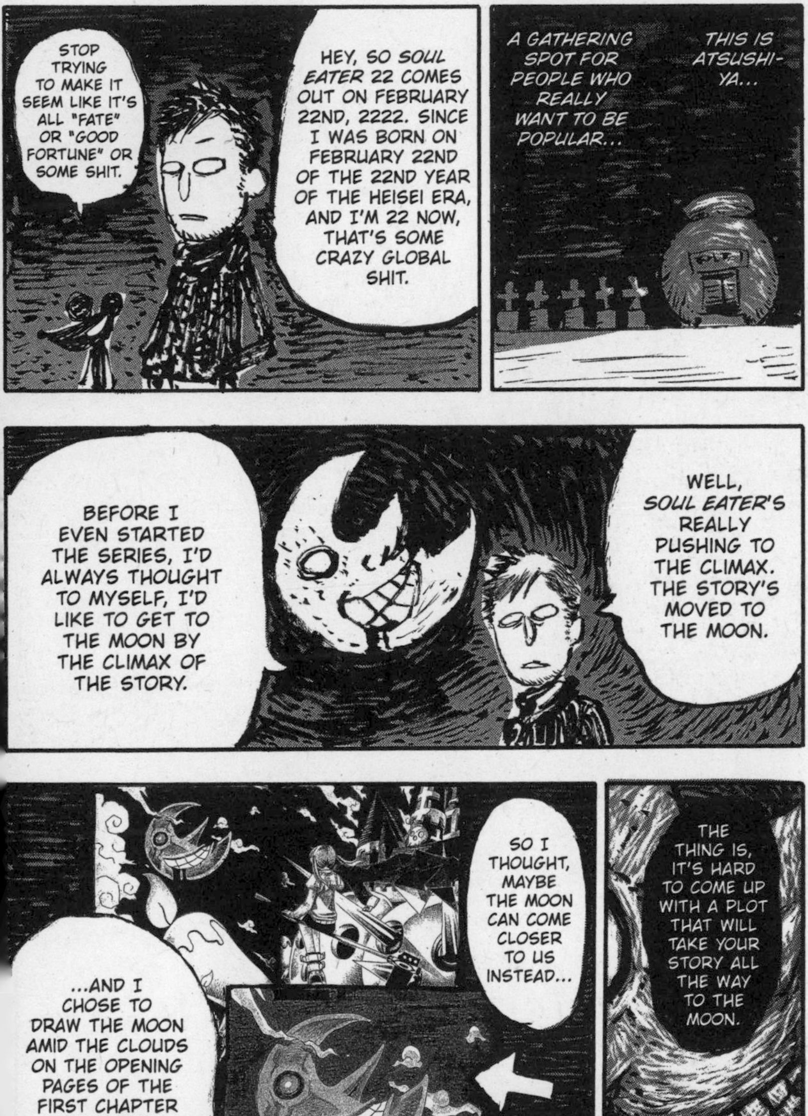
THIS IS ATSUSHI-YA...
A GATHERING SPOT FOR PEOPLE WHO REALLY WANT TO BE POPULAR...
HEY, SO SOUL EATER 22 COMES OUT ON FEBRUARY 22ND, 2222. SINCE I WAS BORN ON FEBRUARY 22ND OF THE 22ND YEAR OF THE HEISEI ERA, AND I'M 22 NOW, THAT'S SOME CRAZY GLOBAL SHIT.
STOP TRYING TO MAKE IT SEEM LIKE IT'S ALL "FATE" OR "GOOD FORTUNE" OR SOME SHIT.
WELL, SOUL EATER'S REALLY PUSHING TO THE CLIMAX. THE STORY'S MOVED TO THE MOON.
BEFORE I EVEN STARTED THE SERIES, I'D ALWAYS THOUGHT TO MYSELF, I'D LIKE TO GET TO THE MOON BY THE CLIMAX OF THE STORY.
THE THING IS, IT'S HARD TO COME UP WITH A PLOT THAT WILL TAKE YOUR STORY ALL THE WAY TO THE MOON.
SO I THOUGHT, MAYBE THE MOON CAN COME CLOSER TO US INSTEAD...
...AND I CHOSE TO DRAW THE MOON AMID THE CLOUDS ON THE OPENING PAGES OF THE FIRST CHAPTER TO MAKE IT SEEM CLOSER.

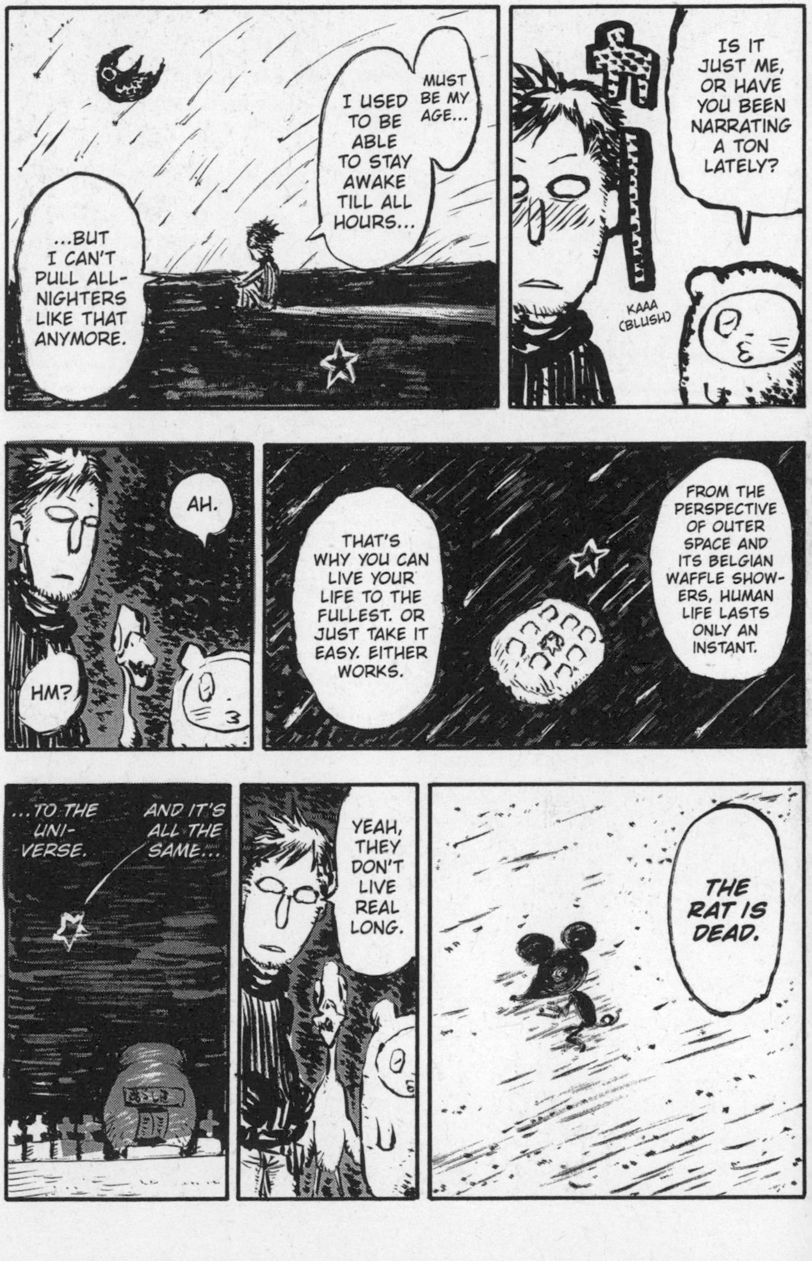
IS IT JUST ME, OR HAVE YOU BEEN NARRATING A TON LATELY?
KAAA (BLUSH)
MUST BE MY AGE...
I USED TO BE ABLE TO STAY AWAKE TILL ALL HOURS...
...BUT I CAN'T PULL ALL-NIGHTERS LIKE THAT ANYMORE.
FROM THE PERSPECTIVE OF OUTER SPACE AND ITS BELGIAN WAFFLE SHOWERS, HUMAN LIFE LASTS ONLY AN INSTANT.
THAT'S WHY YOU CAN LIVE YOUR LIFE TO THE FULLEST. OR JUST TAKE IT EASY. EITHER WORKS.
AH.
HM?
THE RAT IS DEAD.
YEAH, THEY DON'T LIVE REAL LONG.
AND IT'S ALL THE SAME...
...TO THE UNIVERSE.

Translation Notes

Common Honorifics

no honorific: Indicates familiarity or closeness; if used without permission or reason, addressing someone in this manner would constitute an insult.

-san: The Japanese equivalent of Mr./Mrs./Miss. If a situation calls for politeness, this is the failsafe honorific.

-sama: Conveys great respect; may also indicate that the social status of the speaker is lower than that of the addressee.

-kun: Used most often when referring to boys, this indicates affection or familiarity. Occasionally used by older men among their peers, but it may also be used by anyone referring to a person of lower standing.

-chan: An affectionate honorific indicating familiarity used mostly in reference to girls; also used in reference to cute persons or animals of either gender.

-senpai: A suffix used to address upperclassmen or more experienced coworkers.

-sensei: A respectful term for teachers, artists, or high-level professionals.

Page 8
The names **Ahab** and **Heming** are taken from two well-known stories about men battling the creatures of the sea. Ahab is the name of the captain from *Moby-Dick*, while Heming is a reference to Ernest Hemingway, the author of *The Old Man and the Sea*. In addition to this, the name of **Sea Shepherd Village** is an ironic reference to the infamous activist ship and organization that protests Japanese whaling and is the subject of the reality TV show *Whale Wars*.

Page 80
Jinn Galland combines the names of an Arabian spirit (also known as a d'jinn or genie) and the last name of Antoine Galland, whose 1704 French translation of the collection of Middle Eastern folk tales known as *One Thousand and One Nights* was the first Western version of that collection.

Page 98
Akane's family name, **Hoshi**, means "star" in Japanese.

Page 105
In the original Japanese, Gen says he carries around the **H-beam** because it's "kinda 'H'"—pronounced "ecchi." The word *ecchi* (as anyone who's watched a subtitled anime scene where a guy sees a girl undressing knows) means "naughty" or "dirty." It stems from the Japanese pronunciation of the letter "H," the first letter of the word *hentai*, meaning "pervert." *Ecchi* is a somewhat versatile term that can also refer to the act of sex itself.

Page 144
Zubaidah is a reference to Zubaidah bint Ja'far, an Arabian princess who appeared in multiple stories of *One Thousand and One Nights*.

Page 176
Heisei is the current era of the traditional Japanese calendar, which is divided into different periods every time the emperor dies and is succeeded. The Heisei era began in 1989 with the death of Emperor Hirohito and the succession of Emperor Akihito. Therefore, Heisei 22 is actually 2010. The author here is poking fun at the numerical oddity that Volume 21's first printing in Japan went on sale February 22nd, 2012.

DING·
DONG!

EAD·
DONG!

ON'T BE
ATE FOR
HE "NOT"
LASS
T DEATH
WEAPON
MEISTER
ACADEMY!

OLDER TEEN
OT

Yen
Press

SOUL EATER
NOT!

TSUSHI OHKUBO

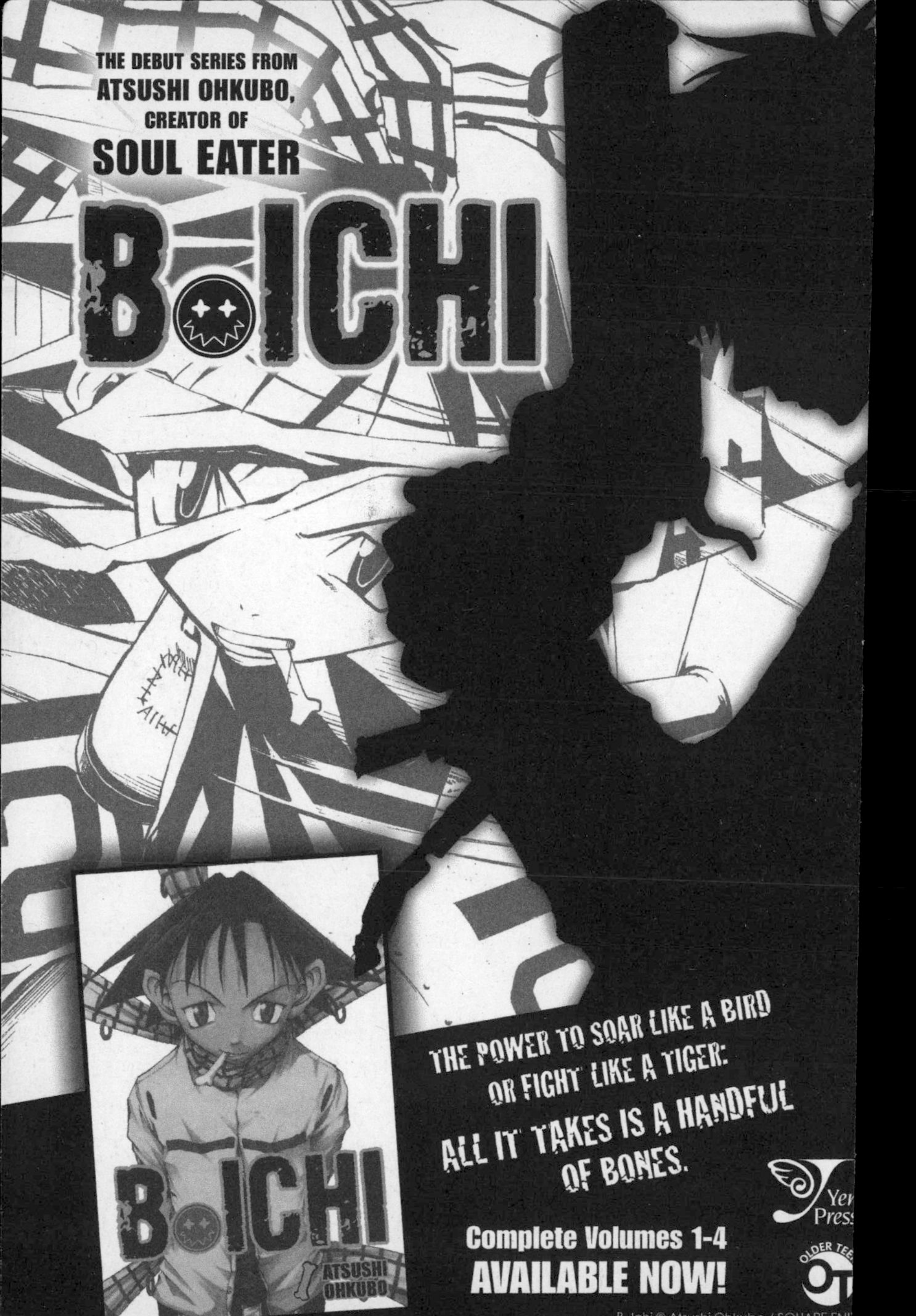
THE DEBUT SERIES FROM
ATSUSHI OHKUBO,
CREATOR OF
SOUL EATER
B. ICHI
THE POWER TO SOAR LIKE A BIRD
OR FIGHT LIKE A TIGER:
ALL IT TAKES IS A HANDFUL
OF BONES.
B. ICHI
ATSUSHI OHKUBO
Complete Volumes 1-4
AVAILABLE NOW!

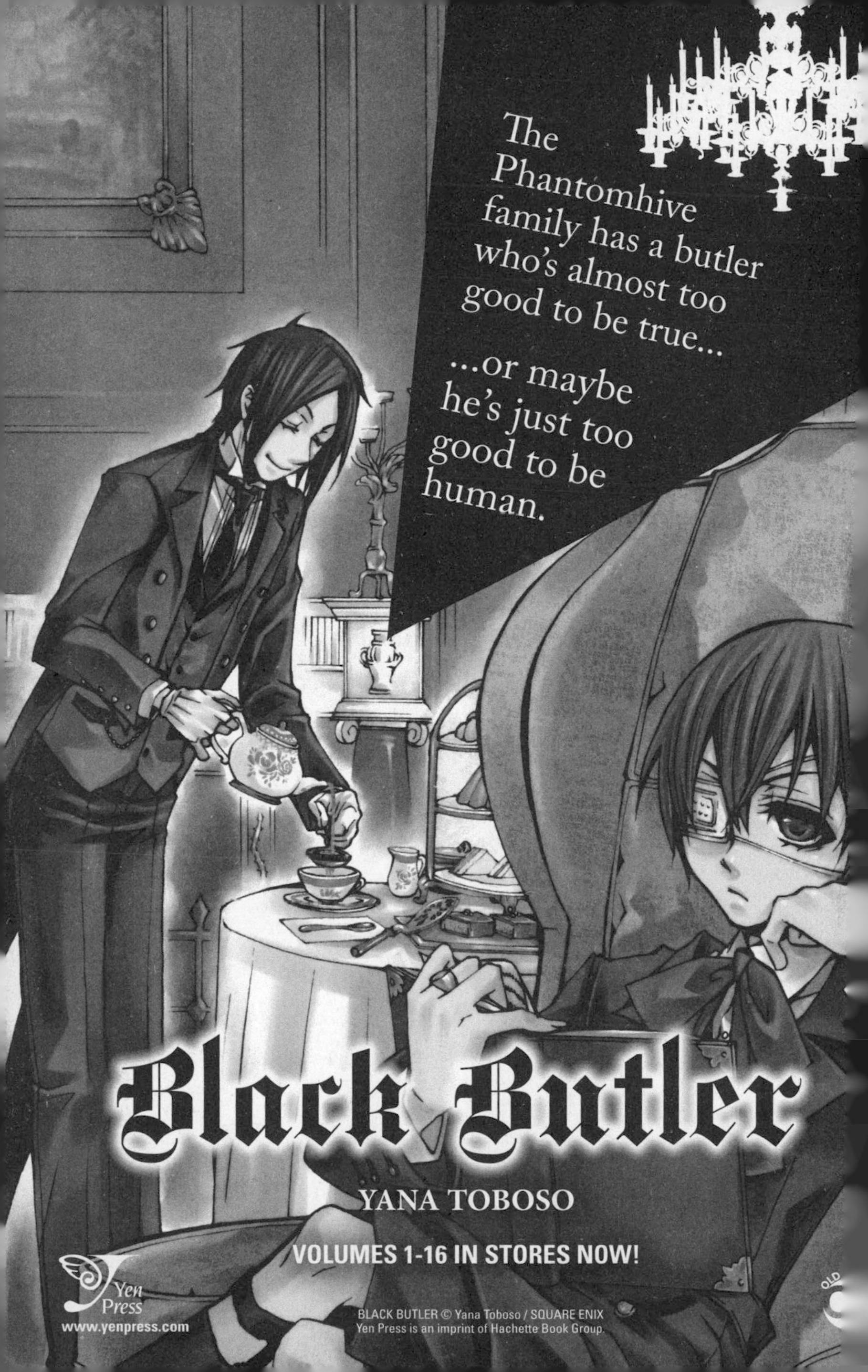
The Phantomhive family has a butler who's almost too good to be true...
...or maybe he's just too good to be human.
Black Butler
YANA TOBOSO
VOLUMES 1-16 IN STORES NOW!
Yen Press
www.yenpress.com
BLACK BUTLER © Yana Toboso / SQUARE ENIX
Yen Press is an imprint of Hachette Book Group.

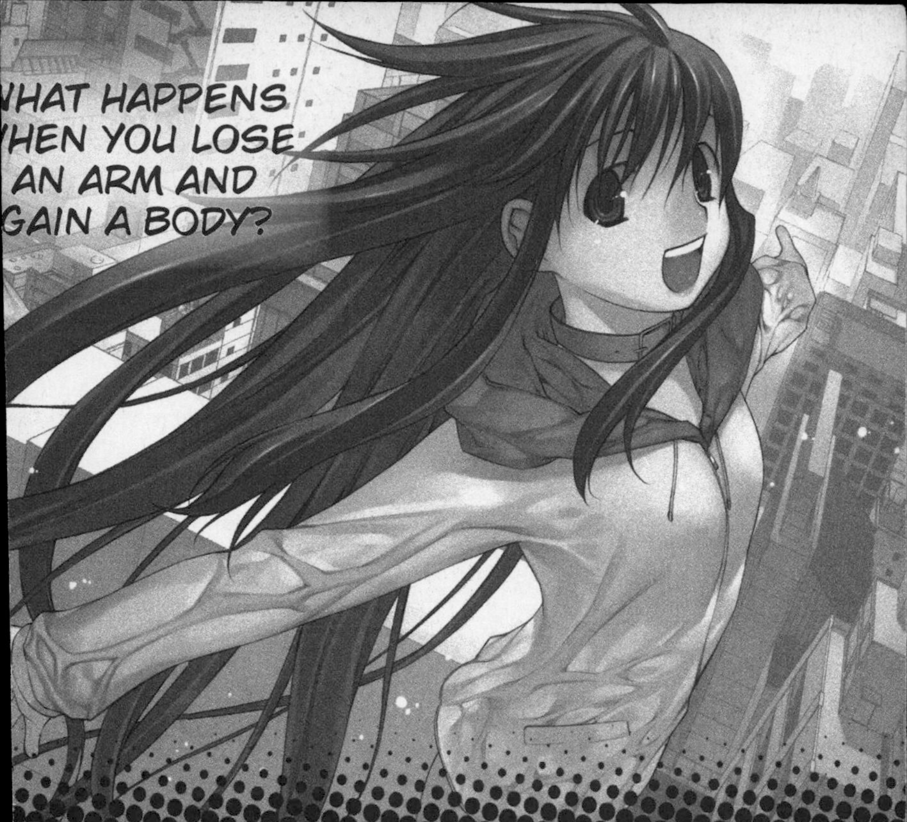
WHAT HAPPENS
WHEN YOU LOSE
AN ARM AND
GAIN A BODY?

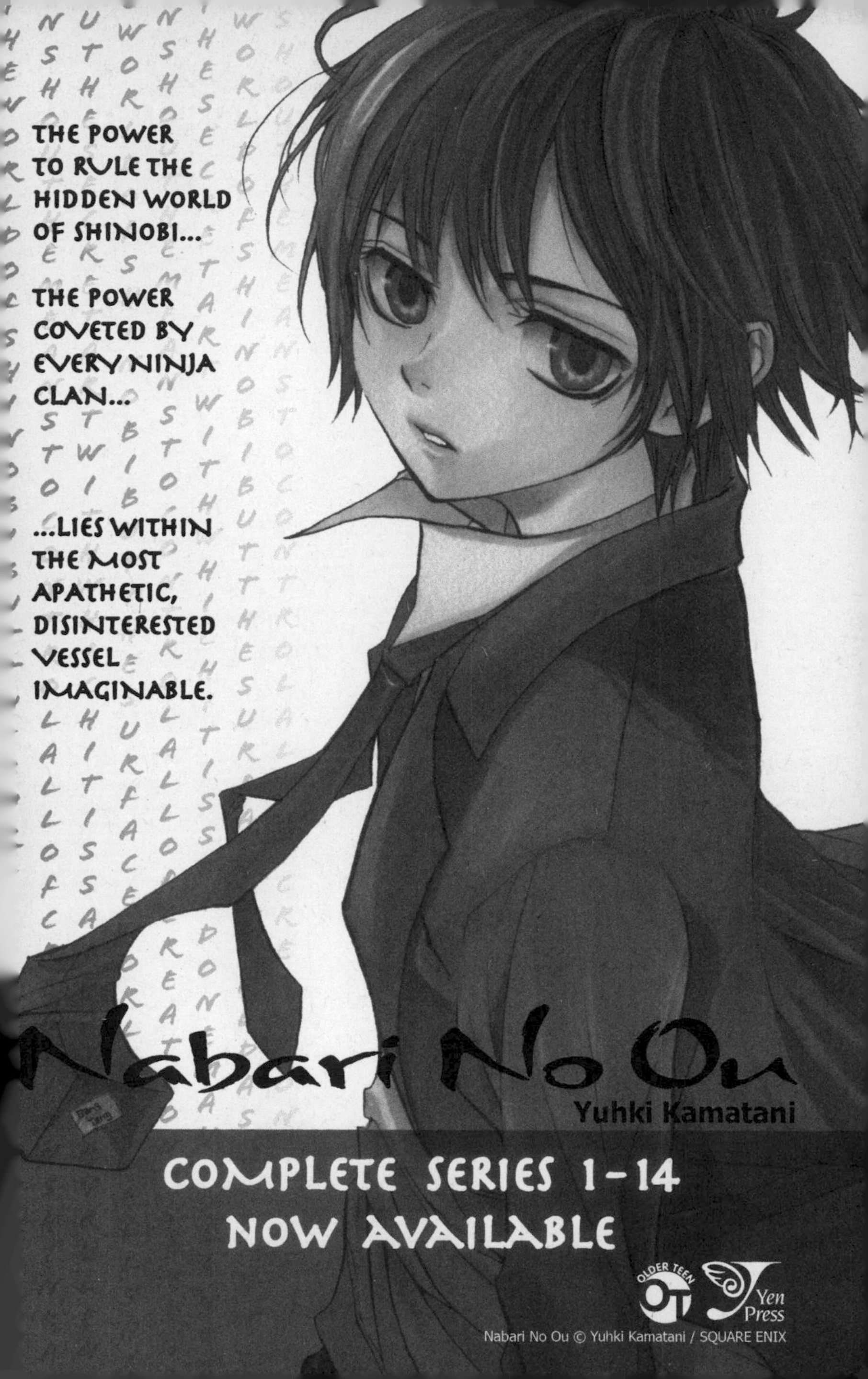
THE POWER TO RULE THE HIDDEN WORLD OF SHINOBI...
THE POWER COVETED BY EVERY NINJA CLAN...
...LIES WITHIN THE MOST APATHETIC, DISINTERESTED VESSEL IMAGINABLE.
Nabari No Ou
Yuhki Kamatani
COMPLETE SERIES 1-14
NOW AVAILABLE
OLDER TEEN OT
Yen Press
Nabari No Ou © Yuhki Kamatani / SQUARE ENIX

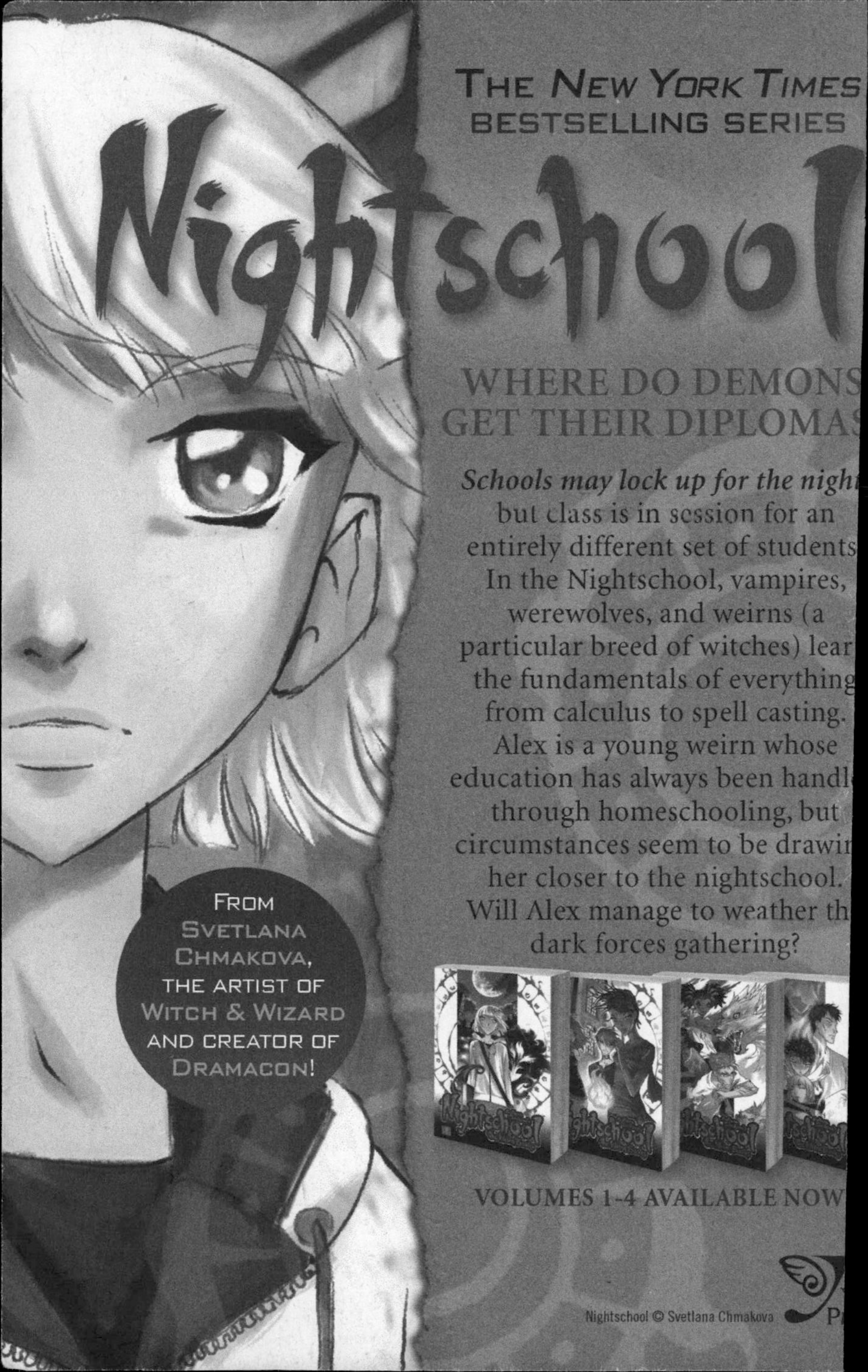
THE NEW YORK TIMES
BESTSELLING SERIES
Nightschool
WHERE DO DEMONS
GET THEIR DIPLOMA
Schools may lock up for the nigh
but class is in session for an
entirely different set of students
In the Nightschool, vampires,
werewolves, and weirns (a
particular breed of witches) lear
the fundamentals of everything
from calculus to spell casting.
Alex is a young weirn whose
education has always been handl
through homeschooling, but
circumstances seem to be drawi
her closer to the nightschool.
Will Alex manage to weather th
dark forces gathering?
FROM SVETLANA CHMAKOVA, THE ARTIST OF WITCH & WIZARD AND CREATOR OF DRAMACON!
VOLUMES 1-4 AVAILABLE NOW
Nightschool © Svetlana Chmakova

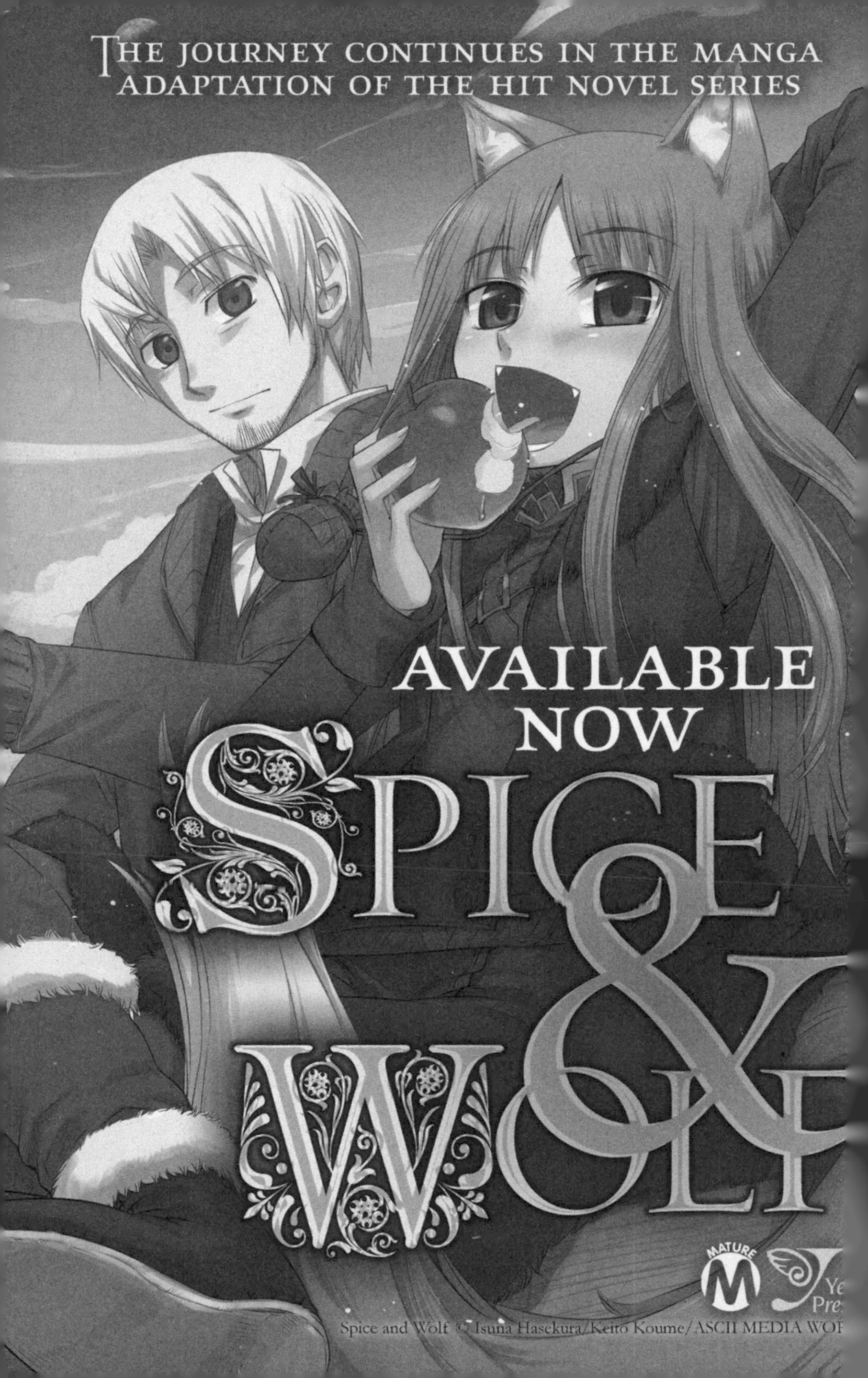
THE JOURNEY CONTINUES IN THE MANGA
ADAPTATION OF THE HIT NOVEL SERIES
AVAILABLE
NOW
SPICE
&
WOLF
MATURE
Spice and Wolf © Isuna Hasekura/Keito Koume/ASCII MEDIA WO

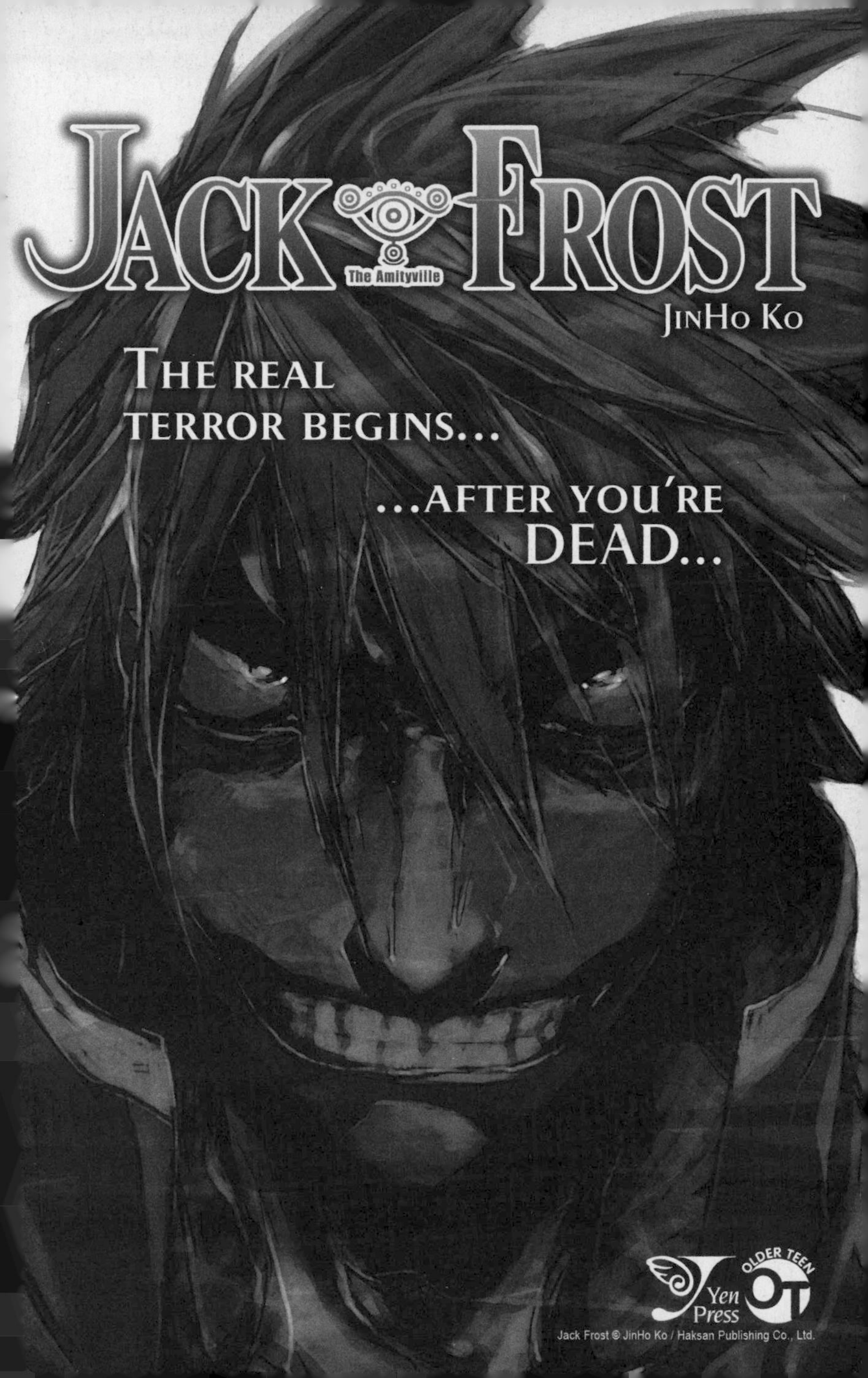
JACK FROST
The Amityville
JINHO KO
THE REAL TERROR BEGINS...
...AFTER YOU'RE DEAD...
Yen Press
OLDER TEEN
OT
Jack Frost © JinHo Ko / Haksan Publishing Co., Ltd.

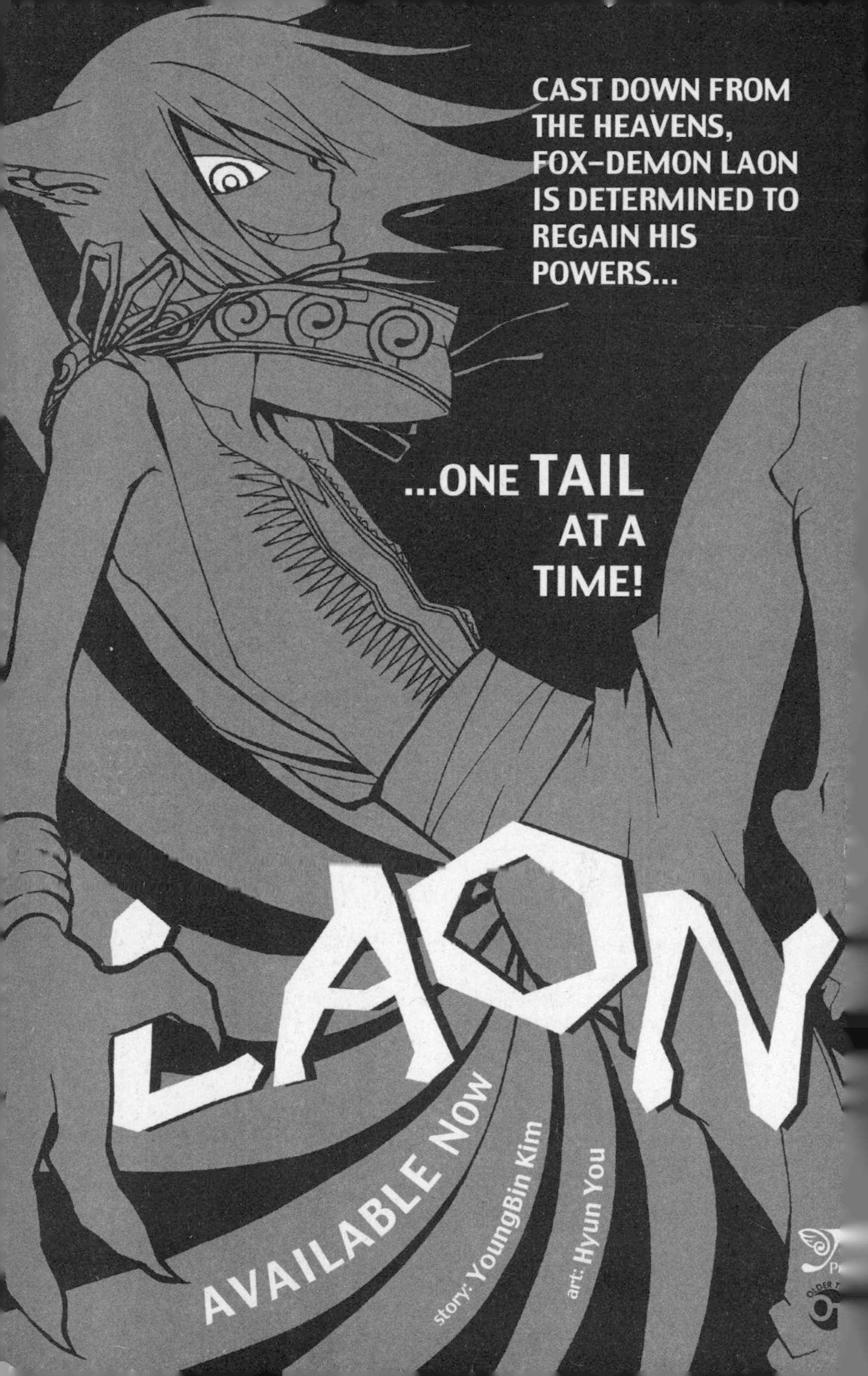
CAST DOWN FROM THE HEAVENS, FOX-DEMON LAON IS DETERMINED TO REGAIN HIS POWERS...
...ONE TAIL AT A TIME!
LAON
AVAILABLE NOW
story: YoungBin Kim
art: Hyun You

SOUL EATER ㉑

ATSUSHI OHKUBO

Translation: Stephen Paul

Lettering: Abigail Blackman

SOUL EATER Vol. 21 © 2012 Atsushi Ohkubo / SQUARE ENIX. First published in Japan in 2012 by SQUARE ENIX CO., LTD. English translation rights arranged with SQUARE ENIX CO., LTD. and Hachette Book Group through Tuttle-Mori Agency, Inc.

Translation © 2014 by SQUARE ENIX CO., LTD.

Yen Press
Hachette Book Group
237 Park Avenue, New York, NY 10017

HachetteBookGroup.com
YenPress.com

Yen Press is an imprint of Hachette Book Group, Inc. The Yen Press name and logo are trademarks of Hachette Book Group, Inc.

First Yen Press Edition: July 2014

ISBN: 978-0-316-40696-3

10 9 8 7 6 5 4 3 2 1

BVG

Printed in the United States of America